Small Water
Trout Fishing

CHARLES JARDINE

Small Water Trout Fishing

B. T. Batsford Ltd · London

To my family: mother Yvonne, wife Carole, children Annabelle and Alexander, but especially Bill Sibbons, 'adopted dad', who taught a generation of small-water fishers.

  This book belongs to them – and of course the trout and the waters, without which the whole thing is superfluous.

First published 1994
© Charles Jardine 1994
All rights reserved. No part of this publication
may be reproduced in any form or by any means,
without permission from the Publisher.

Typeset by Latimer Trend & Company Ltd,
Plymouth and printed in Great Britain by
Butler & Tanner Ltd, Frome and London

Published by B. T. Batsford Ltd
4 Fitzhardinge Street London W1H 0AH

A catalogue record for this book is available from
the British Library

ISBN 0 7134 6942 0

Contents

Foreword

FISHING with Charles Jardine is full of pleasures – the first of which is greeting him at the start of the day and counting the dangly bits on his person. He seems to acquire more each time I see him: there are bottles of float-stuff, canisters of sink-stuff, forceps, snips, scissors – all on those retractable whizzy things.

Another pleasure is being let loose in his fly-box. I remember having great success on the Test with his 'ruptured mayfly' which he let me have for a very reasonable price! – and then there's the pleasure of his advice on one's casting technique: his latest to me was 'take up tennis'! I won't of course; I'll continue to fish and if it's with Charles then I know I'll enjoy it – just as I know I shall enjoy this book.

Bernard Cribbins

Introduction

ONE of the more curious anomalies in this trout fishing world of ours is the tendency to overlook the obvious.

The trout fishing 'revolution' – and it is precisely that – which has occurred since the mid-60s has been phenomenal and mercurial, also minutely documented. Word upon word has been 'fired' at the stillwater 'target'. There has been no let up, and precious few stones left unturned. It seems we are replete and sated by knowledge. Enter the age of the 'gilded lily' perhaps? Not so. As long as there is another season, even another day, we will find a variation to our chosen theme.

But, in this welter of words and chaos of newly found knowledge, a big, ever-growing area has been overlooked – the small stillwater. It is easy and indeed trite to dismiss this significant branch of our sport as a spin-off of the big waters: applying mostly the same tactics and merely refining others to suit these 'Lilliputian' playgrounds. If that is the case then I fear anglers and authors have missed the point.

What small stillwater fly fishing offers is a cornucopia of difference, if approached with an open mind, free of prejudice. It is an area of total interest, endless variety, tactical variance and often extreme excitement.

This book, I believe, is one of the few since Peter Cockwill's excellent offering, *Big Trout Fishing* to be dedicated to the smallwater fly fisher and unashamedly so thus encouraging the angler not to feel inferior to bigger water fishers. The waters themselves are sometimes easier but not inferior, just different.

What is an inescapable truism is the phenomenal growth of interest in this particular area. This is no accident. Indeed, given the almost 'holiday camp' vistas that greet us on reservoirs – yachts, sailboards, walkers, dogs and other leisure pursuers – they offer perhaps a tranquil haven from a world working extraordinarily hard at amusing itself, often to the detriment of peace! This is not 'sour grapes', or humbug, merely observation from someone who likes to escape into a world free of clock-watching, pressure and frantic pace even when on holiday. There are on most small waters (and this is part of their charm) places where you can escape within and without yourself, if only for a few hours – even minutes – so rebuilding and fortifying yourself against everyday mayhem.

Hereafter is a seasonal beakdown of the tactics and theme variations you might realistically encounter throughout the year. Having reached a stage in my thirty-third season when I purely seek pleasure from fishing, I make no excuses at all for giving slant to imitative patterns and styles. I know, as we all do, the effectiveness of lures and I have no axe to grind with them; they have even been 'spirited out' and on to my leader when I wasn't looking, on tricky or 'head-scratching' days; but I confess to being particularly bored by constant use of this type of fly. There has to be more to the sport than pure retrieve rates, colour changes and work rate – and so there is.

And please forgive me for dallying with wildlife and odd instances, characters and all the other minute and major factors which form a whole in this wonderful sport of ours.

As I write this, my third book, I find that it appears I know less now than I did years ago and – though it is something of a cliché – we never do truly stop learning (or is it that those confounded trout are getting cleverer?).

The worst thing that anyone can say to me is 'think like a fish'. A trout has a brain the size of a pea, but still on occasion manages to dumbfound and make ordinary not only our best and most intelligent efforts, but also our fly tying skills. Considering that our sophisticated tackle is a direct by-product of man reaching the moon, this is a sobering thought!

The following is dedicated to the awkward cuss – the trout, and smallwater fishing – unbowed.

Acknowledgements

This book, indeed any book, is not the product of just one person, rather it is an amalgam and eventually 'child' of a closely knit team – perhaps more a family, with all that that entails – even the odd discordant note. But for all that, an enriching journey.

The 'team' on this occasion was huge and, sadly, far and away too large to mention in full – but they know who they are.

However, singled out for special mention far input far beyond the call of duty is my dear friend Terry Griffiths (the Welsh magician of the lens). His help, support and plain sense was always there when needed most.

To the Batsford gang: originally Pauline Snelson, latterly Jim Pipe, and especially Tim Auger for commissioning the work, and their gentle badgering; to editors Sandy Leventon and Chris Dawn of EMAP and Roy Westwood of IPC who have all kindly allowed me to fool about with screeds penned for their journals. Thanks also to my American chums, notably Gary Borger, Al Beatty and Lefty Kreh who have helped me inordinately in understanding some aquatic discrepancies, black holes and Casting Sagas; sage and 'maestro of the blank' Don Green for the rods; Ryobi Masterline's Dick Tallant and Chris Leibrandt for their hard work, leaders and lines; my Nomad colleagues, notably Stuart Cross, Mick Phipps and Keith Bryant who were harangued and generally made to fish in odd places in order to get some photographs.

To the various fishery owners – Roger Daltrey, Marion Mainwearing, Nigel Jackson, Roy Ward, John and Kate Sullivan, Ian James, Barry Bostock and countless others who have helped not just on this project, but put themselves out on my behalf for many years – thank you.

To the hundreds of anglers who have helped, from luminaries such as Peter Cockwill, Chris Ogborne and Bob Church, as well as all the unsung heroes – all of you have made me realize I know little more now than I did thirty odd years ago.

Finally, my family – wife and typist Carole, Annabelle, Alex and Ma, and of course the trout themselves.

All of you take a share in this book. Without any reservations, it would not have happened without your help.

PART ONE

Equipment and Techniques

CHAPTER ONE

Tackle and Technology

EVERYBODY includes it, everybody groans about it, and most reviewers chastise authors for its predictable inclusion. I fear I too will walk the same well-furrowed track.

Tackle – those essential bits and pieces that divest us of hard-earned income – cannot be excluded from a book on fishing. The fact is that rods, reels, lines, leaders and all the other paraphenalia are critical to a harmonious and successful outcome. This problem is further compounded by being so deeply subjective – this, sadly, is unavoidable.

There again, the collecting of tackle (and it would be a rare person who did not own up to just a little 'tackle mania' is deeply satisfying fun. The assembled hoard can be toyed with during periods of inactivity; and gazed at, bringing back joyous or desperate days with equal clarity. And anyway, if there was no tackle to buy, what on earth would we hide away from our loved ones or squander our money on?

The depressing truth is you really do not need very much of it at all for fishing small stillwaters. It is a branch of the sport which positively encourages minimalism. But whatever you select, make sure it is suited to the task it is expected to perform. I have witnessed more crimes in this small stillwater department than in any other aspect of fly fishing apart from (oddly) chalkstream. Quite why is hard to understand, as both the cost of water and the precision required in actual fishing when compared to other areas would suggest it is the one area that positively 'screams' excellence

of material and design. The reality is that your chosen equipment will have to work very hard indeed; with the added spice that you may well be wrestling with a creature the size of a salmon – a big one – in a confined space.

There are other aspects too. Style of fishing comes into the frame. Remember that your fishing should, first and foremost, give you pleasure. Your choice of tackle is instrumental in enhancing this pleasure. Another important factor is versatility – you may want to venture out on to a big reservoir, or fish a small brook or large river. And although you cannot have a 'rod for all seasons', you can at least compromise – a bit. The other feature of tackle progression is how cheap it has become – relatively speaking.

Having started fly fishing in an era that knew only split cane and greenheart, I have watched some of the ensuing developments in tackle with a wry smile. The claims of some manufacturers would have us believe that all we have to do is talk nicely to our chosen system, sit back and let it cast, hook and play a fish. Never forget, deceiving a trout is as much about how you present *yourself* as it is how you present your fish with familiar rod, line and fly. Wood or water craft still counts for something; which explains why that old fogey, derided for

1 Action at Avon Springs. Keith Bryant plays a lively rainbow in exemplary style. The rod is held high to act as a shock absorber

his outmoded tackle and techniques, invariably catches more fish than anyone else! And will, no doubt, continue to do so.

Rods

I well remember my first carbon rod – a Shakespeare President 8ft No. 6 in the early 70s – amidst the usual Pezon-et-Michelle and Hardy fibreglass. It was a revelation, but at a price. If memory serves me right, it cost me just over two weeks' pay. These days it would be comparable to at least a Sage, Orvis or Loomis. Now you can get a rod for half that 70s' figure, if not a whole system, coupled with a degree of reliability. In those dim and distant days, it was a rather pot-luck affair, although technology was advancing meteorically, but compared with today there was an element of risk. Now rods carry a guarantee of some description (if they don't, look elsewhere) and if you are on a budget, then most manu-

facturers have a thoroughly workable weapon in the 9ft to 9½ft category. There are few truly awful ones out there, so rest easy!

Oddly, times have changed very little since a time when my father got the biggest dressing down I have ever heard from my mother, who accused him of spending a week or more's grocery money on a floating line. The line was an Air Cel and cost £15.00 in the late 60s. Today you are getting a bargain.

Of course you could go back further, but urging a re-introduction and a return to the values – dubious ones at that – fashioned by horsehair or silk lines and lancewood rods would be stretching credibility! However, some knowledge of the past does help to obtain a degree of perspective on the sport. After all, although we have changed line systems from Kingfishers Nos 1 and 2 and so on, and HDFs to AFTM, it is very unlikely they would have been different in actual weight from those we choose these days for aspects of our sport.

So, with a sense of history firmly implanted, we move forward. As you may recall, I stated earlier that the business of tackle selection is intensely personal and reflective of the type of water and style of approach you wish to adopt. I can only offer my personal preferences which, to be fair, have changed dramatically down the years.

Being an 'expatriate' chalkstream fisher, my initial efforts were made with Nos 5 and 6 weight systems, invariably split cane rods to 9ft. These were in the halcyon days of an infant Damerham and other similar, then 'new-fangled' small waters, where a 4lb trout was a monster.

Gradually, with the advent of carbon and its more universal adoption and availability, the AFTM for many of us curiously increased; regularly No. 8 systems were used. I remember with joy my first Damerham 'double' to a Hardy Farnborough – now *that* rod could stop a rampaging rhino, let alone anything piscine. Thereafter my system fluctuated given various fads and fashions on the newly opened Bewl Water, known then as Bewl Bridge Reservoir, where most of us adopted a Midlands' approach. Gradually, I found I was getting far less pleasure from heavy lines, and for years after used mostly No. 7 outfits, choosing between 9ft and 9½ft rods as fancy dictated.

My personal 'Grail' was just around the corner. For the last few years, my mainline outfit has been almost entirely based around a No. 6 and recently, almost exclusively No. 5s – sometimes No. 4s.

It is, in essence, a downward spiral in search of not only fun but opportunity of meeting, and defeating head-on, many tactical problems that we so often encounter, and years ago used to frown upon and mutter that they were insoluble.

There are, of course, occasions that warrant a departure from the self-imposed norm – howling gales being just one – but I do feel that I am enjoying my fishing now by using lighter weaponry.

ROD SYSTEMS USED BY THE AUTHOR

● *For light line, very small fly and pinpoint accuracy*: A Sage 490 SP, a 9ft middle-action rod, that takes very happily a double taper No. 4 line.

● *For general use and fishing a wide variety of both fly and line densities*: A Sage 690 SP, a middle-action rod that performs best with the longer-bellied weight forwards or G.F.L. 690 4 pc graphite III – again sage.

● *For stalking where large fish might be encountered and when more beef is required – for instance, casting into the teeth of near gale force wind – and also for continuous sunk-line work including Hi-Ds*: A Sage 790 SP, which is a slightly higher-performance version of the previous one.

● *Other rods that see the light of day during the season are*: A 9½ft Sage Graphite III that takes a No. 6 line and is my preferred choice when fishing the larger small waters at long range with nymphs. And finally, a 10ft Graphite III that takes a No. 5 line and a No. 6 version, which I have found ideal when fishing from boats or, indeed, float tubes when I'm allowed, on the larger types of water. Its length allows for a far greater degree of control and tactical variations.

You may have gathered that I like sage – but others worth investigation are Loomis, Hardy and Fenwick. These are my choices and they are not cheap! I can only stress, however, you get what you pay for. Though, as I said, given the various 'states of the art', you can rest a little easier in your various tackle decisions.

Fly lines

Flaunting tradition, I shall begin with fly lines; for if ever there was a tactic-swinging item of tackle, then this is it.

I feel desperately sorry for the people who labour under the use of just one line, through rulings or bigotry, for they are missing a great many opportunities and demands that trout make upon our various methods.

Floating lines

Obviously a floating line is an essential – as you will see later on – and should perhaps be your first consideration. Whatever you do, get a good one. I have lost count of the times people have asked me during a lesson why weren't they getting the line to shoot properly or perform as it should. Quite simply, two factors were at work:

● Lack of maintenance and cleaning (after every third or fourth trip) given beastly bank-side conditions, your line should be washed in luke-warm, soapy (not detergent) water, then shined with either a chamois leather or soft cotton cloth. Cleaning pads supplied with some fly lines serve as a general line cleaner, which is also a good 'in the field' policy. This will ensure high performance at all times.

● An inferior line. Always purchase from a known manufacturer and opt for the reputable ones. There has, over the past few years, been a veritable fly line 'war' going on – stretch versus non- or low-stretch; PVC versus Teflon and so on.

It is not my business to decide which is right for others – tackle is very personal. I can only say that my trust in reputable lines, known for years, has never been betrayed and I continue to use them, even if it means flying in the face of convention or modernity. There is, though, a problem with recommending named choices

– companies have a nasty habit of 'pulling out the rug' by discontinuing a particular range, making the recommendation null and void. However, with that risk in mind, both in terms of floaters and sinking types, my personal choice would be made from Cortland, Air Cel (3M), Hardy Brothers or Orvis.

In terms of specialized situations, the plot thickens a little. For floating types, my choice would be as follows:

For general use   Air Cel Mastery, Ultra 2 or 3 or Supreme or Masterline Gold.

For special use   Long-range nymphing and dry fly: Lee Wulff Triangle Taper or Roman Moser version.

For delicate operations and very close quarter, light line strategies with nymph and dry fly   The Orvis Spring Creek – or DT 4 Ultra 2 or 3.

This seems to be 'gilding the lily' and so it is; however, you can rationalize the above list into something which suits your particular taste and be assured that it will do the job you intend.

● *Floating and intermediate lines*

a   a floating line will tend to force even the heaviest fly upwards, only allowing it to fall when the retrieve stops. But overall most useful for smaller imitations such as Midge, or any occasion that demands ultra-slow retrieves
b   the intermediate line tends to keep the fly on an even plane which is often preferred by trout, especially rainbows on the prowl

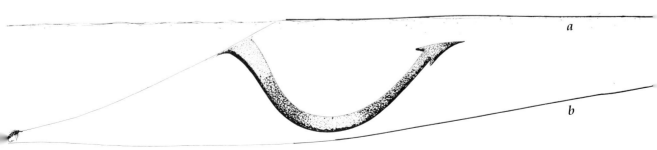

Sinking lines

The sinking line is a veritable minefield of confusion – sink rates, colours – and the whole gamut is cloaked in hyperbole and contradiction. Having tried, at some time or other, most of them, I am left none the wiser and merely retreat back to the comfort of favourite types which suit me and my various styles.

Again, I tend to stick to the aforementioned manufacturers; though, in terms of sink rate, which very much determines tactics on the day and the fly's fishing angle and position in the water, I tend to relate everything to the Wet Cel types (3M).

Intermediate   Surface to about four feet.

Wet Cel I   One foot to about six feet.

Wet Cel II   Four feet to about ten feet.

Hi-D   Ten feet downwards.

However, I am told that Cortland (as I write) have just released a faster high-density line which would make it a fair candidate for high-summer periods of heat-filled lethargy or biting-cold torpor.

But, similarly to the floating lines, there are specialist sinkers that I carry, and you should at least contemplate if the role – to be found on the preceding pages – is applicable to your type or style of fly fishing.

For fishing just subsurface with a floating line control   Cortland Intermediate Sink Tip.

For slightly deeper   The Jim Teeny Mini Tip.

For continuous retrieves just subsurface   Airflo Glass Intermediate (fast or slow) – a very good winter and early season line; the Jim Teeny Intermediate, which is virtually the same as the normal 3M. Or, at the time of writing, the 3M's Clear Stillwater Intermediate.

That really is about it, save for the quaint lack of available sinking lines below No. 7 from the majority of outlets. If, like me, you wish to adopt a light-line stratagem, then seek out an Orvis or Hardy supplier. Both will have sinkers in low AFTMs which are curiously similar in texture and sink rate to the Wet Cel. I wonder why!

Nylon

Because of all the ballyhoo regarding standard monofilament as opposed to the new-wave pre-stretched co-polymers, I thought I would wade in with a few thoughts. First things first: make absolutely certain that any spool of nylon you purchase is as fresh as a daisy, regardless of type or style. To this end I would always purchase from a large, busy shop and select well-known brands simply because the turnover in volume terms is so high that fresh stock is always coming through. Fresh nylon has a true breaking strain generally speaking, and given that its shelf life, especially in some shops where it is assaulted by ultra-violet light almost constantly, is drastically short, it is a risk I am not prepared to take.

On this front there have been, in recent times, spools of nylon packaged in sealed foil or air-tight bags. This, though adding to the price, is a splendid idea. Anyway, what price a lost fish through poor knot and below par b.s.? Quite honestly I have now reached a stage whereby I don't care who the manufacturer is; the only criterion is freshness.

I have a fondness for the reduced-diameter types of pre-stretched co-polymers; tactically they suit my style of fishing. I believe implicitly that the lowered diameter allows a fly to act more naturally and cut through the water far better. I also have the comforting thought of using 8lb breaking strain, yet in a diameter equal to standard mono in the 4lb region – extra power to your elbow. And yet I know many who would not be persuaded away from the standard mono, Drennan Sub Surface Green getting the greatest share of the vote primarily because of its high knot strength and matt finish. The only other contender seems to be Maxima Green, which has been toned down in sheen

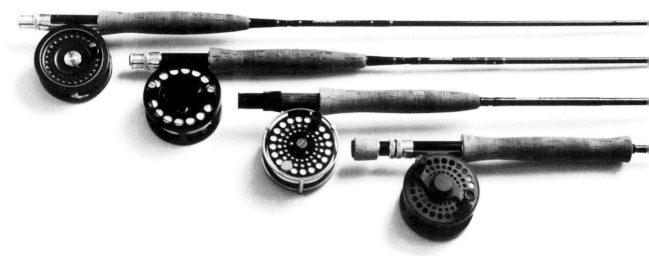

2 Rods and reels – the tools of the trade (from top)
a *the light approach: 9ft Sage s.p. IV No. 4 with matching double taper line (No. 4) and Sage lightweight reel*
b *the all-rounder: 9ft Sage s.p. IV No. 6, Lee Wulff Triangle Taper, No. 6 to 7 line and Loop 1.5 reel*
c *the long-range nymph: 9ft 6in GFL III rod, Ari Hart Orbigo Reel, and D.T.6 and W.F.7 lines*
d *the heavy-duty number: 9ft s.p. IV No. 7, Laurence Waldron anti-reverse reel and No. 7 lines*

since its inception – which it had to be if people wanted to catch trout.

This leads me to the co-polys. The inherent faults lie in both shine and unstable knotting characteristics. Certainly I seek the less reflective types – Drennan Double Strength and recently Orvis Superstrong have reduced their respective surface sheens markedly. Even so a good 'mudding' with Sinkmix is not a bad idea if encouraging shy fish during trying circumstances such as bright days, flat calms or surface-feeding preoccupation.

As regards knots, keep everything minimal. For a junction between two lengths of nylon – a two-, or three-turn at most, water knot is ideal

– and for the hook attachment I would strongly recommend a knot shown to me by Richard Banbury of Orvis. This is a double-threaded grinner knot; in other words, pass the nylon through the eye of the hook twice instead of the usual once, then fashion a standard grinner. Since using this knot I have never had a moment's problem.

The other thing I would urge that you do when using the co-polys is be prepared to change tippets frequently. If the length shows *any* sign of wear or kinking, replace it straight away.

There is, in fact, a nylon that nestles between reduced-diameter, pre-stretched co-polys and standard mono – Orvis Big Game ST (super tough). For holding a dropper and general use, especially if larger than average fish are to be expected, then it really is ideal, and in a short space of time has become a firm favourite with a proven track record. Another of its virtues is it is far less shiny than the other co-polys, again strengthening its case. The knots I use for this nylon are the same as for the previous brands.

For standard mono I tend to be more traditional. For junctions, I opt for double grinner or three-turn water knots, for tethering the fly a four-turn tucked blood knot. These over the years have proved most reliable.

In closing, I can only reiterate the need for fresh nylon. I remember once fishing the River Tay in Scotland during March; the hope of a fresh-run springer – the ultimate angling prize – was looming large in the adrenalin-charged mind. I happened across another member of our little party, sitting head in hands in a state of utter dejection on the rocks. I enquired what was the problem, he muttered an obscenity, then related the tale of the lost fish. As you do, I enquired 'how?'. It transpired that the last spool of nylon he was using for leaders was brought ten years previously and had lain in a semi-moribund state in the bottom of his bag ever since. How odd that it broke. Each year dozens of fish are lost because of old, tired nylon. How unfair to the fish that it has to trail this potential 'time bomb' around with it.

Breakages are unavoidable but can be reduced to a sensible level. At the end of each season I throw away *all* nylon spools and buy fresh. You will land more fish as a result.

And finally, whatever you do, do not leave lengths of nylon at the bankside. Cut it up into $\frac{1}{4}$- to $\frac{1}{2}$-inch lengths or, better still, take it home with you. It distresses me beyond belief the amount of nylon I see left on banksides and especially in the car parks of small waters. These people are threatening the sport I cherish – one more dead bird and one more irate conservationist may well be all it takes. Please, I implore you, destroy and dispose of nylon sensibly and carefully.

Reels

The next logical step is a reel to put the things on. All my predecessors have said it, and others no doubt will continue to do so – a fly reel is the least important item of equipment. This may be so, up to a point, for them perhaps – not me.

Having mentioned that I grew up in the cane age, I should also add that we invariably played our fish 'on the reel', rather than 'off', and by hand. The reason was simple – we didn't like losing trout. It wasn't some romantic notion of hearing the singing of the clutch, but a frantic attempt to stop the line catching on every damned thistle, twig, reed and bank-bound obstruction known to mankind! It is an aspect of the sport from which I find I cannot shake the mantles.

This, of course, means putting all your trust in the reel's smooth running and abilities to assist you playing the fish. It is a faith that will never waver as long as regular maintenance (as with lines) is carried out: oiling, greasing and washing any grit, sand or other debris from the spool.

RECOMMENDED REELS

The reliance on the reel's engineering capabilities does limit choice a little. These choices are:

- The smaller System 2s by Leeda

- The new Hardy JLH fly reels, though spool arrangement could lead to line pinch

- The Gold Sovereign – again Hardy

- The American, though Japanese-made, Maryatt

- Any by Ari Hart or Lawrence Waldron – both bespoke reel manufacturers

- Abel

- The Swedish-made Loop in either size 1.5 or 2.0, a current personal favourite

The last four are ludicrously expensive. However, Loop have just brought out – as I write – the carbon composite version of the 2.0, bringing it within range of just about every pocket, though I have yet to try them on truly large fish.

Others in the frame are Orvis CFOs and Battenkills, but that's about it and, of course, a fly reel is only as good as the maintenance you are prepared to lavish upon it.

You will find that far fewer fish are lost if you can play fish, especially the bigger ones, from the reel. There is less jerkiness and risk of human error. Though, of course, this is simply not possible in every situation, it is nevertheless a habit worth cultivating if you possibly can.

Leaders

As these will crop up throughout the relevant chapters dealing with specific tactics, I will merely outline the systems that have served me well down the years and treat them with a generalised broad-sweeping brush.

The further you can place a fly from the bulk of a fly line, the greater the likelihood of deceiving the quarry. This theory is now, thankfully, universally accepted. So often people forget that anything floating over the surface will cast a shadow underneath, and fly lines, sadly, are not exempted. So often I have seen trout 'spooked' on both chalkstream and small clear water, because a magnified shadow is cast downward across a wide area. Thus, the thinner the diameter, the less the shadow factor and the more unobtrusive your system becomes.

There are, however, times when tactics demand a short leader – a gusting headwind, pinpoint accuracy, especially with a weighted fly – and all these suggest a 9ft to 12ft maximum

leader (including butt). Nonetheless, generally something between 12ft and 15ft would be considered a good working average, with occasionally above this length being necessary for deepwater nymph fishing or very shy trout and/or extremely bright conditions. They are, though, difficult to cast and need practice.

Given the plethora of types, you would be fully justified in being confused, especially in the face of so much contradictory evidence. I can only speak very personally.

For more years than I care to remember, I have used tapered nylon leaders. Initially these were Platil in the 60s and 70s; latterly I use the Orvis Superstrong variety in various lengths, either 9ft to 12ft, or 15ft depending on tactics

● *Leaders*

a   a permanent butt section needle-knotted to fly line

b   pre-tapered (loop-to-loop to above a join with a double grinner)

c   the now popular braided butt section

d   Moser butterfly indicator section looped into the leader

e   roll-on bite indicator (for nymph fishing)

f   weighted braided leader (attach tippet to loop for desired length)

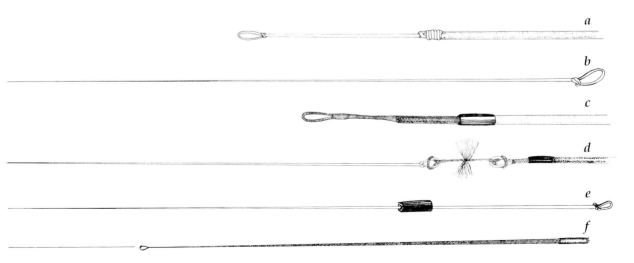

and conditions. I have seen absolutely no good reason to change. They offer turnover and efficiency (if you renew the tippet); are adaptable, floating or sinking at will or on treatment; and, importantly, are reliable and have seldom let me down. If they do, it is generally my own fault for not tying the knots properly.

Their advantages over straight nylon sections and many braids is their turnover qualities; the solid nature adds a little weight when casting into the wind. The smooth transference of energy via line speed passes continuously down to the fly in a more direct manner and, given the build up to various higher breaking strains does, I feel, offer greater overall breaking strength.

There are times, however, when the surreptitious use of a braided leader can alter your chances dramatically – especially if it is weighted. I favour Roman Moser's Copper Twist, Nymph No. 2 Diver and the Airflo *lightweight* Fast or Extra Fast Sink Braid. All three enable small, lightweight flies to descend rapidly and fish depths which ordinarily would be out of the question. Also they allow for a Damsel or similarly mobile pattern to be fished on an even underwater plane. Certainly, on occasion they have meant the difference between fish and no fish and, for that reason, are well worth carrying.

I urge you to have a longish tippet from the braid, which is at best fairly bulky and obvious. As a minimum I would attach 18 inches, possibly up to 3ft or 4ft when 'pulling' rather than 'targetting' styles are required.

As a guide line to sinking capacities (that is, an approximation based on using an intermediate line):

Moser Diver 2 fishes depths from just subsurface to 3ft;

Airflo Fast Sink 3ft to 8ft;

Extra Fast Sink 4ft to 8ft.

In summary of this system, I should warn you about using too fine a tippet with braid; the junction is just too abrupt. Always err to the heavier nylon of your choice; breaking strain, for instance, of 4lb and upwards and *not* lower, as these could lead to lost fish.

Accessories

Similarly to leaders, my intention is to introduce the relevant bits of accessories where appropriate. However, a brief survey of what is available and necessary is not a bad idea.

First, I would urge some degree of restraint. This is difficult, I know. All fishing-tackle shops are like magnets and few of us can resist the piscatorial trinkets waiting to tempt us there. Indeed small items of tackle can almost assume the guise of Chinese worry beads! Yet we can live without most of this paraphernalia. There are essentials and they can draw the critically fine line between success and failure. Right from the start, view everything with an eye to transportation; bags for the most part are an encumbrance and anathema to the bank-bound smallwater fisher. If it can't be housed in a waistcoat ask yourself 'do I *really* need this item?'. Generally the answer will be 'no'.

Occasionally, of course, a long day in the field will necessitate food and drink, and sheer distance makes return trips to cars and/or lodges tiresome and foolish. A bag will be the ideal vehicle to transport lunch and liquid. In a boat, again a bag is near essential. But do please think before dragging around a great canvas bulk that will tend to hamper a nomadic and comfortable style of fishing.

In your waistcoat you should consider the following as essential travelling companions.

Snippers The nail-cutting style of blank-nosed scissors (never pointed as these can inflict a nasty wound if fallen on or caught in clothing). I use the Tiemco black metal snippers; they are quick, efficient and non-reflective so as not to spook trout in bright light. (This is possibly overstating the case but as an old river fisher I am wary of any reflective metal.)

The cutting edge, of whatever design, should be housed on a lanyard, better still, a zinger – a retractable spring-loaded device – for convenience and ease of operation.

Forceps The surgical fine-nosed type are absolutely wonderful. Often I have forgotten these and have found myself very handicapped and earnestly seeking out someone who had the good sense to bring theirs with them. Nowadays, these too I have attached to a zinger, thus preventing my absent-mindedness and its troublesome influence. Like the snippers, I seek out the matt black type available from Orvis outlets. If these are not available, try housing them in a pocket or purpose-designed slip case on the waistcoat; this will also cut down flash.

Priest This is essential. I have seen some neanderthal goings-on by some fishers using rocks, wood and other make-shift contraptions. Your quarry should be afforded respect, especially in its demise. Give it this dignity and use a proper implement; and make absolutely certain it is heavy enough. One blow should be sufficient, even for a double-figure fish – if it's not, get a heavier priest.

It occurs to me, writing about dispatching the quarry, some people are unsure where to aim the priest. Direct the blow immediately between the eyes along the top where the brain is situated, and *not*, as some imagine, the juncture between head and back in line with the gill cover.

Marrow scoop This can be fun to carry and occasionally essential to continued success. It remains, though, a great truism that first you have to catch a fish in order to use the implement – and if you caught the fish do you need the assistance of further information? Sometimes, yes, trout, especially grown-on gravel-pit or larger-water (10 acres upwards) specimens rely on almost exclusively living organisms. Matching these and knowing their ways is essential to fly choice, depth assessment and geographic location of the quarry. A scoop can tell you almost all this, or at least give vital clues.

My personal marrow scoop has been made from a syringe body to which I have attached a length of winemaker's flexible clear tubing. This plunger/suction method – rather than the insert-and-rotate method – is not only kinder to fish but can, if done very carefully, allow fish to be released back into the water, where practised and allowed.

Floatant Again an essential. I carry two types: a fly floatant such as Gink or Fly Flote, and Mucilin or Permagrease for lines and leaders. The fly floatant is secured to the waistcoat again by a zinger – sure it makes me look like a Christmas tree but it does make for quick, easy accessibility when anointing a fly, even on the verge of night.

The line and leader floatant is housed in the waistcoat but separately from the leader sinkant, which I either attach by zinger or in a small accessible pocket. To place the two together is inviting opposites both of which will influence proceedings when you least want it.

For the sink mix I use either Orvis Mud, Dick Walker's fuller's earth mix or Cul de Canard U-45, which is arguably the best available at present.

Hook hone This is a carborundum tool for edging points, is of occasional use and falls into the essential non-essentials. The new-wave ultra-sharp etched hooks are notoriously difficult to re-point and perhaps best thrown away rather than carefully manicured. But for favourite flies and forged hooks (hand-made), a hook pointer such as the E-Z-Lap Diamond is a handy gadget.

Tippet dispenser Having, on umpteen occasions buried my hand in my waistcoat pocket and come up with a spirogyra of nylon, a tippet dispenser is a very good idea. The easiest operated and most unfussy is the LA Calvin or wallet-type from J. W. Outfitters (Lathkill tackle) from America, which dispenses nylon neatly with ease and reliability. It also allows you to choose the type of nylon spool you prefer.

3 *Stuart Cross models the alternative carrying sling to the usual Gye net – the ideal capacity and set-up when hunting big trout*

4 *The Gye net and sling popularized by Peter Cockwill. A perfect arrangement when searching for 20-pounders – and of course, lesser sizes*

Nylon lubricant A new product, as I write, has become available called Knot-Perfect, which in essence is a nylon lubricant. Initially I was very dubious, regarding good old-fashioned spittle as all you truly require when tightening a knot. I have to say that Knot-Perfect by George Gehrke is actually better and beds knots down far more securely – even the co-poly nylons like double strength which ordinarily *should* be pulled dry. Again a good investment.

Fish bass (stringer) This is generally a good idea, and Peter Cockwill's handled variety is excellent. Choose from a burgeoning population of either woven nylon, hessian with insert, or good old Egyptian reed types. Wychwood, the Oxfordshire-based company, have just brought

out ('93 season) a purpose-designed one with shoulder strap which embodies all their customary ingenuity and excellent design combined with a lifetime's workmanship. This looks set to be a real boon, especially for mobile fly fishers. Don't use plastic or bags; these less than aesthetic items can, on a hot day, literally 'cook' your trout. The deterioration level is appallingly fast.

Small torch You might, especially if an avid evening fisher, consider a small torch. Groping around in the half light for lost tackle is no fun and can lead to expensive losses. A pen torch or even the goose-neck variety specific to fly fishing will both provide a sufficient light source for getting around and finding things, and a

5   *My favourite style of landing net transportation. Carried on a simple clip or more speedily disconnected Velcro fastener*

certain peace of mind – and all for very little space or additional weight.

Fly box   The design is entirely personal: some prefer suitcase-sized hinged-lid affairs; others the orderly Fox Box retainer system and a host of permutations thereafter. There is a design to meet every taste, fad or fancy.

My 'vest' holds two varieties, an ethafoam swinged-leaf (four surfaces) Wheatley which holds various nymphs: one side reserved for leaded, the other unleaded, and a De Wit plastic compartmentalized style for dry flies. The De Wit box is American and can be obtained fairly easily by mail order from Kaufman's in Oregon.

I also use a De Wit for carrying various Tadpoles, Woolly Buggers and Growlers –

pretty they are not, but effective they most certainly are.

Polarized glasses   Now to an item which on the face of it would appear never to catch you fish in the real sense but, if left behind, may well render you blank in a variety of circumstances. Not only are polarized glasses a boon tactically but, from a safety aspect, an essential – a wayward fly veering off course, even a fraction of an inch, can inflict terrible damage if eyes are not protected. No matter how good we think we are at casting we all make mistakes occasionally, and we should make certain they are not injurious. A pair of glasses will give you that all-important peace of mind. I carry, perhaps curiously, two types – a pair of ridiculously expensive Serengeti brown-lensed types for general fishing and a pair of yellow-tinted Optix HLT 3 (high light transmission) for stalking and general low-light fishing. Orvis offer an extremely good and reliable alternative, and the yellow-lens type afford excellent underwater visision, even on dull days, as do Polyspecs. Choose wisely, as a poor pair could damage your eyes. Conversely, not wearing any at all may prove more calamitous.

Nets

Each year a great number of fish are lost through one very avoidable cause – too small a net. After all the words and discussion, still fly fishers overlook, or worse still shun, the obvious benefits of a capacious net. I would go so far as to say that a trout lost through too small a net aperture is an act of cruel folly – especially as on many occasions it will be towing a fly and length of line in its wake due to breakage. Even if this doesn't happen you will have missed a golden opportunity and conceivably a fish of the season or indeed your lifetime.

The choice is of course entirely personal, some preferring the fixed-handle type – for years I have toted the Hardy Super Light net about and seldom regretted its reach or capacity, its only fault is in being somewhat cumbersome when stalking and constantly on the move. Others prefer the 'Gye' style – Peter Cockwill, big fish hunter supreme among them. However, having been totally baffled by the carrying sling system on more than one occasion, my personal choice is now a simple clip attachment on a sea trout-sized telescopic, round-headed net made by Sharpes. This net I prize above all others. It is light to carry; has a good reach; enables trout (and sea trout and salmon) to be landed from any angle and, finally, is sufficiently robust to dig fish out of weeds and other underwater obstacles. You may well have another favourite but please ensure it will incarcerate a very angry 10 or 12lb fish relatively easily.

Clothing

These items will be introduced at the appropriate time of the season, but the general business of waistcoats and rain gear can be touched on here. As far as waistcoats, or vests, are concerned, the perfect one for me has yet to be designed. All seem to have a shortcoming or two and, in general, are actually uncomfortable to wear when fully laden. I am at present scouring America for different designs. With luck I shall find my ideal vest, or at least amalgamate those intrinsic good points of a clutch of them and produce my own – pocket design, position and comfortable fit, especially across the shoulders, should be central. Designs which best fulfil these criteria are Orvis, Touchstone/Piscatoria and Bob Church, among others.

Regarding waterproof clothing, things are rather better and only restricted by outlay. There is simply no excuse for being cold and wet given the choice available. Goretex, Cyclone, Ventile and so on have ousted wax from its top position. The drawbacks with waxed cotton are its steel-like grip on movement in cold weather and lack of ventilation in hot. Thereafter your choice can only be guided by price.

Hats, I suppose, nestle into clothing, and certainly they must be viewed as an integral piece of tactical tackle. A brim is vital to reduce glare and aid vision. It actually doesn't matter whether it is attached to flats bonefish cap (which I prefer) or trilby-style safari, or baseball cap design. But whatever you do make sure it will cut out overhead glare and enhance vision and keep eye strain at a manageable level.

6 The stalker's set-up. Keith Bryant in readiness to intercept patrolling or targeted fish. Everything is in its place to make 'snap' or quick casting utterly efficient

CHAPTER TWO

Approaches to Trout Fishing

Dry fly fishing

THE idea for this chapter is to strip away any mysteries concerning tackle and tactics for small or large stillwaters. In the context of this book, it should be seen purely as one of guidance. Each year many people venture from the small to fish the larger reservoirs and are utterly confounded. There is some advice here for such folk, or indeed anyone wanting a simplistic introduction to various approaches.

Dry fly tackle

Starting with the rod, this ideally should be between 9ft and 10ft, taking a No. 5, 6 or 7 line – the general factotum of the stillwater world! Arguably the most appropriate would be $9\frac{1}{2}$ft for a No. 5 or 6, though any system is workable so long as it is not overly heavy (No. 8 to 10) or light (No. 3 to 4). The best action is middle to tip.

For the beginner the 'no-nonsense' single-fly approach is the one to adopt. This will, in turn, allow full attention to be paid to tactics and presentation, which are the key elements in this sphere of fly fishing.

A workable leader should be between 12ft and 16ft long; if too long then problems with 'turnover' may be experienced, and this is one area where accuracy and clean turnover are the routes to success. However it is inadvisable to drop below 12ft, especially if operating with line at the heavier end of the spectrum, as the close proximity of the thick line and the wide shadow it may cast downward (which we tend to forget) can spook wary trout, especially in clear water and bright light.

The accessories are, once again, few – but important. You will need a reliable floatant such as Gink or Orvis Hyflote; Permaflote is also extremely effective, though not as instant. It can, however, be an asset prior to fishing. By dunking the flies in the liquid and allowing them to dry (for approximately 24 hours or overnight) they will then float like proverbial corks and only require reanointing when completely saturated.

Leader sinkant – be it fuller's earth or a proprietary brand – is a must for degreasing the last few feet of leader close to the fly or flies.

Before leaving tackle preparation, it is worth remembering that a means of drying off a damp fly or cleaning it after a hooked fish has re-modelled it into a soggy mass is not a bad idea. Masterline Dry Fly Powder and Orvis Dry N'Float are among the best; though quite the best, but difficult to obtain is the treated, flattened fungus amadou available on the Continent, and a chamois leather can be handy also, especially if using CDC patterns.

Mucilin, Permagrease or Masterfloat will all ensure the high-floating properties of fly line tips and leader butts and a swift strike, so often crucial in this type of fishing.

Fly choice

People have been eager to perpetuate the myth that in order to be a successful dry fly fisher it

FLY CHOICE	
● Bright conditions	
big wave	Orange and Black Hoppers, Orange Emerger/CDC all size 10
medium wave ripple	As for big wave Hare's Face Midge, Orange and Black Hopper size 12, Orange Emerger (Pearl) sizes 12 and 14 (Bob's Bits)
flat calm	Sparkle Gnat, Orange Emerger (Pearl) sizes 14 to 20, CDC Midge sizes 14 to 16, Bob's Bits sizes 12 to 14
● Overcast conditions	
big wave	Claret, Red, Green Hoppers size 10, Elk Hair Caddis size 10 or 12
medium wave	As for big wave plus Haystacks size 10 or 11
ripple	Hare's Face Midge sizes 12 to 14, J C Pearl Raider (claret and red) size 12
flat calm	Sparkle Gnat sizes 16 to 18, High Para Hare CDC Midge size 12, Hare's Face Midge sizes 12 to 14, J C Pearl Raider (claret and red)

is essential to know a great deal about entomology. This is not so. Stillwater trout, though selective on occasion, are remarkably opportunistic feeders, accepting a vast array of different-coloured and shaped floating food forms. Colour and size have generally a far greater bearing on fly selection, as do the conditions on the day, with light intensity, wave ac-

D.T. line (floating)

forceps

7　*The dry fly weaponry*

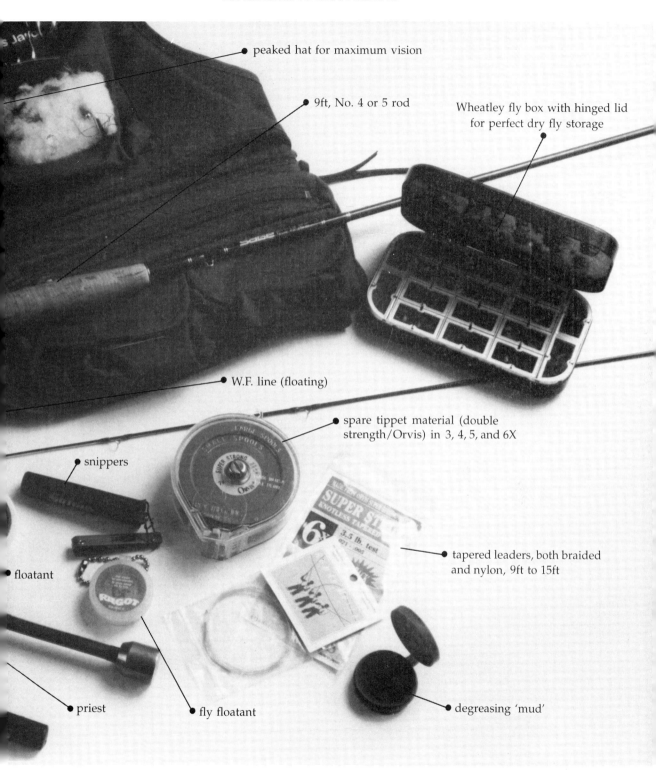

peaked hat for maximum vision

9ft, No. 4 or 5 rod

Wheatley fly box with hinged lid
for perfect dry fly storage

W.F. line (floating)

spare tippet material (double
strength/Orvis) in 3, 4, 5, and 6X

snippers

floatant

tapered leaders, both braided
and nylon, 9ft to 15ft

priest

fly floatant

degreasing 'mud'

tion and size often dictating the correct pattern.

There are, of course, exceptions – large hatches of midge (chironomid), caenis, a 'fall' of hawthorn flies (or heather flies in the north), ants, and large hatches of olives and caddis may all require specialized patterns. But for most of the time a general approach can be fashioned, based on the day and conditions.

If you analyse the list on p. 24, there are actually few patterns you could add. A Wickham's Fancy, Daddy Longlegs and the odd local favourite, one of the 'little black numbers' such as small Black Gnat are all that are really required to cover a host of seasonal situations.

Tactics

As with the dry fly on rivers, what is more important is how they are fished. The lovely thing about fishing the dry fly is that trout tend to give themselves away by rising; all we have to do is to make sure that the next fly they see is our own. This, of course, demands that we take trouble to analyse the rise forms and deduce in which direction that trout is moving in order to plot some form of route and path for our fly. In anything like a reasonable breeze and ruffled surface it is logical to suppose that the trout will head into it, though it is not unusual for the fish to go back downwind or even across it, which can lead to problems. In calmer conditions the route which a trout operates can be infuriatingly haphazard and only close observation of the quarry will offer clues to the correct cast direction. There is also another consideration: the speed at which the trout travels between rise forms can vary dramatically. By and large though, if there is an accumulation of food forms on the water, the progress will be slower than if there are only a few widespread delicacies.

Fishing the rise requires a degree of casting ability with both accuracy and delicacy – key components to a successful outcome. The placing of an artificial where you expect the next rise to be is vital.

However, if you cannot see rising trout or subsurface movement, a dry fly can still be viable, but obviously conditions have to be conducive. A raging heatwave and azure skies are not ideal; conversely, near-zero semi-arctic conditions are not promising either. Oddly enough rain can put a dampener on sport (excuse the pun) – whether the raindrops confuse the trout's image of the surface or depress activity, it has a contrary effect on our floating-fly aspirations.

If you are fishing the dry fly with no obvious movement on the surface, then it is a good idea to select a two-fly leader: an attractor to raise the fish to the fly, such as a Daddy or Bright Orange Emerger (both often get takes) on the point, whilst about 3 ft above on a dropper, a smaller more sombre pattern, such as a Hare's Face Midge. The trout is attracted to the large halo of light distributed by the contours of the larger pattern, and is drawn up through the layers, either taking with a momentous splash rise or turning away and in so doing taking the smaller, drabber pattern.

This approach can realistically be used throughout the whole lake in sedentary manner but, for best results, the style does rely on a nomadic way of fishing with the angler being prepared to walk the shoreline making casts in every likely area or known hotspot, be it a bay, in shallows, along weedbeds, indeed anywhere that just feels right.

The biggest problem when fishing blind in this manner is that trout have a nasty habit of rising when you are least expecting it. So it pays to try and keep concentration at optimum level for as long as possible and, as with nymph fishing, having frequent breaks to stave off eye strain and fatigue.

Stealth, of course, has its role to play. So often fish are frightened from their natural hunting grounds – the food-rich shallows – because of heavy-footed anglers! With dry fly, the nearer we can fish from our position, the more 'hook-ups' we get. This may, on occasion, require you to kneel – even casting across land into the margins. If there is natural cover, use it! Many a trout has been encouraged to rise closer and been deceived by an angler obscured by reeds or bankside vegetation. Oddly, even wading can help, if undertaken carefully, by lowering the fly fisher's appearance out of the trout's cone of vision.

Another attendant (though river-perceived) problem is drag, which can be equally ruinous to stillwater presentation. Try whenever possible not to let your fly drag roundwind, aided by large bows in the line. Either re-cast, mend or walk carefully down the bank, maintaining a straight line as you go. It should be said, however, that often a fish can be enticed into rising by twitching a dry fly along the surface area to create an erratic wake. This goads a trout, especially when done immediately in front of a rise form. Look out, though, for the same savage takes.

This leads me into the timing of the strike, which can only be achieved realistically with experience and practice. Oddly, trout will vary from day to day. Sometimes they will sink a fly then engulf it subsurface, which naturally demands a reasonably lengthy wait; on other occasions they gulp the fly straight down. If a trout is feeding directly in front of you and coming towards you, wait until it gets its head down, otherwise you risk pulling the fly out of its mouth. As a rule of thumb, as soon as you see a trout movement or straightforward rise near to the fly, or the fly's position if you cannot see it, lift the rod tip. Mostly, you will feel a satisfying 'thump' of hooked fish; even if you miss, you can re-cast and get another 'bite of the cherry'.

Another important factor is nylon strength in relation to fly choice. With small patterns, choose as fine as you dare, even 3 to 4lb b.s. double strength. On the bigger patterns you can, however, go as high as 5lb Sub Surface or equivalent mono in order to 'turn over' bulky flies such as Daddies. But remember, the fly should always move with the surface, which in turn calls for as low a diameter as you can get away with, given the size and presentation requirements of this particular pattern. Also the fishery rules should be strictly adhered to!

Points to remember

● Keep things simple – a single fly, sometimes two, fished as delicately as possible, accurately.

● You don't necessarily need rise forms to fish dry flies, but if fish are observed, deduce which way they are going and at what speed, aiming your fly a little ahead of them wherever possible.

● In rough conditions, use a larger dry fly; in bright calms, fish as small and fine as you dare.

● Keep out of sight and tread carefully, fishing constantly on the move.

● If you see any surface movement near your fly's position, lift gently; it may have been your pattern that was accepted by the trout.

● If in doubt, throw out a Daddy Longlegs; even if you are having a cup of coffee, you will be amazed how often a trout will come up and take, often in seemingly impossible conditions.

● *Skating dry fly (Elk Hair Caddis)*

Lure fishing

Nowadays admitting to lure fishing is tantamount to treason, carrying a piscatorial penalty and ostracization to fly fishing wasteland; yet it remains probably the best opportunity for a newcomer to secure their prize. And let's be honest, most of us at some time or another, have surreptitiously slipped on a face-saving attractor. Yet fishing an attractor can be as satisfying and subtle as any other form of fly fishing; indeed, we shouldn't let dogma and purist principles persuade us otherwise.

The key lies in adaptability and a willingness to vary style, technique, depths and retrieves. It also pays to be reasonably systematic. Of course, a random approach often works, but if you are prepared to exercise some degree of system that will not only cover depth and holding spots efficiently, but also do so perming your fly style and colour options.

Tackle

Most rods between the $9\frac{1}{2}$ and 10ft, No. 6 to 8 with a bias towards No. 7 to 8, are ideal in a variety of situations, though perhaps precluding the ultra-deep lead-core styles. There will be a degree of adaptability also with nymph and, to some extent, dry fly – a rod for all seasons (and styles).

With regard to reels, the wide-spool variety are most useful in eliminating tight line coils. The other criterion is spool cost. The one important feature of lure fishing is the positioning of your pattern, because so much depends on retrieve speeds – some fast, some slow, some even hand-over-hand continuous. You need a fly line that will position your fly exactly where you want it. This not only calls for a variety of lines, but spools on which to hold them which are properly designed, easy to put on and take off, and cheap to buy. Without question, the one reel that fits these criteria is the Leeda LC Series, of which the choice for lure fishing would be the 100 size or the hoop carbon model, a lineshooter by Bob Church.

polarized glasses

8 The lure fisher's armoury

28

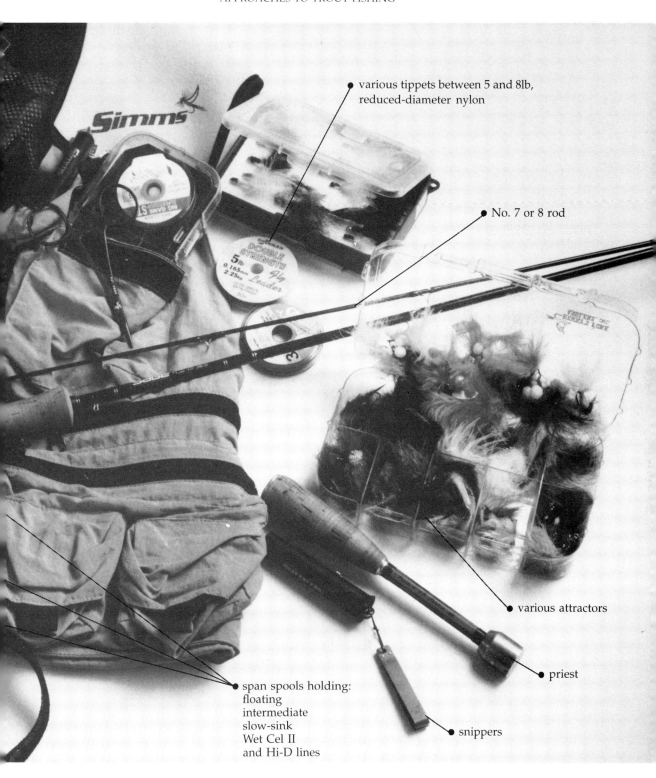

various tippets between 5 and 8lb,
reduced-diameter nylon

No. 7 or 8 rod

various attractors

priest

span spools holding:
floating
intermediate
slow-sink
Wet Cel II
and Hi-D lines

snippers

And so to lines. The most useful profile is a weight forward for the newcomer; the shooting head being more suited to the experienced caster. Certainly the weight forward's handling is very much easier, even at the loss of some distance, but you will need to carry a few line types to suit and reach the various levels, fly styles and trout's fickleness:

Floating line This is for surface fishing, especially with wake-making patterns such as Muddlers, but also Fry.

Intermediate or neutral Used for fishing just subsurface, particularly for trout feeding on daphnia (in dull, overcast weather), damsels and various other high-level situations. A sink-tip can also have a role, especially in Fry fishing.

Slow sink This is optional as there is not a great deal of difference from the intermediate. This may be seen as a luxury, and crossover styles exist, though for slow retrieves where trout are feeding between 5ft and 8ft down, there can be few better lines.

Medium sink This is an essential line for the lure fisher, and arguably the most suited to a variety of situations. Retrieved quickly on touchdown, it will fish near to the surface; after 10-second countdown, 4ft to 5ft down and so on. It is also extremely useful for midwater feeders, 10ft to 15ft, where trout so often feed throughout July when 'harvesting' daphnia and essential for winter fishing.

Fast sink and high-density types These, though important, are less so than you might imagine. They come truly into their own when utilizing buoyant flies and ultra-slow retrieves (Booby fishing), though from a boat they are vital to cold- and hot-water techniques such as 'strip and hang'.

Having touched on floating lines, I must confess the times of usefulness to the attractor and lure fly fisher of 'dry' line are very much less than his nymph-orientated comrade. Far more useful are the various intermediate and neutral-buoyancy lines which can fulfil a great variety of roles from

marginally subsurface up to mid-water (10ft to 15ft). Thereafter, a Wet Cel II or medium sink is a consideration, and especially useful for reservoir fishing in brightish conditions where fish are feeding on daphnia, and general early season use when fishing ledges or fairly steep banks, gradients, drop-offs and plateaux. It is also a handy line on small stillwaters when a lower depth or a continuous retrieve is required.

These days, Booby fishing – fishing a buoyant fly just off the lake floor – is a standard method in extremes of temperature (very cold water or escalating heat) or, indeed, during any period when trout 'plant' themselves in deep water and stoically refuse to budge. This type of fishing does specifically call for fast-sinking lines, with Hi-D being the favoured choice. I am uncertain whether this type of fishing and line is universally useful, but sense and fishing records would dictate that this fourth type of line is almost indispensable in many instances and on many waters.

This may seem a prodigious amount of expense and overkill, yet the fact remains that a change of line type can often mean the difference between a blank or limit – they are *that* important.

Leaders are, of course, important, but not as vital as in nymph fishing. However, you should keep things simple, even to the extent of using nylon lengths straight through – in other words, 12ft to 14ft of continuous nylon of say 6lb b.s. As in other forms of fly fishing, good turnover will be best served by a knotless tapered leader, but they are not essential in this type of fishing, even braided sinking leader (Airflo lightweight system) proving tactically interesting.

A word of warning though, if using a long braid loop from the fly line tip – this will arrest the sinking rate and cause the leader to hold up in the water level whilst the belly sinks. If you don't want this to happen, either use the above sinking leader or a nylon butt which cuts through the surface rather more cleanly.

As an approximate idea as to breaking strain

of leader equating to lure size, you can see 5lb b.s. Drennan Sub Surface or 8lb Orvis Super Strong as basically standard for a variety of patterns, especially those between 10 l.s.–14 and std 8–14, with 8lb for size 6–8 l.s. and for ultra-large tandems and heavyweight 10lb when allowed. This is not because of trout size, but purely turnover of fly and the constant hingeing of the pattern as it travels through the air, perhaps weakening this vital link.

There are other requirements, though not essential, that should be considered. These include a line tray if bank fishing (or long-handled net) and a stopwatch. By timing the line's descent and retrieving after say thirty seconds, then forty and so on, then possibly repeating the procedure with a different colour, a really accurate and thorough search can be made of the immediate vicinity.

Retrieve

A feature of lure fishing has always been its perception by anglers as a monotonous 'cast-out-pull-back, throw-thought-on-the-back-burner' type of retrieve. Nothing could be further from the truth. To fish an attractor in a persuasive manner, a whole gamut of variations is required. Also you should never lose sight of how your movements on the line may be affecting the fly's passage through the water; indeed, the movement of marabou differing greatly from that of hair wings, even the wings alter the movement.

The best way to proceed during a day's fishing with no obvious signs or pointers is to see things rather similarly to accelerating in a car – going up through the gears until peak speed has been attained, then back down again. This can be done with all the following retrieval methods.

9–11 Hand-over-hand continuous retrieve. This retrieve is perfect for damsel-type patterns or indeed any that need steady continuous movement

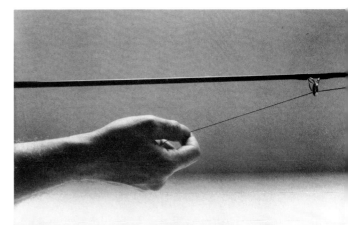

Stage 1 – with the rod handle (keep free of clothing if possible) clasped under the armpit, start the draw on the line with the right hand

Stage 2 – bring the second hand into play once the desired length of line retrieved initially has been reached. Repeat, though now with left hand

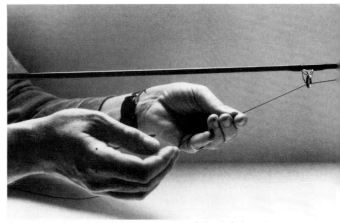

Stage 3 – the end of the sequence of the left hand – merely repeat as necessary at the desired speed

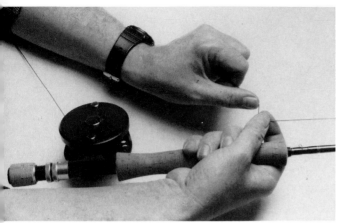

Stage 1 – grasp the fly line with the left hand with the line running *across the thumb*

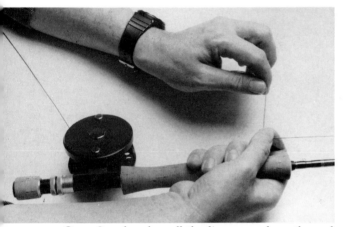

Stage 2 – sharply pull the line away from the rod hand, no more than a few inches

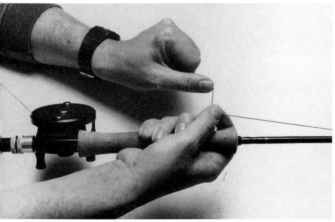

Stage 3 – the effect should be a series of twitchy jerks – sorry, it's the only description possible!

Figure of eight Hand winding, offering either a slow or medium constant movement giving rise to an undulation; extremely useful when using long marabou-tailed patterns such as Tadpoles.

The figure of eight is one of the most overlooked and universally useful retrieval rates to the attractor fisher, and can offer an almost continuous movement of the fly, at varying speeds as required (actually a fast figure of eight can be deadly). By slowing down the winding movement and interspersing it with pauses, it provides the mainstay of Booby fishing.

Pulling The next, and perhaps most variable and widely used retrieve is the pulling method. At its slowest, it can be ponderous and enticing – slow, long draws of the line hand, say 12 inches, interspersed with pauses, activates patterns such as Tadpoles and Poodles and Feather Dusters to a deadly degree. It is especially good for hairwing and featherwing patterns – such as Sweeney Todds and Black Chenille.

Used in shorter (3- to 11-inch), more jerky movements which, in turn, speed the retrieve rate up a notch or two, you then obtain a slightly undulating movement, rather than a flat plane of retrieve. These are often interspersed with a figure of eight, which is good during early season, especially with small marabou patterns and for Tadpoles on a medium sink.

The fast pull – long 12- to 14-inch stroking movements of the line hand – made continually is perhaps the most familiar, yet, for me at least, remains the least effective type of line movement. This could be because it tends to make the movement of the fly continuously erratic rather than variably erratic (which I personally find more successful). This is a small

12–14 Left: Twitch retrieve

15–20 Right: The classic figure of eight retrieve, with the fly line coming straight from the butt ring to the retrieving hand

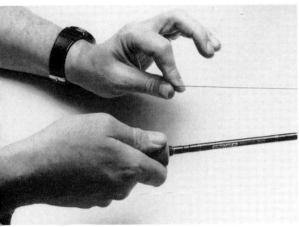

Stage 1

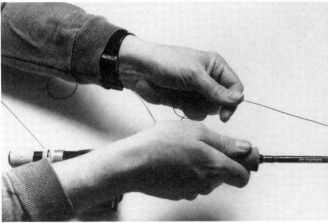

Stage 4 – hold in readiness for the second 'twist'

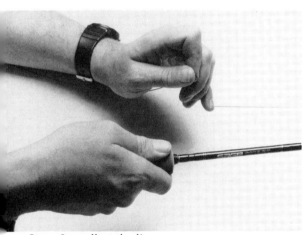

Stage 2 – collect the line

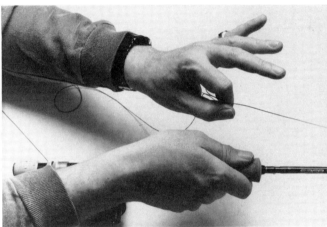

Stage 5 – either keep the line held in the palm or allow it to drop to the ground

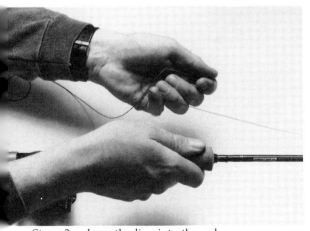

Stage 3 – draw the line into the palm

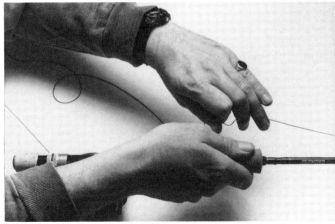

Stage 6 – the beginning of the next hand twist

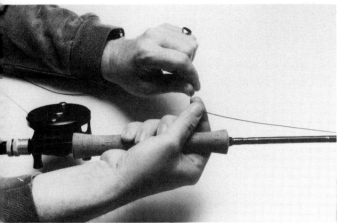

Stage 1

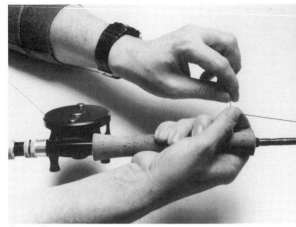

Stage 4

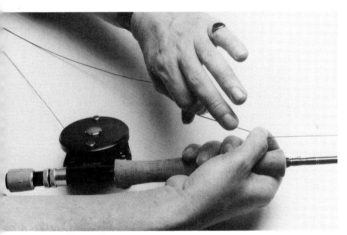

Stage 2

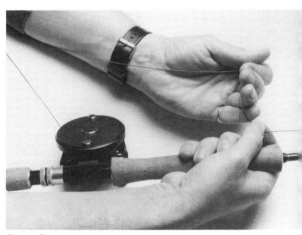

Stage 5

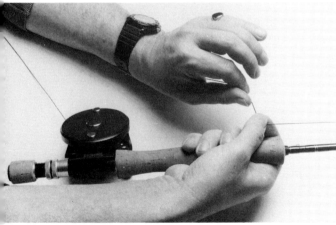

Stage 3

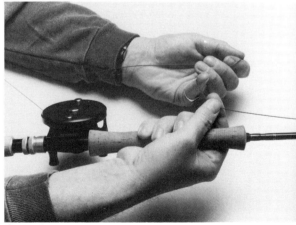

Stage 6

21–27 Closed figure of eight. This is my preferred type of retrieve for nymph fishing and for keeping control of dry flies. Usually only suited to ultra-slow to medium rates of pace

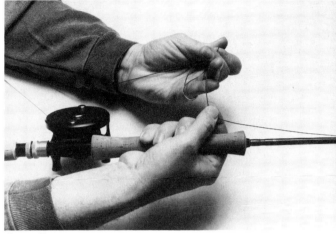

Stage 7 – now repeat

point but nevertheless important, as trout appear to follow then sidle off in a rather disappointed manner.

Having said that, there are times when the stripping fast speed of retrieve is deadly, particularly if you are Muddler or wake fishing with a floater. The 'quick, stop, quick' mode does entice trout to follow and hit, especially after the fly has rested then started up again.

Hand-over-hand Next on the agenda comes the hand-over-hand continuous retrieve. Again this adapts to slow, medium or fast modes depending on situations, conditions and personal preference. This type of retrieve will not tend to win you friends or influence folk about you – it does have the ability to raise the hackles of any nearby purist (sorry for the pun), yet it is effective (and used widely in America for dry Sedge and Stonefly tactics!).

All you do is take the rod under one arm and retrieve with both hands at a speed or mix of speeds required – even variations of 'slow, slow, quick, quick, slow' during a cast being fished out. How do you strike? Well, this confused me as well for some time. Invariably of course, given the constant movement of the pattern, a trout will hook itself, but if a further flourish is needed, then you keep pulling and sweep the body to one side or the other and create an acute angle in the fly rod and resulting striking movement.

The 'FTA' This only leaves the FTA retrieve – its accurate translation should be sought from one Chris Ogborne, but I think only a moment's analysis is actually needed to decipher it. Basically it encompasses all the retrieval methods mentioned, at varying speeds during one retrieve. It does tend to suit marabou-based attractors rather than semi-imitative lures. It is

also a type of retrieve more at home with recently introduced fish, rather than native or grown-on specimens.

For my part, I still prefer to fish my fly fairly slowly. It is habit, yet I remain aware to situations, perhaps even on the same day, when a radical departure to 'Mach 2' will work a great deal better.

Take

Knowing what to look for is half the battle, and you should never form the impression that every take is a full-blooded 'thump' on the rod tip, or a jarring jolt to the senses – often they can be as subtle as with a nymph or as visual as with the dry fly.

Of course, usually fish hook themselves, yet if the line feels just plain heavy or even if the line changes angle between the rod tip and water level, it could be a fish – so lift! When floating-line fishing with fish-imitating lures, you may only see a 'bulge' in the surface or a draw on the line – again, lift.

Before leaving the take, a word about long-plumed marabou-based patterns – indeed, any fly with flowing 'locks'. You may experience a series of 'taps' or 'knocks' as the fly progresses through the water. Keep retrieving, whatever you do; don't stop, or the trout will lose interest and turn away. Wait until you feel that solid thump, which may take a while to happen. With all types of retrieves and sunken line, keep the rod tip at an angle to the retrieved line, so avoiding 'smash' takes, which tend to occur when the rod tip is pointing straight down the line.

Places to fish are as varied as the methods and will be looked at in further depth in Part Three. However, there are few areas that do not respond to this style of fishing, or indeed few conditions.

Which fly?

The eternal question, 'which fly?' will, sooner or later, become a burning issue. Broadly speaking, it is a far better policy to adopt a systematic approach as opposed to collecting a pot-pourri of patterns. By selecting, for instance, a Cat's Whisker – the original being white with a fluorescent lime-green body, then adding a black version, one all white, orange and yellow (perhaps even lime-green) – in sizes l.s. 8 to 10 to 12 and std 8 to 10, you have a system.

You can do the same with Vivas or Tadpoles. There are, however, a couple of standbys which do not equate to this systemization and should be carried. These include Muddler Minnows (the standard being overall the most useful), Boobies in the systemized colours, Appetisers and Zonker Rabbit or Mink, and these should meet most needs and cover most eventualities.

There is another ingredient to the whole equation, covering both tactics and fly choice – confidence! You must have confidence that the system will work, and as long as you are prepared to search the water thoroughly, trying various depths with one colour, then doing the same with another, then you would be extremely unfortunate not to experience success.

The key to effective fishing with lures and attractors is constant experimentation – with lines, speed of retrieve, depth, even angles – changing the rod from one side to another. Far from mindless, it is an absorbing and chal-lenging pursuit of our quarry and, it should also be remembered, imitative in its own way, especially when tackling fry-feeding trout when a close copy of both food forms and movement (or lack of it) is vital to success.

I leave you to form your own opinions of lure fishing as a method. For me, a fly – almost any fly – is a 'lure', and my conscience is clear. Oh, and remember Dick Shrive's wonderful axiom 'keep pulling – they don't know it's feathers'.

Nymph fishing

Given the almost universal success of a lure, especially during the early months of the season, we often forget the all-round deadly aspects of nymph fishing. I would be the first to subscribe to the view that lure fishing can have its artistry and artisans, and be a far cry from the monotonous, laborious and repetitive act that is so often depicted. And yet there is something decidedly more enjoyable about deceiving your quarry on a representation of the natural world, no matter how impressionistic the interpretation may be, and in some cases, facetious.

Tackle

The whole concept begins with the tackle. All too often the method flounders almost as soon as it has begun, purely because of inappropriate equipment. The method's pivotal aspects are delicacy and subtlety, and your tackle choice should echo these factors.

The beauty lies, however, in the lack of equipment actually needed – efficient and successful reservoir nymphing is (or at least should be) a simple uncluttered affair. In most instances, a 9ft, 9½ft to a maximum 10ft loading with a No. 5, 6 or No. 7 line is ideal, with the 9½ft being the most useful; though many nymph fishing addicts use a DT 5 as previously outlined.

Rods The rod should be a medium-taper inclining to an action of the central ferrule to the tip – rather than pure tip or fast action – and definitely not the slower taper with the rod's action being in the butt section. This will only tend to fashion a wide loop and be difficult to handle in a breeze or when trying to cast a long line.

Reels The reel is of entirely personal choice and mostly secondary importance. As long as it encompasses both the line and about 100 yards of 20lb backing, it will do, though it is advisable to have some form of drag system and incline to a rim-control type rather than the enclosed-spool varieties. Whatever you do, keep the system in good working and running order by periodic cleaning, greasing and general maintenance.

Fly lines For the nymph fisher, perhaps the second most important item of equipment – possibly having equal billing with the rod – is the fly line. There is no getting away from the fact that you get what you pay for, and what is required in nymph fishing is total reliability – reliability in casting ease, turnover and taper design, handling quality and, most importantly, buoyancy.

The one saving grace in nymph fishing is that you really only need one line – a floater. You may care to dally with a sink-tip, and an intermediate or slow sinker can be wonderfully effective, especially in adverse weather conditions such as high winds and cold water – or the opposite of flat calms and searing heat with rising water temperature. However, the most universally useful is the floater and, indeed, the most adaptable, given the various conditions we encounter.

The profile or line taper is a matter of personal preference, though some aficionados favour the double taper because of its ease in handling, changing direction or holding a considerable amount of fly line in the air at any time.

Weight forwards have become universally popular because of their shooting ability and distance attributes; yet they are often the subject of misuse. If using one do ensure that at least the back taper, if not the rear section of the belly, is in the rod tip's ring before re-casting, otherwise loss of distance will occur through a collapsed cast, and you will find yourself buying two or three lines per season because of severe cracking in the running line.

It is possible to reach a compromise between the two, in the form of Ultra II Specialist, Cortland 444 s.l. and the Triangle Taper which offer distance ease and a longer belly for presentation. All these are worth investigation.

Having mentioned line, I should also mention Mucilin – this floatant is almost as vital to the nymph fisher as fly patterns. The annoying truth is that even the best fly lines sink (just a bit) at the thin tip end. This can lead to lost fish for two reasons: a delay in striking because the line has become stuck in the glutinous surface film, and missed opportunities as fly line tip and leader butt did not register a take because they had sunk. In both cases, a smear of Mucilin would have rendered the submerged sections instantly buoyant and once more fishable.

Leader Another vital component is the leader. This is the 'tactic decider' of the system: it will allow you to fish deep or delicately, create accuracy or subtlety just by altering length and diameter to meet the water (and trout's) requirements.

A simple system can be fashioned and the important initial factor is to understand leader length and balance. Any leader is awkward to handle in adverse conditions, the problem worsens the longer the nylon section becomes. Initially, at least, use a leader length you feel happy and comfortable with. There is no joy or satisfaction to be gained by being constantly plagued with wind knots, poor turnover and having it continuously caught in bankside vegetation. An ideal starting length is 12ft – try not to make it less as this will place the thick fly line perilously close to the fly and risk 'spooking' trout.

The simple make-up is to purchase a pre-

intermediate line

floating line

9ft to 9ft 6in, No. 5–6 rod

stomach pump
for trout autopsies

forceps

pol
sur

28 *The nymph fisher's gear*

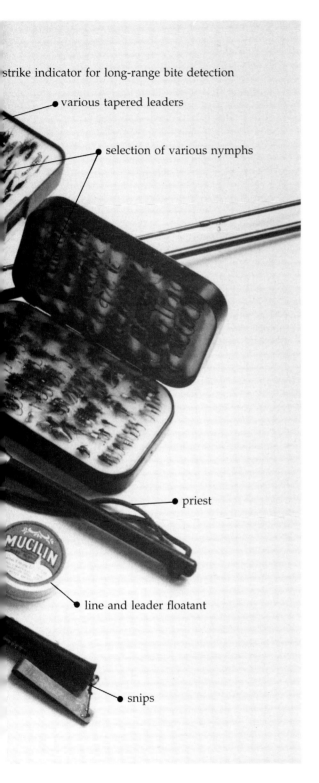

strike indicator for long-range bite detection

various tapered leaders

selection of various nymphs

priest

line and leader floatant

snips

tapered knotless type and, having once accustomed yourself to this, then add a few feet of matched tippet nylon, ie 4lb b.s. leader, 4lb tippet (or 3). Not only will this give you a 14ft leader but also extend the purchased item's life expectancy over weeks – sometimes months – instead of days.

Given the now wide availability of various knotless tapers to 16ft (Orvis, Normark, Platil, Scorpion etc), it would seem sensible to adopt the policy initially, gain an understanding of leader dynamics, then seek out your own personalized system.

Another important factor is tippet size in relation to fly choice. A l.s. 8 leaded Damsel Nymph on a 3lb tippet would be courting disaster, from two areas: the leaded fly constantly hingeing on the fine nylon will stress it and weaken the fragile section; and the limpness of fine nylon will not allow for a clean turnover of the leader, generally the fly landing closer to you than the actual fly line. Conversely, a small fly on a heavy-diameter nylon is unworkable due to poor presentation.

The problem has been solved to some degree by super-strong, reduced-diameter co-polymer nylon (pre-stretched) so a much heavier breaking strain can be used without sacrificing a small, limp diameter. However, as a rule of thumb, and using standard mono (Drennan Sub Surface or Water Queen), the corresponding nylon works out roughly thus:

l.s.	6 to 8	—	std	6 to 8	6lb b.s.
l.s.	8 to 10	—	std	8 to 12	5lb b.s.
l.s.	10 to 12	—	std	10 to 14	4lb b.s.
std	10 to 17				3lb b.s.
std	14 to 20				2lb b.s.

Two other points are worth mentioning concerning leaders. First, if fishing around or near to the reservoir floor, ensure that your leader is double the estimated water depth. A leader on a floating line always fishes back at an angle, so if you think the depth is 6ft then the leader should be 12ft, if 8ft the leader should be 16ft and so on. Once you get into depths over 14ft then the newcomer would be advised to use sinking line. Secondly, no matter how tempting the idea of fishing several flies at once may be, even if it is allowed, keep things simple and initially use a single fly only – you will not be troubled by droppers fouling up and tangling, point flies caught on droppers and many other tangle permutations.

Your motto should be 'it is far better to fish a single fly well than two or three badly'. You will actually catch many more trout if you adopt it.

NYMPH FLY

A working nymphing fly box should contain at least some of the following:

● Pheasant Tails in various sizes – l.s. 10 to 12, std 8 to 18, sporting different thoracic colours (peacock herl, hare's ear, orange, olive, claret and red seal's fur (sub)

● Hare's Ears in similar sizes including Wadham's (round-the-bend type), Barden sparse and lightly hackled, gold-headed for deep fishing and some containing different fluorescent floss tails

● the odd corixa, bloodworm and damsel nymph imitation

● Invictas or amber nymph – for Caddis

● Midge Pupa dressings, the most important patterns in your box. These need not be sophisticated or complicated, but should cover various underwater levels ranging from (1) *surface film*: emergers and suspender nymphs just below, and lightly dressed spiders and sparse, simple seal's fur (sub) dressings; (2) *midwater* with slightly heavier dressed (body) typical midge dressings ie Deacon Mono Midge down to (3) *the bottom layers* and the heavy Varnished Buzzer, indeed any pattern weighted in the thorax or tied on a heavy-iron hook (Tiemco 2457 grub) using water-absorbent, hard materials such as floss etc.

Fly patterns

Nowadays nymph fishing has moved a considerable distance from the days when it meant pure imitations of trout food. Now all kinds of artificials are classified as nymphs: Montanas, Stick Flies with fluorescent tips and all manner of gaudy variations – even Boobies now apparently come under this heading.

In truth you need very few patterns to start with; indeed, if you canvassed most anglers and asked them how many fly patterns they used and/or found effective throughout the season, it would be surprising if any one of them had used many more than a dozen different types. Once again, simplicity is the key. If pushed I would suggest that you could actually manage on a Hare's Ear in various profiles and dressings throughout the entire trout fishing calendar. It wouldn't be so much fun though – often we change for change's sake.

You could go further than the basic list opposite and add shrimps, hoglouse, various sedge patterns, but by keeping the box general in its scope, a greater proportion of insect emergence and activity is covered – suggestively, as opposed to slavishly. The only addition should be a couple of heavyweights – a Montana or Cased Caddis pattern to enable the early season bottom-feeding trout to be covered effectively – but that, honestly, is more than enough.

More important than your fly choice is where and how you fish them.

Locating trout

Locating trout on a lake is the very nucleus of our sport – and sometimes it is easy. Trout have a wonderful habit of rising, which tells us where they are and on what they are feeding – if the fly fisher is observant. However, for the majority of the time, nothing will stir the featureless waterscape, save for the odd swooping swallow or martin – a clue to there being a hatch of midge or olives, but of little use in specific fish location. Here the angler must try and figuratively polarize himself beneath the waves and attempt to decipher the relevant information. This simply takes practice and comes, sadly, only with experience, for which there is no short cut.

And yet there are clues to location for the nymph fisher other than swallows, rises and experience. By noticing the bank you are standing on you will obtain a reasonable working knowledge of the reservoir bed. If it slopes gently, then the chances are it will continue to do so underwater. These shallow gradients are ideal for promoting weed growth and insects such as pond olives, corixa and shallows-loving midge species (light olive, blue and black). Conversely, if your bank layers and contains gullies and other faults, then these usually continue under the water surface too, offering an interesting blend of shallows and deeper channels – again ideal for a number of different insect species such as hoglouse, deepwater midge (black, ginger/orange), red and dark olive corixa, cased caddis and so on.

Other visible bankside areas which may have a bearing on fish-holding spots subsurface are old hedge lines, withies and fence-post lines.

Then we come to those classic areas, dam walls – always worth a try – and bays which are worth fishing from their mouth, into and right the way round, and of course the all-important peninsula which, perhaps coupled with the bay entrance (mouth), offers the best opportunities to ambush upwind-feeding rainbows, be they rising or deeper subsurface. All should be fished confidently and thoroughly at all levels.

Tactics

Now to the tactics. Again, I can only reiterate that you should keep it simple. Indeed, by careful choice of location and a degree of watercraft and quiet on your part, you won't often have to cast very far. The fish, especially towards evening and around dawn, prefer marginal feeding, and all that they require are noiseless banks and in they come. Indeed, given little angling pressure, they will seldom be far away in the majority of conditions. The more people there are (especially wading fly fishers), the farther out the trout get pushed.

The first important decision you will make is an educated guess as to what level the trout may be feeding. Working from top to bottom, the surface film-feeding trout will rise or bulge, making a movement in the water and betraying its presence. All you need do is select a lightweight pattern that will stay in the surface area – if it drops even a matter of inches, the chances are it will be ignored. Lightly dressed Midges or Hare's Ears are ideal choices. There are two tactical options open to you: casting towards the feeding activity, making sure your fly is in the trout's feeding line and in front of its last feeding position, and attempt to track its progress, leaving the fly to fish for itself – in other words, static, as in dry-fly fishing; or fishing ultra-slowly in a figure of eight through an area of trout feeding. Either way, a take (the trout accepting your artificial) will be betrayed by a surface swirl. Seldom if nymph fishing, in any style, will you feel the trout or have the fish hook itself; mostly it is a visual rather than tactile affair.

Fishing just subsurface to the bottom in shallow water is ideally done with a side wind, preferably for a right-handed caster, coming from the left-hand side; indeed, it is one of the classic nymph-fishing siuations. Casting a longish line and allowing the wind to drift the line in a gentle curve, you – the angler – do little other than keep in touch with the drifting line, leader and flies. This is one style which often finds trout hooking themselves – but don't bank on it. Initially, as the fly starts to sink, takes can occur. This is known as taking 'on the drop' and will register by the leader or fly line darting forwards along the surface. More often though, as the fly line drifts around in a curve, the line will appear to stretch, go straight, or feel oddly heavy – at *all* these signs, strike.

Restricted to one style of nymph fishing, and for searching water in a methodical way, be it top or bottom, then fishing the curve, or odging if there is little or no wind – walking a curve into the line – is by far the most versatile approach in a variety of conditions. Coping with deep areas and flat calms with a nymph is different again, and perhaps the most demanding of all. Both require long, ungreased leaders and both are completely visual. Takes to either can be subtlety itself, being more twitches or tremors on the line, more reminiscent of shy carp or roach than 'devil-may-care' rainbows.

When fishing deep areas with weighted patterns, it is far better to opt for heavy-ironed hooks with little if any lead, than heavily-leaded patterns. Takes appear to be far more confident, possibly because of the balance of the fly when the trout pick it up. Of course this does require

a longer waiting period for the artificial to reach the required depth, but it is time worth spending with a good many takes coming 'on the drop'. The area to try this style should have a reasonable depth and ridges, and probably have the wind behind you. The retrieve rate should be an ultra-slow, almost static mode, keeping the fly as close to the bottom as possible. For this style and the curve there has been a recent trend to using sight bobs or bite indicators. These are a positive boon, and there are two types which stand head and shoulders above others: Roman Moser's Butterfly Junction – a small section of braided leader looped both ends, containing a fluorescent polypropylene insert in the middle – greased up will float readily, or the Orvis Roll-on Adhesive Indicator – which comprises fluorescent buoyant foam pads which you simply roll on to any position on the leader that you require.

The tendency when using an indicator is to slow down the retrieve yet more, making them also viable for flat calm nymphing. However, be careful of wake factor (surface disturbance by the relative bulk) which is magnified to an alarming degree in such conditions; even the fly line and leader barely moved resembles a miniature tidal wave. This, in turn, suggests ultra-slow retrieves and slow-sinking patterns,

4

3

2

1

● *Nymph fishing*

1 *initial cast*
2 *line starting to belly*
3 *the deadly curve*
4 *too deep curve – either mend or re-cast*

of the type that will penetrate the generally thick surface film – a sparse Hare's Ear tied short on size 10 or 12 std hook, or a Mono Buzzer being ideal.

Very often a degreased leader and buoyant nymph such as an ET or suspender, just cast or left in an area of known trout movement, will actually bring fish up to the fly. This highlights yet another point, other than simplicity in the tackle system, and that is variation: never stop trying different retrieve rates, water levels and areas. With nymph fishing you must keep an open mind.

There are some other important factors to throw into the nymphing equation. First, attention span: no matter how astute you feel you are, concentrating for much more than a half to three-quarters of an hour at peak level is very hard, and mentally debilitating. Try to have frequent rests and then you will keep your reactions and instincts sharper over protracted periods. Secondly, be aware of water and weather. Shallows soon warm up and are ideal places to nymph at the beginning and towards the end of the season, whereas deeper areas flanked by weed- (and food-) rich shallows are a better option when the water warms up. Also the brighter the conditions, generally speaking, the deeper your pattern should be fishing. Finally, always keep your eyes open for hatches of insects, feeding swallows and martins, concentrations of food areas such as windward shorelines, dam walls, foam lines – anything, anywhere, in fact, which gives the appearance of harbouring food. Trout will seldom be far away, and I assure you your first trout deceived by the subtlety and guile of nymph fishing will be a truly memorable experience that will have you bewitched for the rest of your fly fishing life. Most important of all though, it is fun.

Over the years there has been a mystique drawn up around nymph fishing, seemingly placing it on a higher plane than other forms of fly fishing. Do not be put off, it is not as difficult to master as many would have you believe.

Points to remember

● Keep tackle, flies, leader and technique simple.

● Initially only use one fly.

● Stick to the floating line.

● Keep retrieve rates varied but, if in doubt, use a slow figure of eight. Better still, allow the wind to retrieve for you by fishing on the curve.

● React to any signs of movement on the surface and keep an eye open for likely-looking places.

● Tread quietly, keep on the move and go in search of trout, casting into likely areas, and do not become tied to one spot.

● Always ask advice from the lodge, rangers, wardens and fellow anglers about recent activity from trout and insects, and best areas.

Playing, landing and despatching the quarry

Everyone, it seems, is eager to dispense sage-like facts and information to newcomers on rods, reels, general paraphernalia, leaders, flies and volumes of know-how – me included. Few ever tell you what to do when you finally secure your quarry. What should you do to avoid a potential disaster and the utter dejection of losing your hard-earned prize?

The playing and landing of trout may seem academic to most of us, but to a beginner it is a maze of frantic movements and lightening-quick decisions and reactions. So what can you do to avert impending disaster?

There exist two prime methods of playing a trout: 'via the hand' and 'off the reel'. There are definite merits in both styles when used in various situations.

The hand strip

This method relies on the angler's ability to get any loose line under control as soon as a trout is hooked. The chances are you will already have the line travelling across the index finger of your rod hand during the retrieve anyway, and by instinctively clamping this retrieved line against the cork rod handle at the first sign of a take, you are effectively in control from that moment. Thereafter it is a simple case of give and take. If the trout suddenly takes off for the lake's centre, just allow the fly line an easy passage between the index finger and cork handle. It is also a very good idea almost to feed it through with the line hand, which will take out any kinks, loops, or line twists created during the retrieve.

Once the fish has stopped, or you feel you can gain some line, start to haul with the line hand, gently at first, then back through the passage between cork and rod hand – feeling for what the trout's reaction might be. Once you have some idea as to its next action, increase your authority on the fly line. Throughout the fight, whether using this method or 'from the reel', you must keep your rod tip up. It is, in effect, a shock absorber or spring which will cushion any sudden movement or lunge from your quarry. Rarely should it drop below 10 o'clock (2 o'clock if you prefer), better still 11 o'clock (1 o'clock).

To this end, it is also worth mentioning that keeping the rod tip at an angle to the line during a retrieve will also help to avoid smash takes for the same reason – rather than pointing straight down the line which, unless you know your tackle and a trout's reaction implicitly, will positively scream 'lost trout'.

Once the upper hand has been achieved, keep a gentle, firm pressure on the fish, even at close quarters, but do not overdo it, as applying too much pressure at an acute angle when a fish is close to your position on the bank and about to be landed risks tearing the hook hold.

Rods also play their part, especially concerning the last element – close quarters. A fast-actioned (tip) rod can tear hook holds a great deal more easily than a softer 'middle' variety, so use caution when a fish nears boat or bank when using the faster distance-orientated rod.

The secret when playing trout is always to maintain a constant pressure – if possible from one direction, continuously altering the angle of the rod. Switching from side to side can loosen hook holds dramatically and often lead to a securely hooked trout, which otherwise would have been landed, being lost. If your hand gets tired, support the rod handle along the whole forearm.

Playing from the reel
This is now largely considered 'old hat' in the wake of the reservoir revolution. With the opening of Grafham and the wholesale movement to distance casting and a good deal of shooting head work, it is purely impractical to do so. However, for close-quarter fishing, and especially when encountering large trout, the ability to play your fish from the reel can be a decided advantage. First, the line is stored out of the way from stray twigs, nettles and other bankside problems, and secondly, a good-quality (engineered) reel, well oiled and shown a modicum of care will smoothly and efficiently give and take line, probably more easily than your hand hauls. Thirdly, the improved braking and controlling facility you have by employing either the drag system and/or finger-tip pressure on the spool is to your advantage.

The problem with this method is returning retrieved line to the spool on first hooking a fish. The easiest way – if possible and without too much line lying slack – is to let the trout's first run take out the loose coils in its initial rush. However, do not allow slack line to develop between your rod tip and the trout. Having got the line back on to the reel, similarly to the hand line method, 'give and take' should take place if the fish wants to go for a jog around the lake. Let it take line, unhindered, from the reel, merely either pre-setting the drag system or using the palm or fingertip pressure to the rim or revolving spool.

Once you are playing your trout by this method – and this is especially appropriate if it is a specimen – one of the most comfortable positions to adopt is with the butt of the rod resting either on the chest or stomach. This will offer a great deal of support and also be very comfortable. But do ensure that the reel fitting on the rod is up-locking or has a fighting butt, thus taking the revolving spool away from any likelihood of getting caught up in clothing.

In fact, both with this method and the hand strip, it is a good idea to practise away from water. All that is required is another willing party to run around pretending to be a two-legged trout. It sounds strange, but it does actually work! And a good working knowledge of the playing styles will evolve.

Alternative ploys

There are, of course, special instances when variations on a theme are required. A trout heading for tree roots, weedbeds or other underwater obstructions must be stopped if disaster is to be averted. Side strain is your key weapon, but it does necessitate you put the rod parallel to the water and clamp down on the line, putting as much strain as you dare on the terminal tackle. It is, though, surprising to most people just how much force you can apply to a rod and terminal tackle as long as it is held

upright or at an angle. A straight pull, however, will immediately give way with a resounding snap!

Another very helpful playing ploy can be used, especially if you need to get the fish to the surface and keep it there, either because it's got its nose buried or the need arises to guide your fish from and *over* a weedbed. Initially it is vital to get all the line taut and play from the reel. You then put the rod high above your head, together with the other hand; this additional height seems to drive the fish upwards.

If a trout does become entangled in weed, a very old river trick often works. Let the line go slack and wait a few seconds, then take the slack up and make the line gently taut. Then hit the cork handle with a short bump (or repeated bumps) with a fist made with your free hand. This will send shockwaves down the line and set off huge vibrations which trout hate, causing them very often to bolt from the weed cover. Do not overdo it, however, a couple of short, sharp bursts is all that is required. If

29 *Landing – gently 'to' and 'in' the net. Whenever possible use knotless meshes as this will cause little harm to the trout, should you want to release them*

it doesn't dislodge itself after that, I fear it really is stuck.

Netting

Netting, by comparison, is far easier. There are several points, though, which make for a happy outcome. First, always bring your fish to the net and not vice versa. Secondly, if at all possible, sink the net first, bringing your quarry over the rim, then lifting once the fish is inside the frame. Again, refrain from swiping at the fish – no matter how excited you are. Thirdly, if it is a large trout, do not attempt to lift the net encompassing the fish by its handle as this will put intolerable strain on the joint between handle and net head, and is liable to end in disaster. Instead, try to lift the fish from the water by the head only, and by twisting it on its side, you will fold the trout safely into the net bag's security.

Remember too that your trout, at the sight of the bank and continuous restrictive pressure from above, will be in a highly charged state and liable to panic at any point. Generally this coincides with the angler also panicking in an effort to get the trout into the net too quickly. Always expect your trout to make a last desperate bid for freedom at the net as it approaches the bank. This sudden surge should be allowed to go lightly checked; it will be shortlived and thereafter a gentle netting can be conducted.

The caught fish

If you are intending to return the quarry, use a knotless net and keep the trout in the water at all times, unless it is extraordinarily difficult to do so. Remember, in either despatching or releasing your quarry, afford it the highest respect. If you do wish to retain your trout, make absolutely certain you use a priest to deliver the trout's last rites and despatch it as quickly and humanely as possible. One or two quick, sharp taps just behind the eyes on top of the skull is all it takes. Do not use landing net handles, stones, wood or branches under any circumstances – they are not up the job.

That is playing, landing and despatching. Always keep the fish's well-being paramount and keep the fight quick and efficient.

30 Mick Phipps slides a nice 'bow back to fight another day. If catch and release is allowed, do try and release your fish in the water, ie don't bring them out of the water at any point as this causes them great distress

CHAPTER THREE

Advanced Casting Techniques

IN introducing this pot-pourri of various casting styles, I am aware that I have over-looked, for the most part, the basic movements such as 'pick up and put down', false casting, shooting line and a few others. As I have mentioned in previous books and articles, the fly fisher's cast is notoriously difficult to convey by the written word, and it doesn't get any easier. For anyone wishing either to learn or understand rudimentary steps, even re-discipline themselves in terms of timing, I would urge that they seek guidance from a qualified casting instructor. Anyone holding the APGAI or STANIC will be able to set you on a more efficient path, and make the whole range of movements that are so necessary to tech-niques both a joy and a pleasure. I am constantly surprised at the number of people who re-ligiously entrust themselves to the gentle su-pervision of golf professionals, yet shun the sound words and wisdom of their kinsmen in the fly fishing world. Not only do the move-ments and discipline parallel that of golf, but also the critical business of timing is equally important.

Without overstating the case, an hour or two spent under the watchful eye of a casting instructor is, I believe, worth something in the region of two to three weeks' hard and fruitless fishing time, often spent in complete frustration. There can be, of course, no compensation for learning your 'craft' whilst actually at the water-side; however, I have always felt that this should be of a tactical nature, rather than casting, which can be practised and perfected well away from the waterside and, when fishing, merely be the

instrument by which you allow full rein to your fly fishing skills.

The ensuing problem-solvers are a very per-sonal view of how I overcome those little bank-side hiccups which often bedevil a day's fish-ing. Practice, practice and yet more practice is the only key to real fly-casting perfection. So, with that in mind, I hope the following will be of some use during difficult situations and times when slight variations are required.

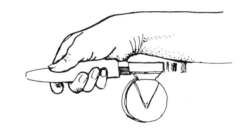

handshake grip

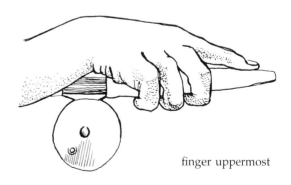

finger uppermost

● *Grips*

Casting into the wind and the need to double haul

Very often the problem with trout is that they position themselves in places that we anglers find very difficult to get at, and you cannot blame them. But these instances do present extraordinary problems when we want to enjoy a successful day. One of the worst problems, and a recurring one, is that of casting into the wind, be it a breeze or a force 9.

The late World Champion, Jack Martin, on being asked how to cast into a stiff breeze, said with customary aplomb, 'you get in your car and drive round to the opposite bank'! There's a lot of sense in that, but the problem won't go away and is further compounded by the fact that trout often favour the windward side, finding any amount of foodstuffs amongst the wave action and general turbulence. Nowhere is this more emphasized than on our concrete bowls such as Farmoor, and indeed the dam walls of any lake system.

Sooner or later you will be forced to face the uncomfortable decision that, in order to catch fish, you will have to cast into the wind. Most of us are less than enamoured (if we're honest) at the prospect – it is seldom easy and, realistically, distance will be curtailed. However, there is a saving grace: trout in such areas are seldom positioned very far from the bank.

As with all things casting, there is a logical reason why you should face nature's hostilities and pitch your fly into the foaming morass. This is the fact that trout are sitting just off the bank scooping the collection of food which has either washed there or is merely stranded, often drowned, by the severe backwash and intertwining of various currents. This not only gives you the reason, but more importantly, the confidence that, even if only the odd cast goes out properly, it will be fishing in areas of trout-feeding activity. It is this feeling that something is likely to happen that creates some semblance of fortitude, perseverance and application in refining technique.

The first thing I would urge anyone who faces the likelihood of fishing into a breeze, even infrequently, is to know the rod's capabilities inside out. This means having a totally balanced system and technique which obeys your every whim and instruction.

Tackle

Your rod and line partnership (and, of course, your timing and discipline) is paramount. Casting into a wind is about narrow loops of line travelling through the air. If you and your tackle cannot fashion these, then I fear depressing times ahead. The rod action should be middle-to-tip (medium/fast taper) or tip (fast taper). I personally prefer the former, though I am aware that the fast tapers provide continuously tight loops when so required – Loomis IMX, Sage III, Church/Powell and Hardy Sovereign X are all contenders, as indeed are any rods producing straight tracking (movement in the air) which possess a fast/medium taper. But a rod alone will not do the job.

Curiously, lines have little significance in the final outcome. A Lee Wulff Triangle Taper may give you a slight cutting edge – as may the Teeny Casting Line or the Church Missile Taper – but the difference is marginal. Added to this is the belief that the stronger the wind, the heavier the line, which probably suggests a Beaufort scale 8 needing a salmon-sized 10 or 12.

It is technique rather than line size that will project your cast leader and flies just that little bit further. I am not suggesting that a light No. 4, No. 5 or even No. 6 will overcome the problem. But there is seldom any need to go beyond No. 7 or No. 8 even in the stormiest conditions. What really makes the difference, and affects the cast, is you. There can be no avoiding the fact that the best tackle in the world will never make the difference if you don't know how to use it. And casting into a wind will find any (even the slightest) weakness in casting style you may have.

The trouble, however, with fly fishing is that

we need these bits of nylon to create an illusion, and this lightweight, gremlin-infested section can cause untold trouble in a head-on breeze or wind. No matter how well your fly line has gone out, the leader has an exasperating habit of blowing back on itself, cutting down dramatically on distance. The logical answer, when using any fly line, even a floater, is to cut down on leader length and use some form of taper that will transmit the energy provided by the rod and line speed down to the very leader tippet – in effect, a good straight turnover.

Don't be worried about reducing the leader length down to 12ft (or even 9ft) – if necessary using a pre-tapered shop-bought knotless type. If you feel that this leader length is too short with a floating-line system, given the depth of water you want to fish and reach, then change to an intermediate, retaining the same leader length. Curiously, intermediates, be they Scientific Anglers Masterline or Airflo, seem to cast well in a variety of conditions. All this necessitates a thorough working knowledge of the double haul.

The double haul

The rod tip assumes water level; with the line hand positioned up by the butt ring, thereafter pulling the line smoothly to the corresponding hip as the rod hand goes through the familiar arc in front – not forgetting natural drift at the vertical. This almost nonchalant stab upwards with the rod tip helps, I find, with this and many other casts' effectiveness. The line should now be travelling semi-vertically from the rod tip – this movement compounded by both natural drift and the line speed of the single haul providing tension. The line moves upwards to such an extent that the line hand is almost encouraged and pulled back up to the butt ring by the line's momentum upwards and behind. The single haul is repeated. Now comes the departure: the line hand, rather than remaining at the hip, floats back up to the butt ring of the rod which now assumes the casting position of about 1 o'clock.

The timing required to affect both downwards single haul, then in the same movement to float back up to the butt ring, is precise, unhurried and smooth and requires a good deal of practice. Any jerking, either with line or rod hand, at this point will simply set off a vibration

● *Single- and double-haul*

1 the pick-up – line hand should be near butt ring
2 haul downwards with line hand
3 start of the double-haul – continue line hand upwards in direction of the arrow
4 final pull – once the line behind is straight and under tension pull downwards again thus generating more line speed
5 the release – don't forget to release the line high (in normal circumstances)

along the line, loading the rod behind and causing significant loss of power just when the rod should be absorbing it.

You will notice that, due to the increased line speed, less time is required for the fly line to straighten. So, unless extreme lengths are developed in the backcast, as soon as the floated line hand has reached a position of nose level or by the side of the rod hand reel face, it will be time for the conclusion – the haul downwards in conjunction with the rod's forward movement.

Correct hands and feet

The rod hand should, at this point, add no more power and merely operate in exactly the same manner as for all other casts – a power 'snap' or 'tap' forwards in order to propel the line behind in front, finishing with a gentle follow through. The line hand, however, should move in conjunction with this movement, smoothly and forcefully downwards to the hip area, where the first haul finished – in other words, the line hand has made a 'V' configuration,

trembling down the last side of the 'V', finishing at the sharp angle. The point of release should harmonize with the power tap – as the tap forwards is made, the line hand should have reached the hip, either releasing the line at this point or repeating the exercise for a further sequence.

To quote American casting aficionado Mel Kreiger, it is a 'down-up' movement with the line hand. I would also add that it is a down-up-down movement then release. And if you harness that whilst imagining a 'V' – the base being the rod – the final manoeuvre clamping down the slope finishing at the 'sharp end', there, in essence, you have the double haul.

But what will this do? Two things: first, speed up the line travelling through the air, and second, tend to close the loop, creating a tight loop both back and, more importantly, forwards. To this end the position of your feet can help dramatically. But before proceeding, whatever you do, start with rod tip down to the water surface, preferably just above it – by inches.

● *Casting into the wind*

1 *drive the line as high behind as possible*
2 *start the haul downwards*
3 *release low, with your rod tip near to the water surface*

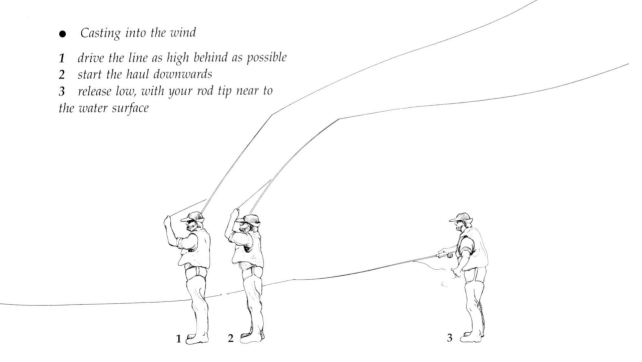

1   2   3

Of course, this does not necessarily call for fancy footwork but you will achieve different results by which foot you lead with and place balance upon. If ever I feel my overhead loop needs closing up, without hesitation I lead with my right (ie if the rod hand is right; this is vice versa for left-handed casters). There is a tendency, if leading with the left, to open up with the shoulder and as a result, the rod arc. The whole movement then creates a wider loop, anathema for casting into a breeze.

The reason for the line hand's sympathetic foot making the difference is a narrowing of the rod's arc overhead. The smaller the rod's travelling distance, the narrower the loop – unless a perfectly stable and stiff wrist is maintained, coupled with ultra-precise timing, then a rod's movement can be longer. Anyone seeing Lefty Kreh or Ed Jawarolski from the USA cast would vouch for that. For we mortals it is simpler to restrict the overhead movement.

The backcast

Oddly, the next stage is positively aided by a wind; that is, the straightening of line and leader on the backcast. However, there can be a problem – timing – because the vagaries of wind speed will straighten line or leader sooner or later. Whatever happens this will be out of sympathy with usual conditions, and must be catered for.

The other important factor concerning the backcast is to project the movement upwards. This will give you the trajectory needed to fashion the forward movement. But again it does rely on a relatively closed style with the rod hand during the initial movements – and a controlled or stiff-wrist style.

I should add at this juncture that casting into the wind, indeed in the majority of situations, is dependent on you not 'breaking' the wrist. This does not mean having a gap between forearm and rod butt, merely that ruinous limp hingeing at the wrist can ultimately destroy any cast, causing the rod to lose any direct authority. Now the ultimate movement – the forward cast.

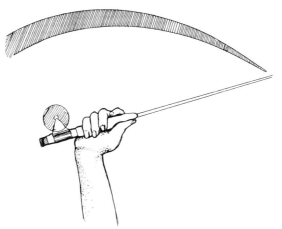

● *Wrist break – loss of loop control*

The forward cast

With rod tip positioned near to the vertical and inclining behind and the rod hand approximately in line with the eye, the fly line and leader straight behind, the forward 'snap' or 'tap' of the rod tip can begin. The trick, if you can call it that, is to be conscious of the rod tip and do all the work with this area, relegating the rod hand almost to the subconscious.

As the great man Lefty Kreh insists, 'the line goes where the rod tip stops'. His whole casting philosophy is 'speed up – stop' – simple, but oh so effective.

Curiously, there is an area of calm air just above the water – though several authorities disagree scientific evidence would support this theory. This is due primarily to wave action, the air speed decreasing over the wave troughs, allowing for a marginally calming influence. Quite simply, you must get the fly line to seek this calm area by running the line on a low and, importantly, flat trajectory by driving the rod *tip* fast in the intended direction. Instinctively your initial reaction is to drive the rod lower by stopping later. Having recently been privileged to get first-hand experience from the maestro Kreh (and his extraordinary creation of narrow loops), I would say that this aspect is the single most important. A narrow loop will pierce a head-on wind; a wide one will not. It is that straightforward. This will necessitate a short but fast rod tip movement on the forward movement.

However, this is where we leave the traditional late power stroke or delivery behind. If we are to believe the philosophy that a 'fly goes where the rod tip stops' (to use a 'Krehism'), this would ultimately mean that when we aim the rod tip downwards, stopping late, then the fly line will hit the water prematurely. So aim directly at your chosen area through using a short but fast power stroke. Reality, though, can play some funny tricks and it is often the late downward stroke and late release which gets the line to shoot low and fast.

There is another way which, though looking

● *Low and high trajectories*

1 stopping the rod in and around the vertical will ensure a high backcast
2 never be afraid to look behind and see when your line is travelling (N.B. be careful not to use the shoulder and open up the loop, however)
3 in most circumstances go for a high release point – if you make a wide power stroke in the direction of the arrow you will open up the loop and seldom achieve distance, or good turnover

preposterous, does actually work. That is, to make the forward 'tap' or 'wrist snap' driving the rod hand and stooping to allow the rod hand to end up a few feet above the water. This will ensure the fly line travels along the calm between wind and water. It is essential, though, to ensure the line, both behind and in front, travels along the *same* plane and does not curve to the side. You need all the energy to be channelled along this one plane.

Curiously, the business of casting into the wind has more to do with confidence and good casting style and very little, if anything, to do with brute force. Don't turn your back and cast across fields; you will only end up losing power on the forward movements. So often this style is the familiar approach, and as yet I have seen few trout on dam walls or in fields. Certainly casting does take practice and application, but it is time well spent. Learn it and your catch rate will increase significantly.

Turnover

A clean turnover is the final flourish to a well-delivered cast. In essence, it is the rod and line's way of telling you how well you have utilized their combined resources.

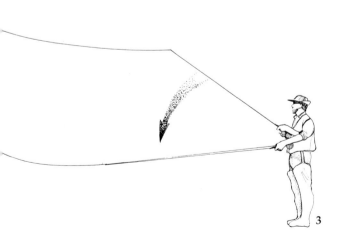

There are those who feel, in stillwater terms, that distance is everything and turnover and presentation are secondary considerations. However, if they stop to think of the times when their leader failed to straighten and how much line had to be stripped back in order to regain control of the fly again, they may just feel that casting a shorter but well-presented line would actually lose them little if any distance at all.

Another virtue of a straightened leader and system on touchdown is on those occasions when a fly is taken on its descent or free-fall path. In essence, fishing commences as soon as straight fly line and leader have landed on the water. The number of times these takes occur, either as the fly drops or on the first pull of line, testify to that.

It could be argued that with a sinking line, especially a fast-sinker or Hi-D, turnover is far less critical than with a floater or intermediate. Again if you consider just how many times a trout takes either on the drop or after only one or two pulls at the start of a retrieve, then you will also realize that obtaining clean turnover is every bit as important as with a sinker.

Achieving clean turnover is simply a matter of adhering to some fundamental principles and fine tuning, and also the minimization of perhaps one of the most common casting problems, particularly when striving for distance.

The tailing loop

The tailing loop is primarily when the leader and thinner portion of fly line drop below the shooting main line on the forward cast. This not only leads to mid-air tangles and occasional wind knots, but also decrees fold-backs and poor turnover on touchdown – seldom will a tailed loop ever straighten once it starts to go back on itself. In essence, you are bringing forward two sections of line and that is how it will land.

Usually tailing loops are the result of too little line speed overall – in which case, you should increase this by either single, or better still double hauling – or making the forward cast jerky and sudden, rather than a gradual progression of accelerated rod tip speed, or by keeping the aerial loop too tight (although tight loops are a weapon of distance, accuracy and efficiency, they can be too close together). To overcome this you should ease the rod tip downward slightly on the final delivery of the forward cast by pressing down on the rod handle with your thumb. This will tend to open up the loop a fraction, without sacrificing tip or line speed. Do not punch the whole hand forward as a fist, as this tends to force the loops together, dragging the leader into the fly line on the forward delivery. This slight opening of the loop is also desirable when fishing long leaders and teams of flies, allowing them an uninterrupted passage through the air.

There is, though, another aspect which can help turnover dramatically – feathering. This is a familiar action in coarse fishing of achieving a regimented descent when using a waggler or stick float, obviating tangles, and is conducted in exactly the same way and for the same reason in fly fishing – turnover.

Feathering

It was Steve Parton who first brought this aspect to my attention, and all it requires is that the shooting fly line be allowed to run through your hand immediately prior to landing, causing a partial retarding of the aerial line. This, in turn, causes the leader and fly line tip to turn over due to a hint of resistance. It is also very useful when employing a shooting head, enabling even quite high AFTMs to land with a degree of delicacy.

Role of leaders in turnover

All too often the dynamics of terminal tackle are overlooked in our quest for better presentation. Mostly this is based on a penny-pinching policy of making do with straight sections of single-diameter nylons. This variety will never turn over as well as some form of taper. Of course, in certain conditions – following breezes, beneficial cross winds and so forth – you could almost dispense with a rod and use horse hair; the system would still straighten, but these instances are rare.

It matters little whether you prefer braided leaders or the more widely used nylon. What is important is to understand why a taper helps. The reason is simple. A continuance of energy is created by the forward cast, which should proceed – uninterrupted – right down the fly line to the fly. That, quite simply, creates turnover.

If the junction between the fly line and leader is very abrupt, then there is significant energy loss; it is for this reason that a taper is desirable. Also, the bigger the leader butt (or more akin to the fly line tip diameter), the better the transmission of energy, even to the extent of opting for 24 to 26lb nylon butt sections (braided loops work in exactly the same way).

Though nowadays outmoded, one of the best leaders ever devised – essentially for river fishing (though the theory applies to stillwater too) – were the Ritz tapers of varying diameters of nylon stepped down in knotted lengths. Similarly, river leaders, which demand precise, clean turnover, are still best made of nylon, and though complex, can utilize three different types of nylon: semi-stiff for the butt section, a stiff (Tynex, Mason, Sparton) 2ft intermediate section, the semi-stiff section tapering to a different tippet of limp, 'soft' nylon.

Essentially, these days, the world is your oyster be it braid or nylon. But, from a casting standpoint and given a variety of situations, tapered nylon still comes out on top due to far less air resistance because it is much denser in its make-up. Braid (unweighted) can 'hold up' and be inaccurate in certain conditions due to its far greater surface area and density. By choosing various systems for different occasions, a working compromise, however, will be reached, which will offer you better overall turnover, which in turn will put many more fish-catching opportunities your way.

Good turnover is within every angler's reach

and will benefit every facet of fly fishing – all it entails is merely attention to some casting details and a little practice.

Points to remember

● A straightened leader and fly line will always outfish a crumpled heap of line.

● Be watchful of tailing loops; try not to punch forward abruptly with the fist, but instead open the travelling loop a fraction by 'pressing' on the rod handle.

● Wherever possible, used a balanced, tapered leader system.

● Practice makes perfect! Even for five to ten minutes in a park or garden, done as a routine (minus a hook, of course – using a wool substitute fly), will help technique immeasurably.

A mighty blow from behind

It is strange to imagine, but it is often much more difficult to cast with a wind blowing from behind rather than in front. You may reasonably ask why this is. Often the length of cast attained flatters to deceive, and if you stop to consider the occasions when leader tangles, dropper tangles and wind knots were at their demonic worst, on balance I would suggest the majority occurred when a healthy blow was driving from behind. There is a very good reason for this – the old hoary problem, turnover or, rather, lack of it.

Although a following wind can add considerably to our distance and, eventually, turnover – or at least appear to – the secret is in harnessing its good points whilst defeating its bad. Certainly most of us (if we are honest) normally seek this type of wind in actual fishing; indeed, tactically speaking, especially in very warm weather and higher water temperature, a move to the leeward can produce fish, through various current movements.

The real problem in this deceptive, flattering wind, is turnover, not on the forward but on the backcast. What happens is that with any given windspeed, with the line being projected back into wind at less than the actual windspeed, the fly line (and leader) meets a soft, but more or less impenetrable, barrier and is unable to straighten fully. If the line speed is considerably lower, it may even stand the risk of being blown forward prematurely. This is often a problem for beginners of only a few hours' experience.

Overcoming the problems of a backwind requires that we once more look to three basic casting elements:

● line speed build-up and its resultant kinetic energy;

● actual placement of the line on the backcast via the rod tip;

● timing to allow it to straighten before being brought forward once again.

Line speed

The single most important act is to drive the line back fast enough to pierce the wind. This will often need additional line speed and that can only be created by the single or, more usually, double haul movement with the line hand; so a working knowledge of these movements is vital.

Placement of the line behind

This tends to be slightly different for this cast from any other. Generally speaking the trajectory should be slightly lower or on a horizontal plane, rather than projected upwards. We are not looking for quite the same time lapse as in other conditions; indeed, in healthy wind strengths force 3 to 5, this will quite probably hold up the line's progress – almost buoying the backcast, creating a quasi-defeat of gravity.

So, when projecting the line back for the formation of the backcast, rather than projecting high, drive the rod tip so to position the line on a vertical plane or, indeed, slightly down-ward (the rod tip stopping at between 1 o'clock and 2 o'clock), remembering to speed up and stop the rod tip.

Another factor which will help the backcast enormously is to watch the line going behind, this will require that the balance of weight is more to the left foot (if you are a right-handed caster) so you can glance over your shoulder. There is nothing wrong in watching the line go behind; indeed it is the only sure way of telling if your timing is spot on (or not) and, of course, being able to make amendments where necessary.

Forward cast

Now to the forward cast. Here again, you need a slight change of position, with the line straight, reducing any chance of wobble or unsteadiness along the fly line length. Project the forward cast slightly upwards, the rod tip accelerating and stopping on a higher climbing plane. This will give the fly line loft and high trajectory, and not only offer much longer distances (the wind picking up the climbing line enhancing the flowing kinetic energy – almost floating the line in a purposeful manner) but allow the whole system – line and leader – to straighten and land softly.

The one area where you will have a constant wind or breeze blowing from behind is in loch-style fishing and, of course, there are many resultant problems which emanate from this style, especially when employing more than one fly and single-minded perverse droppers. The need, therefore, for a straight backcast is vital for a satisfactory presentation.

If the wind is blowing almost hammerlike into the shoulder blades, you are probably left with little option but a stratagem of roll casting. However, given that the longer the line projected behind, the more chance for potential problems, it is advisable in the case of stiff breezes and a soft 'wall' of air behind, to throw a shorter backcast with the added 'punch' of a line size above the usual, so as to 'load the rod' more quickly over a shorter period and also have the extra weight to puncture the soft 'wall' to the rear. It also thwarts any chance of 'chuck and duck' which might have occurred if the line was stopped too low on the backcast, then again, low on the forward cast.

Taking just a little trouble to understand both casting and physical elements will enable you to create possibly the longest casts you have made – in a controlled manner. The whole operation hinges on defeating the wind strength on the backcast and utilizing it on the forward movement.

Points to remember

● Build up the line speed sufficiently to project the line back and 'puncture' the wind.

● Ensure that both line and leader are straight before bringing forward. This may require a working knowledge of the double or single haul.

● Aim slightly downward or horizontally with the backcast, rather than upwards, then bring the line forward. To make the first cast, aim higher than normal, giving loft to the fly line, which in turn will allow for quite long, uninterrupted casts.

● Always, when casting, wear eye protection.

Changing direction

Trout have a nasty habit of rising in one place then, after what seems only an instant, rising somewhere else. This infuriating behaviour leads to the necessity for us to change direction. If ever there was a technique dedicated to catching more fish – whether boat or bank fishing, river or lake, big or small – this is it. The simple truth is, it is not difficult to master. So often the cast is seen as a continuous series of overhead movements until the angler works his way round to the point of the line's release – generally to a blank surface and long-departed trout.

Changing direction in one continuous movement

It is perfectly possible to lift and re-present in *one* continuous movement, as long as some simple guidelines are followed.

Stage 1 Assuming you are fishing for a rising fish to your left that has moved on to the right, the rod tip, if fishing at a proper angle to the line, will already be in the right place, namely *just above water level*. From this point make the backcast in the usual way, though projecting it higher will offer a longer time period in which to make the altered final delivery angle. The depressing truth being 'what goes up, must come down', the nearer it is to the bank the greater the chance of it getting caught up.

The cast might also benefit from an increase of rod tip speed and line speed to ensure that the line is completely straight behind and, importantly travelling upwards. It is this upwards momentum of the line which allows you the time to re-present in another area without the loss of any all-important line speed.

Stage 2 With the line travelling fast and high behind, you merely target your quarry and aim the rod tip in that direction, once the line has straightened behind, simply re-presenting with the usual forward movement of a 'hammer tap' (or, as Mike Marshall would say, 'a paint brush flick') forwards on the rod tip.

Stage 2A If further line needs to be extended, ensure that it is done *after* the movement forwards has begun. This is vital if power loss is not to occur behind and collapse the whole movement.

● *Changing direction*

1 initial cast
2 swing the body and rod in direction of the arrow and, with the line on the water, point the rod tip at your target
3 lift and cast as normal

Stage 3 Always remember to deliver the cast as high as you possibly can, so avoiding a premature touchdown and a spooked trout.

There are, of course, refinements that can help to create an efficient cast, and most certainly a thorough working knowledge of at least the single haul (better still, the double) is required to execute the manoeuvre effectively. This acceleration of the line leaving the water surface ensures that it travels fast enough to load the system in a short space of time and allows a quick delivery in another direction through a wide area. I cannot emphasize enough the importance of this cast's need for a high-projected, high-speed travelling line to effect a satisfactory conclusion.

Some years ago, I thought it necessary to have my feet positioned in the direction the cast is finally to be made. I had not considered the

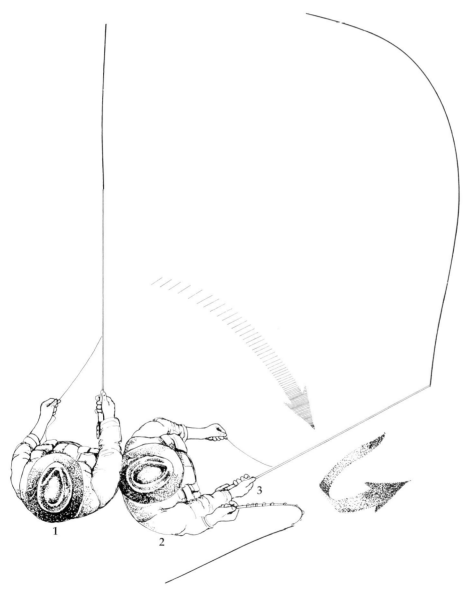

time I needed to change direction ultra-quickly. When boat fishing with dry flies, emergers or nymphs, feet don't enter into the equation; rod tip and line-hand movement does. That scenario works for me but, as in all things, there is another version which may work for you. It may not be greatly different, but could vary significantly.

An alternative method

Stage 1 Again, I am assuming a completely tight line between rod tip and fly, for argument's sake, to your right. From a previous cast you move the angle of the rod tip and body to the direction you wish to make the next cast.

Stage 2 Bring the rod, single hauling as you do so, upwards to fashion a normal overhead cast, ie high speed, high line.

Stage 3 Once the line is straight behind, bring it forward in the normal way to the target, with either the original amount of line or shooting more if necessary.

A problem with this method can occur if there is a wind blowing from right to left with the line positioned on the left-hand side and, though not dangerous, it is potentially troublesome. It may be that you find yourself adapting one or other cast for a specific situation.

Potential problems

The particular 'dont's' in changing direction are: not to allow slack line to develop on either the lift-off from the water or in the backcast – though this also applies to almost all casting manoeuvres; and not to false cast. This repetitive movement can cause untold trouble with overhead movements ending up, as likely as not, with the fly line clattering into itself or the rod as you 'work the angle' and generally making the whole object of the cast untenable and ineffective. Remember there are two movements: the lift-off to the backcast and the forward delivery with or without a shoot.

Changing direction is one of the most effective casts in the fly fisher's repertoire; be it boat or bank, more fish will grace your net once it has been mastered.

Points to remember

● Always start with the rod tip as low as you possibly can – just above water-level ideally. Maintain a taut line between yourself and the fly. The backcast should be aimed high and fast. Deliver your fly in the forwards movement *at* and *above* target to allow for line straightening, shooting and turnover.

● Practise with short line and small angles, working up to the longer line and wide angle.

● Don't forget your eye protection (glasses), even when practising.

PART TWO

The Imitation of the Trout's Natural World

CHAPTER FOUR

Introduction to the Natural Fly

IT may appear superfluous to place this section, both at this juncture and, some would say, in a book covering small stillwaters. Certainly I would concur that in a great many instances on many small lakes, we are doing nothing more than masking the obvious 'pellet syndrome' with artificial flies, which trout know nothing about – or indeed get a chance to. Noise, 'plopability' and movement are the trigger to the trout's feeding response.

But aren't we missing something? The true spirit of fly fishing must rest somewhere in the imitation of the trout's natural world. We may, of course, be deluding ourselves – a great many times I believe this to be true – yet there is something deeply satisfying about noticing the aquatic forms, watching their actions and relevant points and then setting out purposefully to recreate these in various materials at the fly dresser's disposal, finally adding that oh-so-important 'it' factor – the suggestion of pulsating life through our own actions, via our fishing tackle. This for me will always be the essence of the sport.

An instance of this would be the damsel nymph. I studied these solidly for a year. Sample netting, drags with a rake and other organized culls led me directly to a range of patterns fusing Peter Cockwill's life impression of a long marabou tail and David Fynsong's eyed version – the result, a Distressed Damsel. It works on two counts: a wicked movement in the abdomen – where the natural moves – and detail in the thorax – where I feel the important thing is realism, especially in the bulbous eyes.

I have tied in colours ranging from straw/ golden olive through to near-black olive, with even a bright fluorescent lime-green version. All faithfully match nature's colours. Study of the insect has not only led to a range of patterns and fishing retrieves, but colours I would never have dreamt were available in the natural world. But importantly, I now fish such patterns with ultra-confidence, the net result being a far more effective fly.

There are times when this study of the trout's foodstuffs will also unravel feeding mysteries and, believe me, trout on any expanse of water soon wise up to what's available and 'imposters'. The time duration for a trout having left the cosy and sheltered life of being supported by men at the fish farm, released into an alien water and taking full advantage and, in most cases, depending on natural organisms, is within and around a week. All of a sudden it makes far more sense to have some knowledge of what the trout is likely to encounter, what it looks like and how it moves. And apart from that, it's just plain fun.

Chironomids (buzzers)

The chironomid or non-biting midge is none other than our old friend the buzzer, member of the vast order Diptera.

As with many things, we fly fishers have things mildly incorrect, as only the female adults actually buzz. Nevertheless, with in excess of 300 water-dwelling varieties to choose from and a distribution ranging from John O'Groats

● *Midge larva*

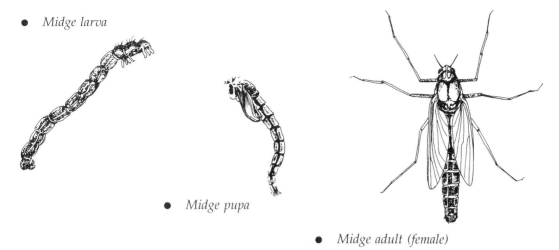

● *Midge pupa*

● *Midge adult (female)*

(and Orkney) to Land's End, we would do this little creature a great disservice in fly fishing terms in belittling its importance.

Simply put, it is the single most overall direct food supply to trout that is imitable. Of course, areas will vary in terms of species' importance, and periods will occur when another species of one specific insect or another will dominate but, on balance, we would be very foolhardy indeed not to look at its lifestyle and imitate it although I have stated that few fish 'lock on' to natural foodstuffs quickly on small stillwaters.

You will find the odd wise fish in such places, very often a traumatized specimen that perhaps has been hooked and lost. These doughty characters will have learned the way of the water and how to harvest it. A mere shadow, a sudden lead-induced 'plop', will have it fleeing in terror. Consider, though, a delicately presented Midge Pupa, tumbling into its area of vision; it is something familiar and, importantly, edible. You will then understand the importance of both matching (to some degree) the trout's larder and knowing something of what lives in its surroundings. Apart from all that it is simply entertaining to look in mud, weed and bushes for clues and specimens.

Larva

Now we get to the 'chicken or the egg' part. Do I start with the egg-laying female midge or the egg itself? Or the resultant change into larvae? Perhaps the larva, because this is the first aquatic stage that truly interests trout; known universally as the bloodworm, which would suggest that they are all red, in fact they come in shades of green, cream and brown. Some prefer a life spent in tunnels, but the imitable ones favour a nomadic free-swimming lifestyle.

Two things earmark this creature as thoroughly acceptable to the trout and well worth mimicking with the fly. First, its colour, which in the case of the red version is very vivid indeed, giving the creature its name. The make-up is similar to our haemoglobin and is called haemoclycin. It serves the same purpose, enabling a tolerance of low oxygen levels and thus a wider range of aquatic habitats; also a varied depth band from a matter of inches down to twenty or so feet. The second thing is the creature's movement. Its wild gyrations are the stuff of piscatorial legend. Pattern after pattern has to be crafted to try and emulate the lithe thrashing, switchback movements – everything from rubber bands (red), balloon shreds, marabou, even chamois leather.

Yet, for all that, the most effective I have used is Mick Williams' Datsun, popularized by that wonderful fly tyer Terry Griffiths, who has almost codified the business of painting hooks red. The Red Hook, or a longshank hook (even size 8) can, on its day be simply devastating. I remember fishing Aveley in Essex – always a difficult water. Trout had gone down and no one was achieving anything. After four hours of 'nothing' I was less than amused. Suddenly I remembered the 'hook'. Out it went on an intermediate line and 15ft leader to 6lb double strength, a steady figure of eight. Bang! Two fish in two casts – one 8lb, the other 6lb. It has since had even greater red-letter days! Oddly the pattern (I can't bring myself to call it a fly) works best in very clear water, preferably with a hint of sun.

I also use another pattern – the Armageddon Worm – though, in truth, the weighted head and blend of fluorescent orange and cerise marabou tail lend themselves more to an attractor than my theory of the colour being the right tone of red at depth. Curiously though, the pattern has worked well where trout have been dining on bloodworm, but is that coincidence?

Pupa

From the larva comes the pupa, the mature pupa only taking a few days before it can journey surfaceward and hatch. This is perhaps the best-documented and most-predated stage of all. Indeed, so well detailed is its life, there would seem little point in labouring farther. However, I would like to offer the following observations.

The first concerns the interim point betwixt larval life and pupation. This has always fascinated me and, I believe, the trout. Caught in between two distinct worlds, the insect will show quite marked characteristics of this by embodying a vivid segmentation between the thorax and abdomen (the late Dick Walker was among the first to notice this aspect) or, in some cases, the rear third is given to the vivid red of the larva whilst the front two-thirds form the embryonic pupa of olive, black or whatever.

The chironomids, when in this state, tend naturally enough to be situated near to the bottom, and imitations displaying this banding have proved very successful. In fact, I would go further and say that the majority of my patterns these days have at least some part in red, be it dubbing strands, ribbing or floss.

Another factor is the pupa's love of exploratory trips to check out the surface. Rather like mayflies, the pupa will actually go on 'fact-finding' missions to see if it's OK to hatch. This is probably a mistake, as trout seem to notice these excursions with equal dedication. When pupae ascend, it is not, I have noted, with a pedantic, querulous rise, but a fairly vigorous swimming undulation – certainly a brisk figure of eight would do nicely.

Now we come to the imitation of their form. It is a jolly good job trout aren't as circumspect as we give them credit for. Shop-bought midge dressings, indeed most I come across, are simply far too portly. Look at any midge pupa and you will see a shiny wraith of a thing, with a bulbous but small thorax and a pair of white whiskers; it may even have embryonic wings and legs attached under the thoracic area. Now compare this with most standard dressings. Most will be overdressed, too big, and most will not be sufficiently translucent. Having previously outlined various patterns, I shall desist here, but would add that recently I have gone back to more accurate tyings, incorporating wings, head plumes and, importantly, enjoying improved success – once the size was also matched.

Emerger

It is hard to know where exactly to place the next part of the midge's lifestyle – is it the pupa in a state of undress or the adult in the changing-room? Suffice to say the emerger – that half in-half out world – is desperately important to the fly fisher.

Most anglers consider the emerger a stage for the reservoir fisher where, of course, it effects styles whenever midge are hatching and being pursued by trout. But it is equally important on small waters. The interesting factor during such times is, once again, the dominance of red – actually an intense orange to be more accurate. Select any colour of either pupa immediately prior to metamorphosis, or a newly hatched adult, and there will be a distinct bright orange about the wings, either fledged or immature and, in the pupa's case, reddish-orange blotches. Their haemoclycin, together with various gases, allows the hatching process to take place. Indeed the red-orange in some adults, notably the orange and silver golden olive, and red midge, is a feature of the wing area for its duration.

The important factor concerning the emerger is not so much what it looks like, but rather where it is. Trout seem to be very particular when feeding hard in the surface; half an inch can mean the difference between success and failure. Nine times out of ten, I look to fish the fly *in* rather than *on* the surface. Several styles work wonders, the Suspender Pupa or, better still, the Halo Emerger, can be truly exceptional during difficult rises.

Adult

The chironomid, having discarded its pupal coat, can be classified a true dry fly, yet I still prefer my flies to fish very close indeed to the surface, either using a parachute or clipped hackle to allow for a flush float.

Entering the equation, both during this adult stage and the previous pupal, is the weather, and it should never be overlooked that any insects, especially midge, find it a much easier task to get airborne on rougher, clear days when the water tension is broken and sufficient warmth is about to dry wings, than on warm, muggy days when the water and air appears almost treacly. These instances often create what must be very anxious, disconcerting times for the pupa, as the thicker water-surface tension often necessitates them having to hang motionless until finally they break through.

When fishing imitations of the dry midge, I have a rule which calls for the flush-riding types in flat calms to small wavelets; one and a half to two turns of head hackle during small to medium waves (offering an almost projectile appearance) and, in biggish waves, a hackle wound through the thoracic area entirely. These are just a few observations upon the chironomid; with so many to cover, one can only be fleeting. I would say in summary, be mean with your materials and pay particular attention to depth control, and you will unlock some of the secrets of the midge. And fish small. Trout respond to food available; it is we who invented hook sizes. If the trout are eating tiny black or green midge, then give them that size of imitation – the trout don't know that you nearly ruined your eyes dressing a size 22 or 24 hook.

Damsels and dragonflies

Since the middle of the 60s, Damsel Fly dressings, in similar vein to Mayfly patterns, have drawn our attentions possibly far beyond actual usefulness. That said, there are few of us who would set foot outside our door without one or two variations on this theme. But, just how important are the damsel and dragonfly naturals to the diet of the trout? In truth probably less than we expect or would like.

Dragonflies

Certainly, in the case of the dragonfly, their importance in terms of the trout's diet is, at best, fleeting and almost entirely based on the nymphal stage.

In many years' 'autopsies', I cannot recall finding any of these 'science fiction-crafted' succulent morsels. I am not for one moment suggesting they are not taken – and in some areas readily, particularly Australia and the USA and especially Canada where in the Kamloops area imitations often as large as 4 l.s. are vital to success – it is just that, given the plethora of foodstuffs available to our stillwater trout, this insect's priority is relegated somewhat low on

● *Dragonfly nymph*

the menu. Indeed, as it is fairly warlike in its attitude – beware pond dippers, the nymphs can inflict an interesting 'nip' – a trout could well be intimidated, especially as some species of nymph attain three inches in length (the emperor dragonfly for example). They are, though, fun to tie and if you are idling your time away at the fly tying bench and you feel the need to carry some examples for the sake of thoroughness, then look no further than either Randall's Green or Brown Lake Dragon, Floating Dragon or Darryl Martin's brilliant creation, the Woven Dragon. Certainly these should keep both you and the trout amused for a while.

Damsels

The damsel – Zygoptera – closely related to the dragon's Anisoptera, both falling under the umbrella Odonata, has exactly the same life-cycle – egg-nymph-adult. The egg, as in most aquatic cases, can be discounted by the fly fisher, with major concentration being focused on the nymph. Certainly the most widely distributed are the common blue and the blue-tailed, with the banded also being widespread, especially in the south. The nymphs, though all varying to some degree, tend to follow the same lifestyle, going through anything up to ten instars or moults.

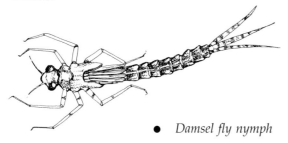

● *Damsel fly nymph*

These are important occasions for the fly fisher, as with each moult the nymph becomes progressively darker. As the nymphal duration often lasts for over two years, this also brings in another equation: during the first nymphal year, the nymph would suggest its winter coloration is straw or soft Naples yellow, through to golden olive, whilst during the second year and towards the end of its nymphal cycle, the coloration is very much darker, erring to very dark olive, near sooty olive and almost black. This huge colour variation also occurs during summer, when progressive darkening occurs, and size increases as the onset of adulthood beckons.

Certainly these tonal variations should be echoed in your fly box. Another factor worth pointing out is the trout's preference for a particular colour on certain days. No doubt this is closely aligned to what is available or on the ascendant, but on many occasions when fishing Bewl Water during the height of damsel nymph activity, I have noticed trout switch their attentions to a dark or light version on a daily or sometimes half-daily basis. It does pay to ring the changes.

Another attractor for Damsel users is the naturals' movement. Not for them laboured crawlings or sedentary travels; instead their whole sleek abdomen can, when threatened or urged, lash from side to side (rather like a newt) and propel the insect at considerable speed. This is one of the two major differences between the damsel and the dragonfly. The dragonfly nymph, rather than displaying articulated movement, relies on squirting a jet of water from the rear of its abdomen, by its three small pointed tails, to propel itself jet-like towards prey or away from danger.

The other difference is the outward appearance, the dragon being very much stubbier or squat, to the damsel's long, leggy elegance. Actually their names say it all: damsel – slender and pretty; dragon – scaly, fearsome and formidable!

However, back to movement. The damsel's

shape, coloration and overall recognition points give it a wide range of key or target imitative points. The problem is that, no matter how lovingly and realistically constructed, it is probably 'that' wiggle which is its trigger and ultimately the trout's seducer. By far the best way to imitate this key point is to choose the correct material: marabou heads the list, with a rabbit or similar fur strip, a close second, and the almost magical illusion of life, seal's fur (in various shades) a vital ingredient. If you have one or two of these components then your pattern will not be wide of the mark.

The natural tends to live most of its life near weeds and reeds – indeed, possibly in an area very localized to that where it was born. I have found it to favour Canadian pondweed, but it will, of course, colonize any type and locale that affords it cover and a ready source of foodstuffs, which can include a wide variety of trout-orientated matters such as shrimps, corixae, various small nymphs and so on. In terms of depth, down to about 15ft is its preferred range with 5ft- to 10ft-wide expanses of weed-strewn shallows being an extremely happy hunting ground.

There are two small yet important factors concerning damsel nymphs. The first is its migration to adulthood, which is always conducted towards a shoreline, be it flanked by sedge, tall grass or reed, whereby it clambers out into our dimension and metamorphoses into the startling, often irridescent adult (as do dragonflies); and secondly, the nymph's size which can vary dramatically, ranging from (in useful fishing terms) a half-inch up to an inch and a half (which is about a size 4 longshank).

Having once hatched into its variously brightly hued adult (male) form, the damsels' use to fly fishers was widely considered to be at an end. That was until Bill Sibbons, the

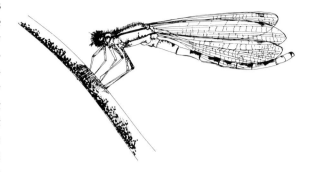

● *Adult damsel fly*

legendary stalker of leviathans on Hampshire fisheries, came up with a pattern and a theory which utilized the adult blue damsel. Bill reckoned that trout become incensed by the 'hither-and-thither' flight of adult damsels around the reeds during high summer, being unable to differentiate properly between above and below the surface, and so constructed an imitation dressed on a nickel hook, ostensibly nymph-like in design, but with the coloration of the adult. It worked, and indeed still does, especially when fished at high speed, just subsurface.

Enter also the American tyers, in particular Gary Borger, whose parachute pattern has worked wherever adult blue damsels have been the choice of the menu. Indeed, I cannot think of many better recreations than lazing on a sunny day, casting out a Parachute Blue Damsel along a weed line, then watching a wall of water and trout explode around it; a minor tactic certainly, but great fun. Incidentally, never fish your adult pattern too far out; the natural enjoys the sanctuary, laying her eggs often actually underwater among weeds.

And so to the various high spots in the damsel's annual calendar. In terms of their nymph-fishing usefulness, this is a year-long occurrence (if your penchant is for winter trout-

● *Damsel fly movement*

a

b

- *Damsel patterns*

a Distressed Damsel – offering a similar movement to the Mobile Marabou Tail
b standard damsel dressing – this tends to be fairly static on the water when retrieved.
NB Note the importance of a long Marabou tail

ing, as well as summer). However, the height of both emergence and trout interest starts in about mid-June, tapering off in mid-September; the real 'high' being July, with morning, even dawn, until about 11 o'clock being their daytime emergence peak.

The one thing that still eludes is the pattern's ascendancy over the trout's interest in the natural. Perhaps it is best not to look too closely at such things and merely to rest easy in the fact that few stillwater trout, especially in small stillwaters and gravel pits, will pass up the opportunity of an imitation – at any juncture of the season.

Crustaceans

Amongst the plethora of foodstuffs available to the trout, fly fishers have a tendency to overlook the very drab. It must, of course, be said that the delicate ephemeral beauty of a mayfly or the jauntiness of the caddis and the often-bright hues of the midge do tend to render bottom-dwelling creatures 'also rans'. But that is just to our eyes; the trout sees things rather differently.

Hoglouse and freshwater shrimp, though being entirely separate from one another and related only by virtue of the fact they are crustaceans, do have a common denominator: they are 'staples' – foodstuff that a trout can avail itself of throughout the year, a constant in its ever-changing palette. In our own terms they would be an *hors d'oeuvre* to the main course, and trout see these sombre beings in much the same way.

Hoglouse

Taking arguably the more prolific first – the hoglouse – this rather flat, mottled crustacean ranges in size from a fledgling 5mm ($\frac{1}{4}$ inch) to a more realistic 10–12mm ($\frac{1}{2}$ inch); I have actually seen them as large as 15mm ($\frac{3}{4}$ inch). The species enjoys a huge distribution on a variety of differing water types. Mostly it is a lover of dark, dank places, where it will forage around the rotting vegetation seeking out algae and other organic particles like a mottled vacuum-cleaner. It doesn't do a great deal of swimming, preferring a crawling regime amongst its food matter.

The hoglouse's threshold of pollution levels is very high, which gives us a very good idea of where to find it and its influence upon our fly fishing styles. It is rare to find solitary hoglice; they are far more likely to be in communities, which of course tends to concentrate the trout's mind a little when feeding at a slothful gait.

The other accommodating point about this

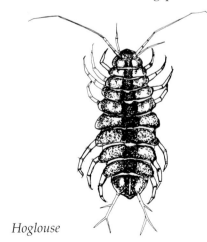

- *Hoglouse*

isopod is the water level it can endure. I have known it to occur – certainly in reservoirs – in areas of up to thirty feet, most notably at Queen Mother Reservoir in Slough, which contradicts the popular opinion of its preference for muddy, shallower areas. It is, in fact, a great survivor and able to endure a vast range of different depths and areas, which makes nymphing viable in a great range of circumstances.

Certainly this fourteen-legged 'critter' can be found on most small waters and English reservoirs, and I have encountered teeming thousands on the great Irish loughs, especially the limestone, notably Sheelin in the south and Erne to the north where it is an extremely important early- and late-season foodstuff and pattern choice.

Another interesting factor concerning hoglouse and trout-feeding behaviour, one that is especially noticeable, occurs at Rutland Water during the midge-rich period of May and June, where repeated autopsies have shown trout to be predating on both midge and hoglouse simultaneously, though more heavily to the buzzer. It would appear that trout take the hoglouse almost as a side dish, whilst tucking into the main course, making the inclusion of a Hare's Ear or specific Hoglouse pattern at some point on the leader a very sound proposition.

This leads me to patterns. There are in fact several direct hoglouse imitations – Peter Lapsley's version, Anne Douglas's and my own personal tying – but at a pinch the good old Straight or Wadham's Hare's Ear will work admirably, but fish them slowly!

Shrimp

The shrimp, though perhaps better known and certainly more readily imitated, enjoys a far less protracted distribution. This may come as a bit of a shock, but certainly their locale on stillwater can be very small or non-existent – indeed, on balance, they favour a far more alkaline type of water. However, where they are present, numbers can be epidemic.

Though vaguely related, the shrimp offers the perfect foil to the hoglouse; being hunched and rounded and rather armadillo-like, compared to the flatness of the hoglouse, whilst being speedily agile, especially when pursued by a predatory trout. Similarly the shrimp has seven pairs of legs, but unlike the hoglouse, their classification 'amphipod' – the ability to use the legs in both directions – explains their athletic performance as opposed to the hoglouse's isopod, which are singular in direction.

There are actually two species of interest to British fly fishers: *Gammarus pulex*, a common indigenous species, and a *Crangonyx* species hailing from America. Although very similar in size and shape – both being armour-plated, multi-legged creatures which can attain a very large size of 25 mm (1 inch), also both show a preference for fairly well-oxygenated weedbed areas, especially those near stones, pebbles or rocks – it is the contentious area of a shrimp's colour that separates them so markedly. *Crangonyx* tend to be a transparent grey, erring occasionally to a very watery grey-olive – almost a smoke colour – whereas *Gammarus* tends to be a much darker olive-grey, even tending to quite very dark olive, with some a distinct orange, erring to amber.

For years the orange colour was attributed to either the breeding colours or a disease,

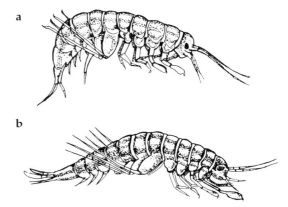

● *Shrimps*

a defensive/curved

b swimming

depending on who you listened to. Indeed, when shrimp die they do turn orange due to carotene being present in their shell – hence orange-fleshed trout. I rather think we were being had! I have come across any amount of shrimp that were a distinct orangey olive; on one lake in particular, the huge (and I mean *vast*) colony of shrimp was a soft orange the whole year through and they were very active indeed. Certainly this allows the fly dresser a much-extended palette to work from, with anything from Brindled Hare's Ear, through olive and hot orange to play with. I would, however, stress that in certain areas – notably chalk-infused streams and lakes which *Crangonyx* favour – Grey/Hare's Ear types are used for preference.

Another myth regarding the shrimp which has been perpetuated is their so-called penchant for swimming upside-down. Actually most of the time they swim sideways or upright, as well as upside-down – it simply matters little. A point worth considering, however, especially in terms of fly design, is their shape. Most fly tying enthusiasts opt for the naturals' 'resting' curved aspect, when in reality a sleeker, extended pose would be more realistic.

As mentioned, the shrimp's swimming action can be very fast, especially when being pursued. One foot- to two-foot long, swift stripping movements, interspersed with pauses, mimic this action very well. But it can be equally deadly on the drop. Because the shrimp is such a familiar form to the trout, the feeding instincts are often triggered by an imitation tumbling into their vision, which makes it a perfect consideration for clear-water stalking. And, though enjoying a largish distribution, on some waters especially large stillwaters, colonies can be incredibly localized, often in bays or weedbeds dotted around the shoreline – and nowhere else in the lake system. However, trout in such areas will react accordingly, making the imitation an important one.

That really only leaves fly patterns and, with such an abundance of juicy features to imitate,

it is little wonder that fly tyers have created a welter of variations. Favourites though are:

● the Patterson Red Spot, which exemplifies the natural's egg cluster (up to 1,000 I am told), held in a brood pouch at the female leg base, which have an orangey hue;

● Peter Cockwill's Hare's Ear, a version of utter simple deadliness – and 'shrimpy' to boot;

● my own Deer Hair type has worked extraordinarily well recently, and Gary Borger's Hair Leg Scud can also be very effective.

The colours should be adapted to suit those most prevalent in your area.

Thus you have two of the most important items on the trout's menu, and not just here; you will find identical shapes, sizes and colours throughout the Western hemisphere. Horrible and dowdy they may be, but they are nevertheless a vital link in fly fishing and the biological chain.

Phantom midges and daphnia

Phantom midge

One of the most familiar, yet overlooked, creatures on low-lying stillwaters is the phantom midge. As its name implies, it is among our most elusive imitatable creatures, yet it is so often critical to fly fishing tactics and trout behaviour.

The insect belongs, as you might expect, to the huge order *Diptera* – true flies – those of a flat-wing lineage, and is closely related to our old friend the non-biting midge – chironomid or, colloquially, the buzzer – though the family group is slightly different, being Charaborous.

It is the outward appearance that gives clues to the midge's name and secretive distribution, being for the most part, throughout its life, transparent. This of course, creates two problems for the fly fisher: first location and identification, and secondly imitation.

Of the first point the plus factor is the phantom's parallel lifestyle to that of chironomids – larva, pupa, adult – and an almost identical behaviour pattern, albeit wearing a different coat. This, of course, makes each differing stage appropriate for imitation. However, the phantom's influence on our sport is not quite so protracted as various other midge species; mostly being active between April and August and, during mild conditions, into September. The peak, though, is in June and July when it can be a vital consideration in tactics and fly choice.

Most authorities suggest that phantom midge are lovers of darkness and, being at their most active, they also hatch at this time. Actual fishing situations, however, would seem not to support this wholly, as many active periods, especially during the peak of activity, can be observed at any time of day. True the insect does tend to be fairly sensitive, making it similar to daphnia in that respect, being near the surface on overcast days, crash diving on bright days and fluctuating on those combined sunny/ cloudy days.

Their affinity with daphnia does not end there. During the larval stage the phantom performs as a practised hunter but, unlike the midge larva or bloodworm, does not reside hard on the bottom, writhing about in decomposing vegetation; instead it hangs vertically at suitable water levels, resembling miniature Egyptian mummies, predating on passing hapless daphnia, and during this time it is able to move quite swiftly in little darting movements. At this stage the creature is almost entirely transparent apart from two black eyes and a faint orangey coloration to the thorax. Another notable aspect is its clear, almost balloon-like thorax and hooked 'nose' by the eye, used for ensnaring its prey.

But, once changed into the pupa, its appearance switches into a more familiar shape: the outline is almost identical to a midge, although the body may be slightly thinner and thorax more bulbous. It is, though, readily identifiable as an opaque, small midge.

Thankfully for fly tyers there is at least some substance to imitate at this stage, the abdomen becoming creamy-white but solid, as opposed to transparent, and the thoracic region becoming a more pronounced orangey brown. The pupa's actions are almost identical to those of the Chironomidae, fluctuating up and down in the water levels until adulthood beckons, some four

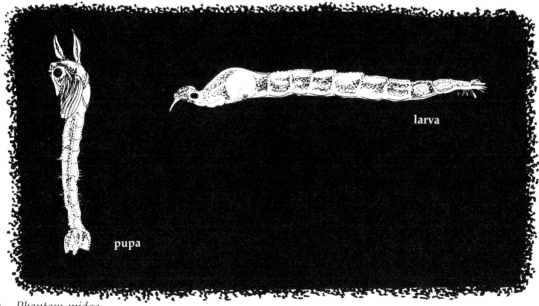

larva

pupa

● *Phantom midge*

to six days after pupation, and they make the final ascent to the surface and hatch into fully fledged adults.

Of all the stages, the adult is possibly of the least interest to the fly fisher; even the pupa perhaps plays 'second fiddle' to the larva which seems to dominate the trout's culinary interest.

Encountering the phantom when fishing can be a confusing business; often there is no tangible reason or clue as to what is happening or why trout should be feeding quite so frantically on the surface or on what. If you encounter this phenomenon, which is marked also by similar trout feeding behaviour as noted with midges – languid head-and-tail rise forms and those upwind furrowing rises through the waves and wind lanes – then the chances are you have encountered some phantom-eating trout.

There are, nowadays, a plethora of patterns to meet this particular challenge. They are specific, primarily because trout, when dining out on Charaborous, become very selective and any old fly will not do. The biggest problem though, when fishing a phantom imitation, is confidence; confidence that something *that* small and transparent will catch trout.

Years ago and still a favourite method on small waters was to fish a phantom larva on an intermediate line. This tactic often worked after the trout had seen every other fly dressing concoction known to man. More usually, though, it is a floating-line strategy that works – fishing to trout seen moving on or near the surface, though possibilities do exist for experiments with Hi-D line and the 'hang-and-hold' method.

Certainly, if you are on the water scratching your head wondering what trout are feeding on or what to try, you could do a great deal worse than the unprepossessing phantom midge.

Daphnia

Not so much a 'hatch', more a 'happening' – 'orange madness' they call it and all because a humble little orange (or green) water flea excites

trout to such an extent that they enter into a gastronomic orgy of harvesting this minuscule crustacean known as daphnia.

To understand this tiny being, look no further than your local pet shop, where great clouds of this little darting creature are sold to ardent fish keepers – it seems that goldfish are every bit as partial to this water flea as trout.

As diminutive as this form is, its importance in establishing trout feeding habits, location and depth is colossal. And its influence is not – as many believed years ago – confined to high summers on reservoirs, but on any water from the beginning to the end of the season.

Realistically they are inimitable, though some have tried. 'Taff' Price conceived a pattern, but I cannot help but think he had his tongue firmly planted in his cheek when he did so because, if you consider fishing Corixa or Midge slightly against the odds, then what chance would a size 18 or smaller have in a veritable cloud of teeming thousands of these crustaceans? Thus reality urges us not to even try to match the 3mm ($\frac{1}{8}$ inch) and smaller hatch. Thankfully though, the daphnia's colour(s) gives us a clue to fly choice, and by understanding something of its lifestyle and preferences, we can gain vital information regarding the depth and manner of fishing our patterns.

Having mentioned the size, which is depressingly small, it should also be pointed out that both kinds – *Daphnia* species and *Simo-*

● *Daphnia or water flea*

cephalus veterlis – are ostensibly transparent, apart from their internal organs and egg clusters which tend to give them distinct colour tones. *Daphnia* are orange-based, and *Simocephalus* a lime-green. This is important, as it will determine the best colour combinations when selecting a suitable pattern. The next important factor is the water fleas' penchant for establishing colonies or 'blooms' – huge groups which tend to move as one, filtering tiny organisms from the water. This perhaps more than any other aspect concerns the fly fisher, as trout will follow these undulating blooms doggedly, and if we are to be successful then we must also alter our fishing depths accordingly.

As you might imagine, the vast groups of daphnia will be situated near the surface during periods of low light – dawn and dusk – and cloud cover, crash diving as soon as direct sunlight bombards the surface. The real difficulty comes on days which produce intermittent sun and cloud, making the vast blooms of daphnia rise and fall with the frequency of a yo-yo. The fly fisher is left with little option other than to chop and change line types in order to keep in touch with these undulations and the trout predating on them, and this may entail using a high-density sinker one minute then switching to an intermediate or floater the next – very demanding stuff.

Yet their location is only half the battle. How do we logically represent this veritable 'fish soup' of tiny daphnia? As previously mentioned, the size is largely inimitable; however, by echoing their overriding colour – orange for daphnia, fluorescent green for *Simocephalus* – we can achieve excellent results. Whether this represents to the trout a great 'gloop' of the crustaceans, or they are purely 'switched on' by the colour, is hard to guess. It is, though, a time very much dedicated to the lure or attractor fisher, with patterns such as Whisky Flies, Chief Needabahs and Tadpoles in orange to cover the preference for *Daphnia* species; and for the green *Simocephalus*, Leprechauns, Fluorescent Lime-green Tadpoles and Punk Rockers.

The loch-style fly fisher can also meet the challenge by using Old Nicks, Jaffas, Grenadiers, Vindaloos and other Hot Orange Palmers and mini-lures and, of course, lime-green attractors as well. Curiously, though, black-based patterns can be very effective during daphnia mayhem, and are often a first choice for fly fishers.

The nymph fisher need not become too despondent, as trout can often be triggered into taking a familiar insect-shaped fly imbued with a suitably coloured 'hot spot' such as a Hare's Ear or Pheasant Tail with a fluorescent green or orange thorax. The key is finding the right depth, and this can on some occasions be very misleading. During evening periods and on those grey overcast days, swathed in misty rain, the trout often start to cruise and rise, 'bulging' in the surface, making us reach immediately for midge pupa patterns. Often, especially in large water areas, the reason for this nymphing rise form is, in fact, daphnia-feeding, and many frustrated anglers and dry nets have testified to a misreading of this parallel feeding behaviour.

It should be said that it does take a while for daphnia species to colonize a water and, even once established, they are given to species fluctuations; however, there is little doubt that, aside from midge pupa, the next most important protein-rich trout food is daphnia, and that also makes it very high on the fly fishers' priority list.

So, next time you see some midge-rising fish, do not be too hasty; give some consideration to this humble water flea. It might just turn an ordinary day into a red- (or should it be orange-) letter day.

Olives

Among our loveliest aquatic life forms are the Ephemeroptera – to we fly fishers: the olives. These wonderfully delicate little flies brighten any day when they hatch, looking for all the world like a miniature regatta of yachts mustering before the start of the race. They were largely the originators of the artificials which started the whole business of fly fishing. Yet I have to confess that compared to midge, damsels, even crustaceans like shrimp and hoglouse, this gentle upwing must be seen as 'second division' – a glorious interlude and an important one but, as its name implies, ephemeral.

That said, there are waters where its emergence is a major and imitable event. Indeed, on acidic, high reservoirs, tarns, lochs and larger stillwaters and gravel pits, it is an important food source. It would also be foolish to overlook the importance of the olives on Irish loughs; both the lake or, colloquially, 'sooty' olive and the mighty mayfly often provide the cream of the fly fishing season.

Their actual lifestyle is similar to most semi-aquatic insects. Laid as an egg either by the female lying directly on or under the water's surface or even (as is the case with blue winged olive) aerially, the egg then hatches out into the nymph.

Nymph

The nymphal stage is the most diverse in terms of appearance, from species to species. Although adults vary enormously in size, colour and markings, their actual appearance is very similar. Not so the nymph, which not only varies in shape from order to order, but also fashions different lifestyles to accommodate differing aquatic habitats.

But before identifying the nymphal shapes, a rationale of species location must be addressed.

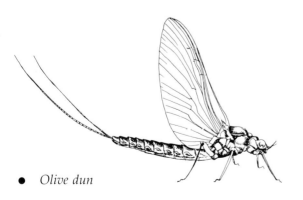

● *Olive dun*

The most common, stillwater species are pond and lake olives and, everyone's friend the caenis – or 'Angler's Curse' – the mayfly, sepia dun, large summer dun, claret dun. Though similarities exist, the nymphs of all seven do vary – some dramatically so – and are worth outlining because of the different styles of dressing needed to imitate them – and indeed, ways of moving about under water, which ultimately affects retrieve rates.

The major types conform to the following nymphal varieties:

● Pond and lake olives and large summer dun – agile darters

● Claret and sepia dun – laboured swimmers

● Caenis – silt crawlers

● Mayfly – bottom burrowers

The nymphal stage lasts for very nearly twelve months, the nymph changing skin (instars), growing in size and becoming generally darker as emergence beckons.

The lifestyles of nymphs are as different as the locations they inhabit:

The agile darter   (of the summer dun, pond and lake olives)   This is a lover of extensive weed-beds and fairly rich water such as Midlands reservoirs and southern and other lowland lakes and gravel pits. It relies on speed and (as its name implies) agility to avoid capture. In fact a fly fisher is hard pressed to imitate the nymph's quicksilver speedy darts, interspersed with rests, and jerkings. However this suits perfectly the 'quick, quick, slow' of a fairly fast, twitched retrieve and don't worry too much about the odd high-speed draw with the line hand.

Coloration can vary enormously from species to species and even within the same family. However, the appearance does remain constant, being fairly thin in the body with a rather pronounced thorax where the wingpads are situated; six slender and quite long legs, and three widely separated tails, approximately the same length as the abdomen.

The laboured swimmers (of the sepia and claret duns) These are different again, being generally a darkish brown colour (both species) and almost tubular in shape, with very noticeable fringes of hair-like gills at the junction between thorax and abdomen. The tails are also distinctive, the three tend to be widely spread, spiky in appearance and the same length as the insect. It is of course the movement which gives it its name, and a slow, twitched figure of eight is perhaps the best retrieve style.

The bottom burrower (mayfly) This is realistically only viable as a nymphal form, in fishing terms, during the period between 18 May and about 20 June – though locale may protract or diminish this, it is essentially a brief hatch period.

The silt crawler The character we 'love to hate', the caenis (or 'Angler's Curse'), has by contrast a long hatch period. As a nymph it is a small,

Caddis – *thought to be the least important of the aquatic foodstuffs; there have been quite a few occasions recently when both pupa and adult have proved important, especially toward evening, from late June to early August*

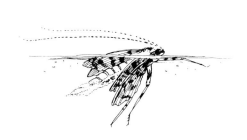

● *The sedge larva or cased caddis – each stillwater species builds its own unique fragment constructed home. Generally a stickfly or 1.6. s.10 Hare's Ear will imitate this bottom-trundling stage. Fishing time: March, April, May and June*

● *The hatching sedge – if you see sudden splash rises, the chances are the trout has chased the pupa to the surface and is feeding on the hatching stage – the Invicta or Muddler is the best remedy*

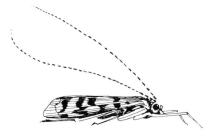

● *The pupa – most species fit into yellow, amber, cream, light and dark olive, in size 18–10. Good imitations are Invictas, Hare's Ears and Muddlers, fished subsurface. The natural has a decided 'stop/ start' ascent movement best suited to a 'strip-stop-strip-stop' return*

● *The adult stage – most familiar sights will be grouse wing, longhorn, cinnamon, silverhorn and red sedges on small stillwaters. All will have roof-shaped wings and fairly prominent antennae. The one depicted is a grouse wing. Try an Elk Hair or Ovipositing Running sedge or Stimulator. Sedges seem always to be on the move and that is how one should fish the pattern*

unobtrusive creature which rests on the bottom but it does make excursions to the surface – to sample the air, as it were. It is at such times than an artificial can be extraordinarily useful, as long as you have the confidence to fish a size 18 nymph; sadly few people have and they miss golden opportunities. In appearance they are short, squat, mottled brown with a very pale underside and a pronounced large thorax, small tails, but six muscular legs. Again it is a pattern best fished slowly figure of eight, from midwater to surface.

Emerger

The next stage, and one common to all, is the hatching process or now-popular 'emerger' state. Without question it is one of nature's masterpieces – from dowdy flattened form comes a creature with wings aloft and of totally different colour and appearance. No one is precisely certain what makes this group of insects hatch out at such specific times, as regularly as clockwork; yet they do, year in and year out. Could it be because of barometric pressure, the angle of the sun, or light intensity? All these possibly contribute to the performance.

What is in no doubt is the trout's intention. The hatching insect takes precious moments to emerge and discard the nymphal shuck on damp, muggy days, and in drizzle this can take a considerable time. The trout, ever aware of such proceedings, waste no time in harvesting this crop of olives in their dishevelled state while they are trapped in the surface film. This explains why tatty flies or well 'picked out' dubbed-body emergers fished absolutely still work so well.

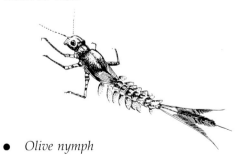

● *Olive nymph*

● *Caenis spinner*

Once free of its nymphal incarceration, the dun prepares to take to the air when its wings have dried sufficiently and fully extend. (They actually work like a concertina and need blood pumped through them to spread out.) Their appearance now looks more familiar as olives and, although they all resemble each other, subtle variations exist, as of course does colour and size. Of all these imitable aspects and clues to fly choice, size is the most important. Even the huge variation in colour schemes and wing and body markings can realistically (in fishing terms) be secondary to size.

But, on an entirely personal level, I do believe wings matter on patterns. Logically they are target points and must certainly be the trigger that alerts the trout to something good to eat as the dun comes within the trout's cone of vision.

It is rare for any of the stillwater olives to hatch singly; it is far more likely that a cluster or considerable numbers will all emerge at the same time. This is referred to as a 'hatch', and can occur at any time and varies from one species to another. But the dun is far more likely to emerge between 10 a.m. and 8 p.m. Caenis are the 'wild card' as they hatch as a dun in the evening and change almost immediately, even on the wing, into a spinner.

Adult

If the insect has managed to escape the attention of the trout, then it will fly off the water and begin its now famous brief life – the Latin title Ephemera meaning literally 'short-lived on the wing'. The nymph's ability to feed is given up on adulthood, and only mating remains as the prime motivation. Most olives now enter an amazingly short period of between twenty-four and thirty-six hours before their ultimate death; and yet, even in this short period of time, the adult will transform itself yet again into what can only be described as its 'breeding coat' – the spinner. This transformation is truly re-markable: the comparatively dowdy dun sheds its skin to emerge, glistening and resplendent with delicate pearlescent wings taking over from drab grey and sparkling brightly hued body from the dowdy olives. This tends to take place away from water and is of only academic interest to the fly fisher. However, the now spinner (or imago – perfect fly) will mate, the female returning to the lake and ultimately, after laying her eggs, a watery grave – death following quickly after the exhaustion of this act. The fly is now referred to as 'spent' and is yet another important imitable stage.

'Spent' fly

Egg-laying is conducted mostly at last light and into the night, and again very early in the morning. In fact, it is not unusual to find great 'rafts' of dead spinner in bays and windward shores at dawn after a heavy 'fall' of spinner (egg-laying activity) the previous evening. In fishing terms this is important as many trout forsake their usual caution and begin to feed in exceptionally shallow water, at both evening time and dawn, scooping up great mouthfuls of spent fly. This feeding activity tends to happen when mayfly, lake (or pond) olives and caenis

- *Olive spinner*

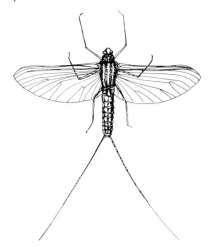

have met their watery end in large numbers.

It is very important at such times to ensure that your fly is correctly positioned: *in* the film, rather than *on* on the surface. Also, deceiving trout that are feeding on spinner calls for a great deal of accuracy, and delicacy. The trout's feeding line will vary only slightly – unless it is maddeningly darting all over the place after caenis – and to miss by one foot is to have missed by a mile.

In terms of artificials, this insect order has enjoyed unrelenting impersonation by fly tyers, to such an extent that there are probably more olive imitations than any other. Yet the reality is that few patterns are needed in order to cope with various hatches encountered – again it is size that is the dominant factor.

Pond and lake olives

There cannot be many sights that gladden the heart or quicken its pace for the reservoir angler so much as the first big hatch of olives. Not that lake Olives are confined purely to our reservoirs; the vast loughs of Ireland, high tarns and lakes of Cumbria and far away lakes of Wales all play host to this natural carnival.

And, if one talks of lake olives, one should also mention the small water counterpart – the pond olive. Actually, separating the two in either nymph or dun terms is a nightmare, there being so little difference as to be marginal or cursory to fishers, fly tyers and fish. The only really notable difference is apparent in the spinner or imago form and then it's nearly all over bar the shouting.

Practically, they can be treated as one. Both belong to the family *Cloeon* – the lake is *Cloean simile*, the pond *Cloeon dipterum*. Clear identification between the species is further hampered by the huge colour variance which the nymph and dun seem to enjoy.

However, for those who are 'sticklers' for such things, the female pond olive dun has two parallel red-brown lines along the underbody, and the male pond olive has two red lines through the eyes. Along the wing leading edge, the pond olive has three to five cross veins, the lake between nine and eleven (I doubt though that trout can differentiate between the two or really care too much).

Distinguishing either the pond or lake olive from other upwinged mayfly species is though relatively easy as they are the only ones *not* to have hind wings.

Now to the bit you're probably most interested in. How do they dovetail into the fly fishing year? The Agile Darter shaped nymph (similar to other Baetid types) lives life at a modest dash throughout very nearly the whole year in either its embryonic form or when fully fledged. However, from about late April onwards they will become decidedly active, notably in depth, racing from marginal shallows of a few feet to wider weed-strewn areas of around twenty feet. You can confidently expect flurries of adult preluding the main hatch from early May, reaching a crescendo on most waters during late May and early June; then again in September.

That said, there can be flurries of activity throughout the flyfishers' season; but May, June and September are when the really big 're-gatta's' take place.

Now to size: most authoritative books will tell you it is of a 'medium' designation, which doesn't help much.

In tying terms, standard shank 14 and 16 hooks are about the right size for either species.

The nymphs' overall characteristics are similar in shape, sporting three tails and quite marked gills along the side of the abdomen. Both species are a mottled/variegated olive ranging from yellowish olive, right through to brown-olive; however, some authorities have ventured that the lake olive is a great deal less energetic and can be found over deep-water weed beds, sporting tubby legs in comparison to its more agile pond 'cousin', which does err to lighter yellow-olive colouration.

I would personally favour a figure-of-eight method of retrieve for both using a long leader (18 ft plus) floating line and a GE Nymph as the imitation (though a pheasant tail or Greenwell's G. Nymph are contenders).

The dun, as with other Baetids, has two tails, there are (as mentioned) only two wings which are a distinctive mid-smokey grey. The segmented bodies on either can vary hugely between a very yellow olive (Peter Gathercole and I found some last season at Rooksbury Mill and couldn't figure out what species they were, and only when Peter took them home to hatch into spinners did he discover they were, in fact, pond olives), right the way through to brown-olive. Some late lake olives I saw (swarms of them) during a September 'tubing' session on Lough Sheelin, were almost black – hence perhaps the Irish term for them – sooty olives.

As to patterns, the evergreen Greenwell's Glory (the tailed and winged version has much to recommend it, but for true-to-life accuracy and attitude, you might care to try a Peter Gathercole olive version taken from my original Duck's Dun concept. This has been deadly over the last four or five seasons when duns of either species have been seen on the water (as mentioned, it is at the spinner stage when most differences occur. I won't dally with the male spinner as they have marginal angling importance; the female, on the other hand, can be vital).

Nor is it just the colour of the female pond and lake olives that separate them. Nature has once again woven her mercurial spell – inside the female pond olive the eggs that most other upwinged species merely lay on the water actually germinate during a two-week cycle and develop into minuscule larvae which, when laid on the water surface, quickly disperse in similar fashion to midge larvae and begin their growing process in the seclusion of water weeds.

Whereas duns of both species tend to be midday or afternoon hatching (though this can get progressively later during the autumn), the spinner 'falls' tend to occur in the evening and, I feel confident in stating, a vast amount lay their eggs under the cloak of darkness (certainly both species favour warm, still periods for egg-laying missions). It is not unusual to find great rafts of spent spinner littering shorelines during the still, mist-swathed dawns of early and late summer. But, be it early or late, the weather pattern must be settled and warm for egg laying to take place.

The female pond olive's colloquial spinner name pattern gives the game away – the Apricot Spinner – and that's exactly what the body looks like – a ripe apricot, flushed with orangey-red ribbing. The hyaline wings are also distinctive, having a yellow-orange leading edge, with delicate brown veining. The female lake olive, on the other hand, has a rich chestnut-brown abdomen with faint-yellow banding. The hyaline wings are almost devoid of extra colour.

I used to think the spinner of either species to be of only academic interest. That was then. Countless occasions over the years have persuaded me otherwise. The spinner can often literally be the 'key' to success at first and last light.

Pattern recommendations for the Apricot would be a Lunn's Yellow Boy or my own imitation based on the Renee Harrop Bodied Biot theme in sizes 14, or better still, 16.

For the lake olive a spent tied Pheasant Tail will suffice, though I would recommend the sunset spinner as being more imitative.

In closing, there is one aspect worth considering – the Emerger or hatching dun – and though the nymph, dun and spinner are all mainstays, the fractionally sub-surface hatching fly has given rise to a plethora of wet fly designs, mostly with an Irish accent. Sooty olives and Melvin olives and other lake olive patterns, not forgetting the wet Greenwell's fished traditionally with a suitable nymph as a point fly, or singly, using the Quigley style of dressing, can be deadly.

I would add that when a big hatch of either species gets under way sport can be frantic. Oddly, I have noticed some of the larger fish in the various water systems come out 'to play' – there just seems something bewitching about those diaphanous olives for fish and fisher alike.

Magnificent mayfly

Fly patterns often reach a status of 'legend' – James Ogden's Invicta; the canon's Greenwell; Dr Wickham's Fancy and Lunn's Particular, to name a few, all testify to this. The natural insect is not generally afforded the same privilege, that is, unless it is the mayfly. Seldom, in the history of angling, has so much been dedicated to a mere month of the fly fishers' season, and then, only affecting a tiny portion of the country's trout waters. Flies, passages in books, study, argument, discord, even clandestine and secret departures from work – all surround this, our biggest upwinged fly. The term 'mayfly madness' was not coined for nothing. And yet its beginnings are humble, solitary and cloistered.

Nymph

The nymph is among the most distinctive of this order. It is tubular in appearance, a fawny cream in colour, with intermittent chocolate-brown abdominal markings, and a distinct dark brown wing case. The body is also distinctive due to the feather gills, which aid its tunnel digging, collecting oxygen and bits of microscopic food. They lie along its abdominal sides, but mostly surround the area between thorax and abdomen.

It is classified as a silt- or bottom-burrower and can spend as much as two years in its burrow in the lake or river bed before emerging. There are two distinct schools of thought about the nymphs' life-span; one leaning to the original theory of a two-year nymphal cycle, and another, which I tend to favour, that there are two distinct cycles – a yearly one and a two-yearly, albeit the same insect genus. Be that as it may, the nymph's imitation has only a short working period; so I must conclude that the argument is largely academic for our purposes. And yet, the Mayfly Nymph's effectiveness far and away exceeds both its short (to the trout's eyes) subsurface active life and area distribution. Curiously some far-flung and generally wholly unsuitable water can be fished confidently with a Mayfly Nymph – from April to October – which makes a mockery of the natural's movements between mid-May and the first two weeks of June.

The nymph is a relatively laborious swimmer, but can put on a surprising turn of speed if danger threatens – a pronounced 'sink and draw' movement of an artificial would echo the natural perfectly. The nymph can make several excursions towards the surface before finally taking the plunge into adulthood. It is at this moment of hatching or emerging that one of the great fly fishing opportunities presents itself, and one that is all too often misinterpreted, misjudged or just plain missed.

Emerger

Whilst emerger fishing on our reservoirs has enjoyed phenomenal interest and experimentation, it appertains almost exclusively to midge (chironomid). However many other insects go through exactly the same excursions, including the mayfly, and are just as available, if not more so, to the trout.

Some years ago I came up with a floating Deer Hair Mayfly Nymph. It remains to this day, one of the more effective flies in my box (at the appropriate time of course). Its function is to mimic the dishevelled chaos of the discarded nymphal shuck's exploding inner gases which create the hatching process and the illusion of metamorphosis. All this hatching and changing appearance takes time – precious time – which of course makes it dangerously available to the trout: on balance, this stage is one of the most important.

Another style entirely at this point of hatching is the classic 'Wet Mayfly' of Irish origin. Some, though looking incongruous and wholly inappropriate, can deceive selective trout readily; the Arrow Mayfly, the Gosling and many more parody this state of hatching confusion.

There is another which can only be described as the 'stillborn' stage and is outwardly similar to the emerging process – the trout's reaction to it being near identical. However it tends to be important only when a really large hatch gets underway, when a proportion of the natural flies fail to hatch and therefore die in the process, either in an advanced state, as a dun with crumpled wings, or half in and half out of the nymphal shuck. Sometimes very accurate dressings of this stage are called for, especially in calm conditions, though thankfully this is not an overly common occurrence and the floating nymph tends to carry on its effectiveness.

Adult

The next stage has had generations of authors reaching for their pens to pay homage to nature's magnificence. A newly hatched mayfly dun has all the pomp and circumstance of a man o'war in full sail. It is an impressive beast, and patterns are legion, ranging from the ultra-realistic to the preposterous parody – and most work on the day.

There are two major types of mayfly – *Ephemera danica* and *E. vulgata*; there is another – *E. lineata* – though this is very rare. *Danica* and *vulgata* are very similar in appearance (only underside marking really separating them) so, in essence, we can treat them ostensibly as the same insect.

The point of which to be aware is how different the overall colour schemes vary. The mayfly in Ireland is a pronounced overall brown, erring to yellow and olive; whilst in the south of England the creatures tend to the classic creamy yellow-tinted body with pronounced chestnut abdominal and thoracic marking and heavily dark brown-veined olive wings. Yet in other areas a distinct brown-olive appearance can sweep over the dun. A constant recognition point is the fly, having three olive brown tails, whilst most other upwinged species have two. Even if colour can be confusing, the size of the insect cannot; it is quite the largest upwinged fly on our waters. So much so that trout can be decidedly suspicious of it when first hatching, and often take some days to acclimatize to the fact that this huge insect is actually good to eat.

However, once trout are really 'on' the hatch, they can become decidedly fussy in how they take the adult, what they see as a trigger or recognition feature, and in what order they take them. Remember, not all mayfly fishing is a 'duffers' fortnight'. Indeed, often a trout will fall into a sequence feeding mode, taking every other fly and missing out one, or every third, fourth or fifth natural. Unless your fly falls into that order, you will not catch. In terms of patterns, the Shadow Mayfly, the Grey Wulff and, for realism, the Lively Mayfly are all proven.

Once the dun has dried its wings and launched itself from the water with lazy yet majestic wing beats, the final stage begins of mating and, ultimately, death. It is during this brief period, lasting between twenty-four and forty-eight hours that another metamorphosis takes place, and the transformation from dun to spinner occurs. The Latin terms are really rather appropriate: sub-imago (imperfect fly) to imago (perfect fly) – for *that is* a mayfly spinner, a perfect fly. It is of academic interest only that mating takes place well away from the river – often spinners will be seen near parked cars, the warmth of the metal or perhaps the shiny surface attracting them – for it is the egg-laying female that presents the fly fisher with yet another golden opportunity.

Spinner

Whereas the dun tends to hatch out during the day – often from eleven to twelve o'clock during the morning, then again in the afternoon from about three to six o'clock, with a short lull, and possibly continuing until evening – the spinner tends to 'fall' an hour or two before darkness and is almost entirely an evening fly.

On appearance, the mayfly spinner could be mistaken for another insect entirely. It has three long blackish-brown tails; ivory white body (abdomen), with intermittent brown markings to the rear; a dark brown thorax; and wings which are clear to the point of looking like electric-blue reflectors with delicate blackish veins. The spinner positively sparkles when compared to the drab dun.

Curiously, the Shadow Mayfly works extraordinarily well during a fall of spinner, but Neil Patterson's Deer Stalker and John Goddard's Polywing Spinner offers a more accurate imitation, as does the late Dick Walker's hairwing spent pattern. The similarity aspect of a good spent pattern must also echo the egglaying stage, or immediately after when the fly, with wings outstretched and at right angles to the body, lies flush in the surface, only twitching with life and exhausted from her egg-laying exertions.

Trout at such times feed lazily and confidently, knowing their prey stands no chance of escape, and often so selectively that only a realistic pattern stands any chance at all.

And so, with eggs laid and trout sated, the whole process can begin again. Life seems to be like that in the natural world; as one stage comes to a close, another starts life.

Snails and corixae

On first impression, snails and corixae would appear strange bed-fellows indeed, but first impressions can be so deceptive. Though largely different, some similarities do exist between these two forms. There is their widespread location over many types of stillwater and rivers, though perhaps less so in the corixa's case. Then you have both their importance in fashioning fishing styles, techniques and imitations. Also there is the, sometimes overstressed, influence they have on tactics. Both have important, though fleeting, bouts of usefulness. I say this in the full knowledge that there are times when both are vital. There is also the fact that they are staple and available to the trout throughout the year. So you see they are inter-related, albeit tenuously.

Snail

It is very easy to fall into the trap of assuming a snail is a snail and so on. In fact, only a few types of the huge array are worth angling attention; of these the wandering snail, Jenkin's spire shell, with perhaps the ramshorns, being the most usual in the trout's culinary attentions.

Snails fall into two categories: pulmonates, breathers via a simple lung, and operculates which are able to seal the entrance to their shell and breathe by allowing water to pass over their gills where they accumulate the necessary oxygen. Trout of course don't care much one way or another; however, what does concern both angler and trout is that most snails have to venture surfaceward to breath. Often this migration to the lake's surface corresponds with warm weather, which 'Taff' Price considers proof that this is why the movement takes place, rather than for recolonization or mating reasons.

Certainly anglers, especially at Grafham, Eyebrook and other lowland reservoirs, have encountered fantastic quasi-'dry fly' sport when snails enter into their migrating mode – if they recognize what it is – during these warmer spells, especially during July and August, using

● *Snail*

deer-hair shaped snail imitations. Of course, not all snail fishing is about the surface; I have encountered, on many occasions, heavy snail predation when tiny Jenkin's spire shells or wandering snails become enmeshed in blanket weed, so much so that the weed positively crunches with their sheer numbers. They are very much a feature of the warmer months, with the ubiquitous Black and Peacock arguably the best imitation of all, leaded or not.

There is even a species of brown trout in Ireland, the Gillaroo, which has evolved a muscular stomach to deal specifically with the hard cases of snails and similarly tough crustaceans. So snail imitations on the lake bed are also important – perhaps more so than the surface. That said, light does play a significant role. Arthur Cove, among the greatest stillwater nymph fishers, believes in an orange-based pattern when imitating the snail, especially during their migration, the reason being that there is a distinct orange hue given off when a snail shell is viewed against a strong light source.

Plotting the lifestyle of the snail serves no great purpose; at first it is an egg (or, in the case of the Jenkin's, it is birthed a tiny adult) and then it has a three-year life-cycle as a shelled adult. However, it is the mollusc's adaptability to various water types and its sheer weight of numbers that make it one of the more important staple food forms, which especially concerns fly fishers during the high summer months.

Corixa

The corixa, though showing the characteristics already mentioned with the snail, is fundamentally different. Its lifestyle can be best described as 'on a dash' – dashing from danger, rushing to get oxygen, the odd rest then off again.

The lesser water boatman, or more familiarly, corixa, came from a larger family known as back swimmers which embraces the occasionally fearsome greater water boatman. The corixa divides into about thirty families which accounts for the vast range of colour variation from water to water.

● *Corixa*

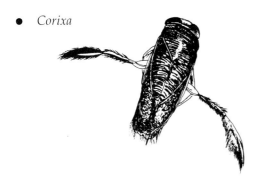

Life for the corixa starts in the spring when the egg is laid, implanted into the stems of weeds. Thereafter the insect will go through five instars or moults. These are particularly important to fly fishers, due to each instar being similar in some aspects to a peeler crab when the shell of each becomes very soft; in the case of the corixa this sponginess coincides with a much lighter coloration, prior to the new coat being formed. This lighter state – or instar stage – is generally a fawny, almost pinky cream and can often galvanize trout into a frenzied feeding preoccupation.

The corixa enjoys a wide range of habitats, but does contain itself among the more low-lying rich reservoirs, lakes and pools, where it will live in weed-fringed shallows of mud or pebbles, seldom seeking out depths much over fifteen or twenty feet.

The actual coloration of the insect varies enormously, and fly tyers and designers often create either silver or white-bodied patterns. Certainly, I have found soft yellow (pale primrose) and cream far more accurate, as well as the aforementioned pinky beige, than pearl or fluorescent white. Another body colour is bright, almost fluorescent golden yellow, which Richard Walker imitated so effectively with his varnish-soaked Yellow Corixa with its striking olive (almost grass) green back. This pattern is an extremely good imitation of a particularly numerous corixa found in alkaline water. The other members of this tribe have the more familiar golden brown and heavily dark mottled wing cases. Yes, believe it or not, corixa can fly. This is often very evident during May and

early June and again in September when great numbers will burst from the water, take to the air and fly for quite long distances. They do this probably either to colonize or mate in a different area, possibly due to pressure of numbers or even because they have a 'sixth sense' of a dying-out habitat.

Of course, the allure for trout and fishermen alike is the creature's darting journeys to and from the surface in order to replenish oxygen – on the way back, their quasi-oxygen 'tanks' flash like quicksilver, alerting the trout to an opportunistic meal.

But, as attractive as the corixa most certainly is, I have found few in trout 'autopsies'; though this is countered by occasions when I have watched trout feeding very selectively indeed on them. I remember one day at Enton lakes, in the shallow corner of the dam on the top lake, seeing marauding bands of trout pummelling terrified instar corixa colonies, and again Eyebrook positively reverberates to corixa plundering – but once more, it appears to be the moulting stage which incites this voracious predation. Curiously, one of the best patterns I have used during such periods is a Golden Hare's Ear, tied with the fur found on the cheeks rather than the mask.

However, in terms of fishing strategem, the corixa does lend itself to imitation and, importantly, in a shape that can incorporate a good deal of weight so it sinks quickly, creating a stalking type of bug for fishing to individual fish, especially 'on the drop'. Curiously, when fishing 'blind', as quick as the 'bug' most certainly is, the best policy is a long leader, floating line and a figure of eight retrieval.

It is also worth adding that the traditional fry-feeding frenzy during autumn coincides with the final moult, and very often fry-feeding fish will suddenly switch their attentions to corixa without their clothes on.

Certainly, as with the snail, there is a fair chance of corixa being present on most waters in England and, if it is there, the trout will tend to eat it at some point – eventually. By this virtue alone, it is a strong candidate for the leader in a 'don't know' situation.

Black gnats and other bibio

One of the hardest things for most fly fishers to grasp is the enormity of the insect family Diptera – flat-winged flies. Indeed, it might surprise most people to find that the humble house fly, gangly daddy longlegs and vital chironomid (midge) are all interrelated. Of course, trout don't care much for family trees; their only interest is in abundance and availability, closely allied to ease of gathering.

Certainly a category that fills this equation is the family Bibio, from the umbrella group Diptera. The word 'Bibio' may not mean a great deal to you, but when dissected into specifics – the hawthorn fly, the heather fly and black gnat – then not only are rivers and stillwaters suddenly and importantly bound together, but great chunks of the season and tactics catered for. And important interludes they are.

Gnats

The 'gnats' cover just about every water type in the country, ranging from upland acidic reservoirs and the heather fly; to small and large stillwaters and lowland streams, the hawthorn fly; and just about everywhere, black gnats.

The gnats are a vital component of our surface-fishing strategies, both in the late spring and the near-dead period that straddles late summer and early autumn – August and September. True to the perversity of fly fishing, black gnats are not black at all, but dark smoky brown.

Another piscatorial problem is size. Given

● *Black gnat*

that a majority of stillwater fly fishers consider 14 small and 16 ridiculous – though this is changing slightly – you may be depressed to learn that 18s and 20s are *de rigueur* to imitate the natural.

Oddly, it is the role of this species that is of most interest to the fly fisher. The male gnats have a habit of swarming in dense clouds near to the water edge, presumably like upwinged males, to attract the amorous attention of any wayward flying female. It is here that their downfall really begins. Due to being fairly poor on the wing, they frequently get blown on to the water and are immediately gripped in deadly surface tension. Because of the density of these clouds, the surface, particularly calm lanes originating from the leeward bank, can become pitted with little black lifeless forms.

Trout, when confronted with a large supply of any item, will select this above all others. Possibly this is not a witting gesture, but one born out of instinctive harvesting. However, some days are highlighted by the trout's refusal to 'play ball' with any other type of fly or its imitation. You will need some tolerably close-copy imitations of which, it has to be said, there are legions, ranging from Halford's tradition, through to Clarke and Goddard's originality. The choice is very much a personal affair though, among the recommended would be the Knotted Midge, Halford's Black Gnat, Terry Griffiths' 'Wonderwing' interpretation, or my own version. All will have their day, as long as they are kept small, and by that I mean size 18 or, better still, 20 or 22. Familiar confused gnat-like offerings for the trout are smuts – reed and the like. They fall out of the perimeter of this family, although they are nonetheless dipterans, and are in fact a similar species often (and descriptively) referred to as 'Black Curse' and occasionally, 'Angler's Curse', which can be confusing as the broadwing caenis is similarly dubbed. The creatures are tiny and size 26 to 28 hooks are about right! Thankfully they confine their activities to those stillwaters that are directly influenced by a river's or stream's close proximity.

● *Hawthorn fly*

Heather and hawthorn flies

It leaves just their fellow Bibios to be mentioned, for oddly enough, both the heather and similarly shaped hawthorn fly are kinsmen. The hawthorn fly's lifestyle and pattern directory has been frequently broadcast, but not so the heather fly, also known (again aptly) as the 'Bloody Doctor'. This ringer for the hawthorn, with only the red top jointed legs really separating them, is a familiar feature in more acidic areas – hill-top Welsh reservoirs, far-flung Scottish lochs and similar locales, and occasionally in the south.

The much-loved and appropriately named Bibio is an excellent general imitation, but if greater realism is required, merely substitute the black trailing bits (legs and hackles) with red, and there you have it.

There is great truth in the fact that seldom is there a day during the season when something small and black doesn't end up as a part of the trout's menu. It is for that reason that the dipteran gnats should occupy not only a space in your fly box, but also find their way onto the leader once in a while.

Daddy longlegs

One of the most unpredictable, yet unmistakable, occurrences in fly fishing is a fall of 'daddies' – people have based holidays around its manifestation, sloped secretly away from work, even sat disconsolate in hotel rooms waiting for this enigmatic dipteran to land on the water in numbers. When this happens, the 'cream' of autumn fishing can explode in frantic activity – but, equally, you can miss it.

Few anglers will not be familiar with this insect's gangly appearance, though they might be surprised to learn that there are well over two hundred different species, and not all crane flies appear in the autumn; there are many that are 'on the wing' throughout the summer months.

Larva

The larva can occur both underwater and in marshy areas and equally be a villain in the gardening plot, colloquially known as the 'leatherjacket'. Though imitated in America, where there are several dressings for the larval stage ('Taff' Price's book on stillwater flies offers the dressing), it is doubtful they are realistically any use at all in subsurface fishing techniques. 'Taff' also refers to the aquatic stage as 'washout' food – wind action creating underwater disturbances and redistributing the maggot-shaped lethargic 'nymphs' some distance from the shore.

That general-purpose pattern of all time – the Pheasant Tail Nymph, especially the long-shank version – would be a sound choice, but then it could equally be so for other washout forms such as cased caddis, alder larva, dragon and damsel fly larva and so on.

Adult

The real fun begins with the emergence of the crane fly proper. Of course, given the huge variety, not all will be found near water; however there are sufficient variations in size, colour and densities to make the fishing of the adult a season-long opportunity. The overall appearance is unmistakable: six extremely long legs, noticeably jointed in two distinct areas, two clear/opaque wings, a carrot-shaped body (abdomen) and noticeably stocky but short thorax. This general shape does not vary between the smallest and the largest – *Tipula maxima* – which can attain a body length of 32 mm ($1\frac{1}{2}$ inches), and is prevalent through August and into early October sporting a fawny beige body.

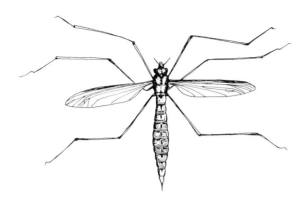

● *Daddy longlegs*

Crane flies are most commonly of use to the fly fisher in mild, muggy conditions, which seem to activate the hatch; often huge colonies will rest in neighbouring grassland and water meadows where they will also mate. The insect is very much at the mercy of the wind – heartening news for the fly fisher – due to its weak flying performance if a breeze does happen to cross the water. The 'trigger', and indeed their downfall, is their long legs which act very much as an anchor dragging the fly down to the water and pinioning it there. The insect's exertions, often noticeably making it 'dance' along, furrowing the water surface, further seal its fate by alerting the trout to the prospect of an easy meal. Frequently, after frantically treading the water, the hapless creature becomes so exhausted that it lies prostrate – only a lucky few dance into take-off – and at the mercy of water, wave and trout, soon becoming waterlogged and sucked into either a watery abyss or a trout's mouth.

This rather sad epitaph gives the fly fisher at least three permutations of fly fishing:

● the skittering dry fly and the use of the natural in some areas (Rutland and Grafham still allow the use of the real insect) and the lovely style of dapping

● the resting or 'spent daddy'

● the damp or drowned crane fly

All of these have spawned specialized patterns and methods.

Equally, the crane fly can offer late spring and summer fun; indeed, recently at both Pitsford and Grafham, there have been large quantities of small buff, creamy white-bodied 'daddies' which have on occasion produced preoccupied feeding by trout, when only a passable imitation would be suitable and chosen.

There are, of course, other shades: one orangey-bodied type exists, as does a striking sub-species, *Nephrotoma crocata*, with its dapper yellow and black-banded body.

Those crane flies that survive all the hostilities then mate, the female laying her eggs on damp ground or marginal mud, where they pupate after about fourteen days. The larva has a somewhat glutenous existence until adulthood the following year.

There are a host of crane fly or daddy longlegs dressings to interest both the fly tyer and fisher – the distinction is appropriate as the appendages are a magnetic draw for any fly tyer. One of the most ingenious of recent times utilizes picture cord, Pantone-coloured buff, to form a detached body. There are, of course, the now common Dick Walker-style and competitive-orientated Hoppers. More recently there has been a large development in weighted dressings of the adult which imitate the drowned insect and trigger a response from the trout by almost 'conditioned reflex'.

The essence though of 'daddy' fishing is a big wave on big, small water and the soft, languid take of a big trout ascending from the depths to engulf noiselessly a drowning 'daddy'.

Terrestrials

One of the most overlooked areas of imitative fly fishing on stillwaters and insect orders are those categorized as terrestrials. It is a loose term and covers a huge diversity of creatures, and yet, sooner or later, they will effect your efforts with a fly rod.

To try and list all the likely terrestrial 'happenings' would be to create a book of great complexity and infrequent usage. There are, though, certain creatures that can determine not only the trout's feeding zone and response, but whether we are to be successful on the day. Indeed, to know them and their lifestyles will catch you more trout. Amidst this plethora, several insects predominate: beetles, ants and moths form the premier league, whilst the second division (and on their day just as vital) comprises caterpillars, greenflies, drones, wasps and bluebottles and the odd grasshopper.

The term 'terrestrial' tells us a great deal. Translated from the Latin it means 'land-based' or 'land-borne', unlike the other trout food forms which are aquatic or water-borne. There is another term which I use and that is 'drop-offs'. This covers any insects that hang around trees – caterpillars, spiders, beetles and so on – and 'drop off' into the water.

One of the key angling elements in this area of fly fishing is the proximity of natural refuges: aforementioned trees growing over the water, tall bankside grasses and, perhaps most important of all, conducive winds – breezes that will pick up poor, or non-flying insects and deposit them on to the water surface. Indeed, there may be a combination of these factors, all of which will effect both number and distribution, which of course will vary from location to location both in terms of density and importance.

Ants

These are among the leading candidates for a starring role in a fly fisher's box. It is hard to imagine anyone not recognizing this creature, yet as familiar as this scurrying six-legged, almost double-bodied shape is, few anglers are

● *Ant*

aware that during muggy, thundery days of high summer, a proportion of ants of a more streamlined shape sprout wings and take to the air in huge colonies. If this happens near water and a 'fall' of flying ants occurs, you cannot mistake it. This prelude generally provokes intense activity from birds, particularly swallows, martins and swifts, and also sea gulls flying overhead will gradually spiral downwards following the descending winged ants.

Once the ants reach the surface, what follows can be a fly fisher's dream come true – or nightmare if you don't have any suitable patterns. On two occasions – both at Bewl Water – I have experienced a 'fall' of ants. It seemed that every fish in the lake rose in a huge orgiastic feeding frenzy – truly an amazing sight. Yet, even amidst this gluttony, trout are aware of imposters, and a reasonably carefully constructed winged pattern is required to deceive rising fish.

There are two basic colours of winged adults: black and mid-brown. Both are reasonably large, the brown one being generally slightly bigger than the black, and the two wings of both tend to be smoky grey. Curiously, only larger ants take to the air – virgin queens and drones – making dry flies smaller than 14 of little use (thankfully).

However, when fishing the dry winged adult, it is very important to ape the aspects of the natural, which tends to sit *in* the water surface film, rather than *on* it, with the heavier lower body (abdomen) often dipping under the water surface and the head and wings supporting it on the surface.

The same could also be said of the familiar ant proper. What you have to realize right from the outset in fly fishing is that, whether you like it or not, trout are scavengers accepting a huge range of opportunistic food forms from newts and small snakes, even mice, down to delicate upwinged olives. If a creature finds itself in the water, sooner or later a trout will eat it. So, given that there are so many ants about, it is hardly surprising that many misguidedly have a bath. These can vary from the small, ubiquitous black and brown ant (size 16 to 20), up to the larger red/brown wood ant (size 12 to 14) and, although colour may be somewhat immaterial in fly dressing and usage, aspect certainly is not. A good ant design should look like a passable imitation of the real thing, having the large bulbous rear segment (abdomen), thin waist and pronounced head section (thorax). Good imitations are the Ethafoam Super Ant, Borger's Para Ant and the McMurry Ant.

Beetles

In similar vein, the beetles, given their huge and varied distribution, can form an important part of the trout's diet, especially on upland acidic lakes, lochs and reservoirs. Indeed, there can be few of us who, at some time or other, have not fished with a Coch-Y-Bondhu – that ubiquitous Welsh beetle, also referred to as the June bug – on a diversity of waters and far from its natural surroundings of Wales and parts of Scotland, where its half-inch-long red/brown back and black body can be very important.

The soldier and sailor beetles are also very common in a variety of watery haunts and yet, though good imitations exist (especially 'Taff' Price's realistic creation), I am sceptical as to its importance and, though many feast on the nectar from waterside plants such as cow parsley and ragwort, I have yet to find either insect in a trout.

This is not so with other beetles, especially the aquatic variety, which are ably catered for by Tom Ivens's eternal pattern – the Black and Peacock Spider.

● *Beetle (coch-y-bondhu)*

Before leaving beetles, mention should be made of the rape beetle – not a scurrilous being, but a lover of that now common yellow plant crop – and its growing importance on lowland reservoirs during May and June, especially Rutland, Grafham and Bewl or indeed any water with close proximity of fields to oil seed rape. Trout really do get preoccupied on these tiny black beetles (size 16 to 18), and often fishing a small rape beetle awash in the film is the only recipe for deceiving these fussy fish. A simple black-shaped peacock herl-bodied imitation is all that is necessary, but once again fished in rather than on the surface.

Ladybirds

Ladybirds too have caught the attention of both fly dressers and fish; Dick Walker created a very lifelike pattern, though its use may be termed 'infrequent'. During very hot summers – particularly during 1976 and 1989 – large colonies get on the water and, though imbued with a poison, they do occasionally get eaten by trout.

Moths

Moths can form a fleeting but occasionally important part of a trout's diet, but with somewhere in the region of two thousand British species to choose from, knowing where to begin is a little painful. However, many imitations have been created, importantly Dick Walker's Ghost Swift Moth and Geoffrey Bucknell's Hoolet. There are, in fact, aquatic moths, existing in a juvenile stage underwater then hatching into adults, including the brown china mark and small white, the latter being discovered by 'Taff' Price. But for the fly fisher the likelihood that an imitation is actually taken for an adult sedge is a large probability.

Of course there are many other individual occurrences that are important, especially for river fly fishers, such as caterpillars (the tree-loving sort) which often become a favoured diet for trout. The green, worm-like moth types are especially available, as they hang precariously above the water surface.

Grasshoppers

Grasshoppers are also relished by the trout, but again are more important for the stream fisher, who can choose from a range of American patterns that are not only devastatingly effective, but range from the ultra realism of Darwin Atkins' Field Cricket through to the impressionism offered by Joe's Hopper.

Lacewings

Lacewings, the delicate vein-winged caddis-shaped insect, a distant relative of the alder fly, with emerald-green bodies, are considered by John Goddard a very important river fisher's terrestrial – and no doubt they are important to the stillwater fisher as well. Trout are apparently very partial to these when they get blown onto the water, generally towards evening time when they will selectively feed upon them. John Roberts' *New Illustrated Dictionary of Trout Flies* offers two dressings.

Other terrestrials

There are, of course, many other types of terrestrials which ignominiously meet their end in the trout's stomach: spiders, beetles – cockchafer, leaf beetles, etc – however, a fly box has to stop somewhere! Yet the fly fisher should always be prepared for an important and trout-preoccupying instance. I have had one fly lying idly in my box for nearly twenty years, but even as I write, it is a must at Rutland Water and is just starting at Grafham. It is the Dronefly, and is almost mandatory on a three-fly leader, be you fishing from bank or boat.

● *Drone fly*

The harmless wasp-like family, which also includes hoverflies, falls into two categories, terrestrial and aquatic, with the most familiar species on stillwater coming from the latter and hatching from a larval stage, known rather unromantically as a rat-tailed maggot, finally turning into the yellow-and-black-banded familiar insect. Imitations of this fly are many, the most notable being from the legendary reservoir angler Cyril Inwood, whose version, like Richard Walker's, placed emphasis on a red head. I do not know why, as the naturals do not appear to have one.

Be that as it may, to be beside or afloat a lowland reservoir without a suitable dressing, would be courting the same disaster as not carrying an ant pattern. You may never use it, but if the opportunity arises . . .

Winter hatches

The chill mid-winter is hardly the time to expect fleets of olives, hordes of caddis and epidemic hatches of midge. Yet, shining amidst the cool depths, life goes on – to be fair, in very much a reduced state and clad in an insect 'torpor'. Yet life does stir. Despite a paucity of species, there are some aquatic forms which can make our winter imitative approach a far from foolhardy exercise.

First though, we should look at the effects of weather and, more especially, temperature, as it is this element more than any other that will determine what will or will not happen. Certainly we can rule out blizzards and 'freeze-outs'; I have known doughty fishers break the ice to fish and indeed, do extremely well, but common sense would dictate there are better conditions. By and large, the weather that we shun in summer can, in winter, be conducive to hatches and fly fishing. I make the distinction 'hatch' purely because of its synonymity with those crystal-clear azure-blue days which combine bright sunshine, little wind and thawing frost as soon as the sun makes its impact. The occurrence to watch out for during these crisp, bright days, are little midges – chironomids. Generally they will be the small, black variety, though occasionally there are flurries of dark brown and dark olive varieties on certain days.

I cannot stress enough the degree of small-ness of these insects – 18 being quite large, with 20, but more likely 22 and 24, being the going imitation size. However, the good news is that, when they do hatch, they have the uncanny ability to promote a healthy rise and trout really do seem to relish them. The hatch duration is, as you might imagine, very short, and real-istically an angler should concentrate his efforts from about 11 a.m. to 3 p.m. with the peak most likely occurring between noon and two o'clock.

Though the pupa will be active, it is the dry fly that tends to be the more 'killing' aspect, at least both the emerger and adult imitations. This hatch can occur on almost any fishery throughout the British Isles – Grafham was particularly blessed with some staggering hatches one year. It must be stressed, however, that they need near calm, better still, flat-calm conditions to encourage the chironomids to hatch.

Of course, not every period through winter is dogged by cold; often we get those won-derfully warm, overcast, moist days driven by westerly airstreams, riding on the Gulf Stream. When this happens, extraordinary insect ac-tivity can quickly get itself underway. Quite what galvanizes the somnolent nymphs into such a quickened pace we can only guess. Per-haps their weather forecasting skills are honed and more intuitive than our own; but, for what-ever reason, you can often witness some quite extraordinary hatches of both pond and lake olive, though the pond olives tend to be more usual.

Although they can hatch on any water where they are present, be it large or small, it does tend to be the more stable alkaline or limestone-infused or southerly clay-based small stillwaters that receive the more reliable and heavier hatches.

This brings me to another critical element –

midge pupa

midge larva

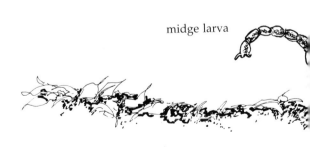

● *Winter hatches*

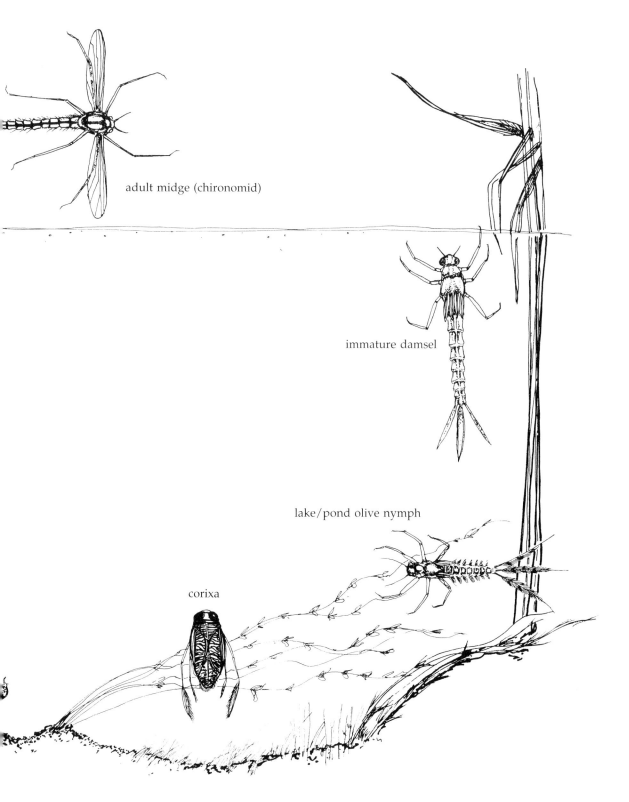

adult midge (chironomid)

immature damsel

lake/pond olive nymph

corixa

water type. This too will fashion and promote life or repress it depending on make-up. By and large, acidic waters fare rather badly during the colder months, if for no other reason than geography, as they tend to be in far-flung corners and colder conditions; life will, sadly, decline in their chill wake. However, chalk and limestone spring-fed lakes and gravel pits tend to do very much better, even during harsh conditions. This is purely down to their stability; they lack the temperature fluctuations of other types. Given normal situations, you can realistically expect water temperatures to operate in a band from 48 to about 52/54 degrees Fahrenheit. This of course has a profound effect on insect life. Most of the staple food forms will not only be present, but importantly, active. Shrimps, hoglouse, snail and corixae will be scuttling (albeit at a reduced rate) around old frost-bitten weedbeds and other areas conducive to their well-being.

However, that is not all. Surprisingly active also during this bleak time are damsel nymphs, perhaps not quite as you would expect damsels to be, but progeny of the eggs laid during the summer will have hatched and, pertinently, will be imitable. These smaller versions of the summer nymphs tend to be much lighter in colour, being a more golden olive, erring often to a soft pastel yellow – even a pale pea-green – and best suited to a size 14 l.s. hook. These immature nymphs, again, tend to be found fairly close to the bottom and especially around old weedbeds.

Of course, in terms of embryonic nymphs, the same could also be said of the upwinged ephemerid – lake and pond olive – nymphs. Again, these tend to be much lighter, a very pale olive, and extremely small, size 20 being about right. And, if we are discussing the formative stages of insect development, then mention too must be made of the bloodworm. This first stage (discounting the egg) of the midges' life-cycle tends to be a quasi-staple food, in as much as it exerts a continuous influence prior to its various pupations throughout the year. During winter, even in quite cold weather, they can be remarkably active, and this gives fly fishers a life-line as to areas and tactics. In the main, activity will be concentrated near to the bottom layers, where the water temperature will be generally a fraction warmer and, wherever possible, concentrate on rotted weed, leaf mould and other silty detritus which the bloodworm – or midge larva – tends to prefer. As to fly patterns, it is an insect stage that at least lends some respectability to Terry Griffith's habitual use of the Red Hook – to be fair, it is a perfect fly for the job.

There are, of course, other insect species, or more accurately, stages, active to a degree. Cased caddis should be trundling their stick and stone homes about with them on the lake floor on most days; daphnia might be journeying through various depths, and phantoms haunting the water layers.

And, given a prolonged mild spell, almost anything can happen. Indeed, once when fishing the Upper Avon during November for grayling, I experienced one of the heaviest hatches of mayfly I have ever witnessed. These, though, are rarities and freaks born from unusual weather conditions. My money is on the tiny black midges, immature damsels, bloodworm, and occasional olive to brighten up a cold, hard winter's discontent.

PART THREE

Tactics for all Seasons

CHAPTER FIVE

Small Stillwater Fishing

FLY fishing is a business of personal preferences, which often take a diverse route and embrace a host of different styles and venues. Conversely, we might be decidedly singular in our piscatorial tastes. The sad fact is that many of us foist our preferences onto others and try to dictate how fellow anglers should enjoy their chosen recreation – we fly fishers can be bombastic that way.

So I begin this journey on fishing small stillwaters mindful of the 'bad press' such fishing appears to incite and, from the outset, to give credit and respectability to an area of fishing that can be among the most demanding anyone could wish for; whilst offering accessible fly fishing in most regions to suit most price brackets.

Many people in the past have been put off or discouraged by the tag of 'put and take', stories of 'stock in and haul out' and, worst of all, a 'fishmonger' mentality. It can be all of these – then so can any water, large or small – but it need not be so. It is we, the individual anglers, who must ultimately create the bounds which govern our fishing – we satisfy no other than our own moral code of conduct. This is as applicable on a small stillwater as it is on a chalkstream or reservoir, where the one guiding motto should be 'never break the fishery rules'. Outside of this we should please ourselves not others and, most importantly, enjoy ourselves.

That said, let me embrace the task of covering a season on a small stillwater. There are so many choices, and different styles and patterns which best suit the various situations en-countered during the season. These choices largely revolve around imitation, but I am a realist, and there are occasions when, quite honestly, you would be sunk without an attractor of some kind, especially during extremes of temperature. These need not be gargantuan or technicolour, but create or provoke an interest rather than appeal on an imitative basis.

But before going into this area of discussion, it is essential to decide what constitutes the various forms of stillwater available. Broadly speaking, anything under about 55 acres is considered a small fishery, though in the larger acreage it is probably more practical to approach them as one would any larger reservoir. More normally however, the upper average will be six down to three acres, sometimes two.

Here another division exists between clear and opaque. There are, in reality, all manner of crossovers – one tactic being suitable on a variety of waters – it is just that specialist strategies have evolved to cater for the specific requirements of one or the other.

These days, with so many small waters operating 'catch and release', with others adopting a 'put and take' policy, a further division – even dimension – is added. Released trout often become decidedly wary in a confined space and certainly demand an amended approach if consistent sport is to be enjoyed.

So, though small stillwaters tend to be placed conveniently under one umbrella, a great variety does actually exist. However, despite this plethora, there are really only two primary tactics open to the fly fisher: a 'blind' strategy, taking in various nymphs and pulling styles, with the aside and spice of rising and known actively feeding trout, and the entirely separate business of stalking and selectively hunting trout in clear water, which can be as near primaeval hunting as you could possibly get. The division is marked, the styles different and often specific to a particular water. This all sounds agonizingly complex – it is not. Indeed, on balance, the tackle required to meet the various small-water styles and demands is far less diverse than on reservoirs – given that the philosophy is not based on 'one line and one rod'.

31 *The gang are here! Members of the Nomads prove that netting fish can be a communal affair. The captor: Bob Lawrence*

A mobile approach to tackle

The secret (if that is the word), is to go lightly. Years ago my father drilled home to me the advantages of a strategy based on a fly box, net, rod and pockets full of a few essentials, over the gargantuan bag viciously biting into the collar bone and the clutch of rods approach. Mercifully waistcoats have since intervened to cut down or at least house the results of our piscatorial gadget-collecting habits.

Nevertheless, a mobile lightweight approach is worth cultivating. Of course, the demands of the two distinctly differing styles suggest different systems and it would be complete folly to suggest the ability to fish a 2lb tippet and minuscule size 20 Midge – as can happen on occasion – could also cope comfortably with the surges and power play of a double-figure fish.

Yet, much will depend on the water you are likely to fish, and this alone dictates tackle selection. There are though, general requirements, common to both areas.

Clothing

Never have we been better off in this department. No longer do we have to withstand early season cold encased in a hardened wax-proof shell (undoubtedly efficient though they are), now that Musto, Wychwood, Patagonia, Nomad and Touchstone/Piscatoria all create lightweight, warm and utterly waterproof alternatives. Waistcoats are also legion, and we all have our favourite designs. Care, though, should be executed in choice as these form the base for tactical operations.

Vision

Another vital component. Hats should be selected for ability to cut out glare from above and, if possible, the sides also. Polarizing glasses further intensify underwater vision, whilst offering important protection. I cannot stress enough how a good pair of glasses enhance the day's enjoyment.

The lightweight system

Because of the generalization, I offer two systems for the small stillwater: a light to medium to cope with tiny flies and small-water nymphing with lightish tippets; the other for boisterous days, encounters with large fish and general distance work.

In each instance, the rod need not exceed 10ft, better still $9\frac{1}{2}$ft or 9ft. The lightweight system should revolve around lines of No. 5 to No. 6 and be a middle-to-tip action. The heavier system should be able to operate between No. 6 erring to No. 7 and again have a middle-to-tip action. This is important, for this type of action will achieve not only distance but accuracy as well as power over a hooked fish at

range, but is not so brutal as to tear hook holds at short range – where most specimen trout appear to be lost.

Obviously choice will be determined by a host of criteria – not least, cost. For years, I have used the Sage Graphite III $9\frac{1}{2}$ft No. 5 and $9\frac{1}{2}$ft No. 6 and No. 7 and lately S.P. IV. They have never let me down, nor have Loomis IMX in similar sizes, although they are expensive.

Alternatives exist however, that do not cost a king's ransom and, though lacking the more subtle nuances and refinements, are nonetheless perfectly suited for the job. Amongst these Bob Church offers some gems such as the IM8 Yellowstone $9\frac{1}{2}$ft No. 6–7 and 9ft Welsh Dee No. 5–6 and IM6 Dovey 9ft No. 5–6 and $9\frac{1}{2}$ft No. 7–8 small fishery and Ogborne 9ft 4in No. 6–7, as well as the more general types produced by Shakespeare and Daiwa. The golden rule is to try before you buy. This is essential: a valid judgement cannot be made by one or two tentative tip waggles in a tackle shop. It must be cast with and loaded – then, and only then, a judgement can be passed.

As to the smallwater fly reel, this must be reliable. Nowadays, with the preference for playing fish by hand so prevalent, engineering and smooth purring spools with adequate braking power have largely been relegated low in importance – that is until the first memorable fish has the spool revolving in an angry blur. I am old-fashioned and play fish from the reel – I just feel happier knowing my line is on the spool and not likely to get tangled in clothing, bankside debris or an awkwardly placed size 10 boot. I also feel that I land more fish because of it; though, it has to be said, periodic maintenance – oiling and washing – is essential for engineering harmony.

Good ones are the Leeda System 2 lightweights, either 5/6 or 6/7, the Orvis Battenkill 5/6 or 7/8 and the Shakespeare Cassette No. 2. All incorporate extremely reliable braking systems, are lightweight and have excellent spool capacity.

You do not need, though, to spend a fortune

on fly lines. Two types will actually see you through a season, with few missed opportunities. Of course, a floating line is essential as many small waters allow this type only. But, I have to confess, I would be lost without an intermediate (or slow sink) when so permitted.

As to types, there are so many good floating varieties about, I would almost settle for anything in the w.f. format, though I do have a soft spot for Air Cel and Lee Wulff's Triangle Taper in No. 4–5 or No. 6–7, or Jim Teeny's floating line – all tried and personal favourites. With an intermediate, three choices exist: the Wet Cel (or Hardy, which is surprisingly similar) or Air Cel's Stillwater Monoline or Masterline: Neutral Gold.

Other lines, whilst not being essential, can tip the balance in the fly fisher's favour. A Wet Cel II (or other fast-medium similar) can be a boon for placing the fly just that little bit deeper, and during last season I had cause to reappraise the sink-tip, having used the Teeny Mini Tip and Cortland's 444 slow-sink version and found both instrumental in catching fish which otherwise may have been missed. But that really is it save for a Hi-D when the going gets tough.

Of the accessories, a good heavy priest, nylon snippers, artery forceps, nylon sinknet, floatant – both line and fly – a hook hone are all vital ingredients of the fly fisher's cache.

Nylon too needs careful consideration. Having constantly fallen in and out of love with the low-diameter high-breaking strain types, I still can't make up my mind. However, the Orvis Superstrong Double Strength or Tectan in 3 to 8lb b.s. are all reliable. And the Drennan Sub Surface Green in 4 to 5lb b.s. in conventional nylon has proven reliability. Really that offers sufficient permutations to effect tactical changes and presentation.

On an entirely personal level, I have gone back to using knotless leaders and joining them to a needle knotted 2 section of nylon or shorter braided loop juncture from the fly line to fashion a leader length of between 10ft and 16ft depending on circumstances. This has afforded me far better presentation and turnover, and I believe, a greater overall tippet strength, the load or shock being spread over a wider tapered and ultimately stronger area than afforded by a straight nylon section.

What is important is to match standard mono with a standard nylon leader such as Plaitil or Normark; conversely, low-diameter nylon to a similar leader type such as Orvis or Scorpion knotless tapered.

With leaders now coming in 9ft, 12ft and 16ft lengths, by carrying a variety, infinitely variable systems of length, construction and breaking strain can be formulated. Knots are also important; for attaching the fly I tend to either a tucked blood or grinner and for nylon joins a double grinner for standard mono and a water (or surgeon's) knot for the low-diameter higher breaking strain types.

Finally the net. Why is it, after all the advice and words that have been dedicated to this piece of equipment, that people persist in using designs simply too small or inadequate for the job? The very last thing you should be considering when trying to land a 8lb, 10lb or larger fish is whether to net the head or tail first. A net should be two things: big enough to cope easily with the maximum size of trout you expect, and transportable. Sharpes made one for me with a round sea trout-sized head in matt black (no shiny bits to frighten fish), with the ability to land trout from any angle and a telescopic handle which allows me to carry it on a 'D' ring between my shoulder blades yet still reach beyond reedy margins.

There are other types: the favoured Gye net and various sea-trout types. Personally I go for anything that attaches to the angler rather than being fixed and constantly picked up and put down – though the 'superlight' types by either Hardy or Bob Church are very effective. Choose carefully, or your choice, if too small, may cost you dearly.

Thus prepared, it is time to go in search of our quarry.

CHAPTER SIX

Spring

March

THE early season, for me, starts from 1 April. I always think of March as a bonus, and because both types of water – clear and opaque – tend to respond similarly, they can conveniently be treated as one.

Unless otherwise stipulated, I would immediately set out with an intermediate line with 12ft leader, and seek out water that shows signs of, or has been previously detected, being between 8ft and 10ft – perhaps not the deepest, but certainly not shallow.

Weather being another dominant feature, I would also prefer to face into the wind. So often in a small water, especially during the early months, the quarry behave in a similar way to their reservoir kin, seeking out the wind-ruffled areas and forsaking the angler-friendly calms.

Curiously, though, the fish can be found reasonably near to the surface; a band between 2ft and 6ft from the surface should be explored first. Rainbows do seem to prefer patrolling this mid-water section.

Cold water conditions tend to call for slow retrieves. A small water is no exception, and most of my faith is placed on the constant figure of eight method. The one deviation that you should be ever aware of is the 'drop' take. As the fly (leaded or otherwise) drops 'free-fall' through the water, the trout intercepts. Takes such as this are detected more easily on a

32   A wonderfully-conditioned Dever rainbow, proving that the modern smallwater rainbow is a thing of beauty rather than a mere parody of its wild relatives

1 Thompson Scissors
2 Hackle Pliers
3 Hair Stacker
4 HMH Vice
5 Dubbing Needle
6 Thread Bobbin

Stalking Patterns

1 Yellow Head
2 Ol' Lead Eyes
3 Wiggle Tail Hare's Ear
4 Sibbon's Speck
5 'Poxy Speck
6 Shrimp (Red Spot)

General Nymphs

1 GE Nymph
2 Phantom Pupa
3 Diawl Flashback
4 Pheasant Tail
5 Wadham's Hare's Ear
6 Gold Head Montana
7 Chalk Springs Brownie

Dry Fly Patterns

1 Elk-Hair Caddis
2 Ducks Dun
3 Bob's Bits
4 Lively Mayfly
5 Stimulator
6 Hopper
7 Ovipositing Running
  Caddis

Midge Patterns

1 Orange Emerger
2 Hare's Face Midge
3 Parcel-String Buzzer
4 Barden Pupa
5 ET Emerger

Damsels and Derivatives

1 Golden Distressed Damsel
2 Dick Walker's Damsel
3 Distressed Damsel
4 Borger's Para
5 Gold Head Damsel
6 Rabbit Damsel

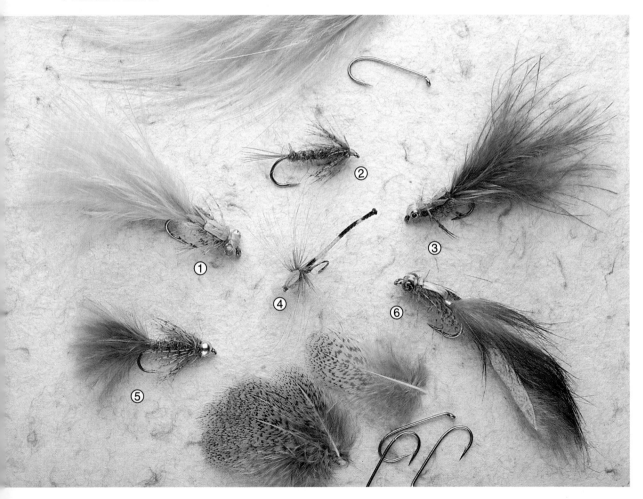

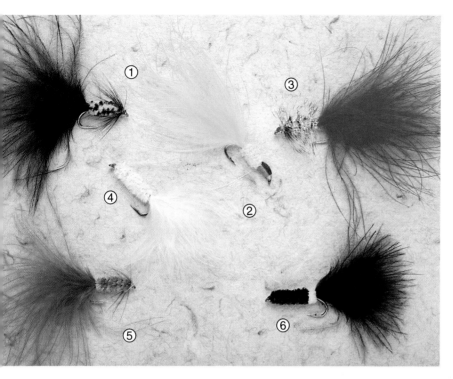

Tadpoles and Derivatives

1 Peter's Tadpole
2 Cooper's Yellow
3 Pink Tadpole
4 White Tadpole
5 Olive Tadpole
6 Green Butt Tadpole

New Wave

1 Gold Head Daddy
2 Red Hook (Datsun)
3 Tube Buzzer
4 Dawson's Olive
5 Idiot-Proof Nymph

Lures

1 Booby
2 Clifton
3 Cat's Whisker
4 NQAL
5 Street Walker
6 Jardine 'Nymph'
7 Doggy
8 Wobble Worm
9 Armageddon Worm

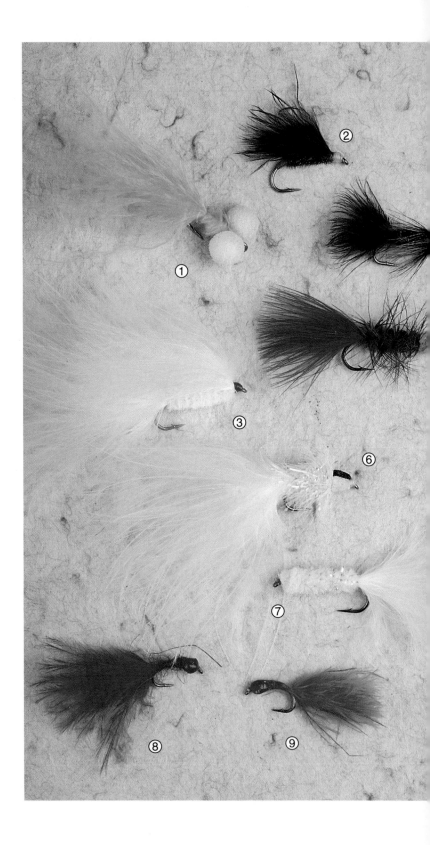

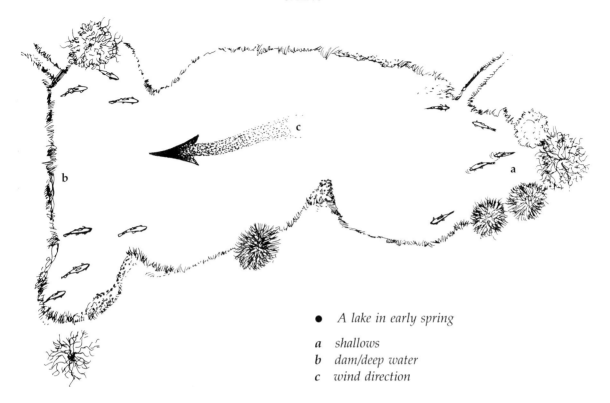

● *A lake in early spring*

a   *shallows*
b   *dam/deep water*
c   *wind direction*

floating or sink-tip, but are not impossible on a sunk line. It is vital that, whatever sink time you allow, be it five seconds or fifty, your concentration does not waver from the area around 6 to 10 feet from the rod tip: if the line moves in any direction, even a twitch – strike!

Another type of take to consider can only be described as the 'first pull – pull'. Having reached the desired depth, the fly fisher commences the retrieve. A take will cause a savage pull and, if great care is not demonstrated, an instinctive and equally sudden reaction by the angler can lead to a 'smash' take. Everything early season appears to be so tactile and you must be aware of it.

Choice of fly

As to initial fly patterns, the ubiquitous black-based variations almost parody themselves in effectiveness, and variations on this theme will help, especially as everyone else will doubtless be using something similar. Recently a slight variation on Martin Cairncross's Clifton did

exceptionally well for me, as did the black version of my Distressed Damsel. However, the ever-faithful Black and Green Tadpole should always be to hand. You may have qualms about such flies. If you have, the NQAL might pacify the more 'purist' amongst us. The Damsel and Tadpole should be leaded; the Clifton unleaded but dressed on a heavy-iron hook.

I am being a pessimist. Not all March days are leaden, inhospitable struggles with the elements, laced with brisk north-easterlies; some are quite pleasant, even balmy. When days like this occur, it is not out of the question to experience something akin to 'normal' fly fishing. Often, even on quite cool, calm, bright days, quite sustained feeding activity will occur from around noon, which can regularly continue into dusk. This tends to occur, however, in the shallower areas of a fishery. The reason behind this is simple: the shallower water warms more quickly under the influence of even a weak sun which, in turn, gives rise to some form of sporadic (though sometimes hectic) chironomid activity. Beware, though, because the creature is often small.

In the main, colours will be black, brown or a near black (almost sooty) olive, and the sizes depressingly small, possibly best imitated on a hook size of 24 or 26 – realistically you can fish 18s, but I would not go much above. Obviously this calls for light tippets, especially the low-diameter type, and an ultra-light outfit.

The problem arises when large trout are in the vicinity. However, if you are careful, and you match and balance your tackle – a piscatorial fine tuning – the chances of a break are unlikely. Hook hold with such small sizes is a problem, and much depends on luck. With nymphs, tying short can reduce this problem; in other words, half-dressing a 14 hook will give you an insect size of 18 whilst providing the holding power of the larger hook.

Two patterns of this demanding type of small-water 'midge' fishing which work consistently well for me are a dry fly called the Sparkle Gnat (a derivative of the Griffith's Gnat)

which is seldom refused where surface activity suggests emergers or little adults are being taken, and the Barden Pupa, which is a raggedy parody of a midge pupa, but lightweight and extraordinarily effective. Fishing is as simplistic as the flies' construction: the Gnat should be greased and cast on longish (12ft to 14ft) light-tippet leader (3 to 4lb Super Strong), anticipating both the course and future rises of a feeding trout, then left utterly static. The Pupa can be treated in exactly the same way, especially if a few of those delicious 'head-and-tail' rises are seen. In general fishing the same leader set-up should be used, degreased with fuller's earth mixture as necessary, then fished either in a classic wind-aided curve or extremely slowly figure of eight style, either into or down wind.

I could not, however, leave March without offering one final heavyweight nymph pattern for those who prefer the long-leader and floating-line type of approach: the Gold Headed Fourwater Fox – an adaptation of Gordon Fraser's deadly Hare's Ear – which has proved utterly lethal during cold conditions in the winter of 1993, often outfishing many a lure. Again slow retrieval seems to work best, and you must be extremely observant when the fly is free-falling on the drop, where many of the takes occur. It is a complete 'confidence' pattern.

There really is no need for other patterns during March. The reward for your perseverance and preparation in the midst of gun-metal water and purple-washed horizons is a rainbow as silvery and dashing as could be found on any reservoir.

33 *Howard Bickerstaff of Silver Creek carefully cradles a rainbow allowing it to regain its strength prior to release – essential for a happy outcome*

April

April for me remains a siren's song. It is probably deep-rooted, traditional – indeed a touch sentimental – but there it is. I grew up in the knowledge and surety that 1 April was the start of the trout season 'proper'. I cannot shake that notion, even in these enlightened times of frost-bitten trouting.

I remember also days in years past, set amidst the budding and rejuvenating Usk Valley, where March and the spring chorus of birds, bulbs and rising brown trout made their spectacular entrance, where our fly fishing world was harmonious and vital. And nothing, as yet, can quite match the adrenalin rush and feverish anticipation of an April day – on any water, for small stillwaters are by no means immune to this often hyperactive behaviour. Yet there are steadying factors:

● the weather, which can be wickedly inhospitable in April. Our comfort and fishing style must take into consideration this fact;

● the quarry themselves, for trout will behave differently under pressure;

● the presentation factor;

● fly choice may, under the circumstances, need extra care and understanding;

● you will not be alone in getting 'spring fever' – other anglers will be equally smitten. This can often dictate your position on a water, especially if you happen to be an inveterate late-comer like me!

Weather

Beating the cold has always been a problem, exacerbated by those sudden bursts of sunshine and warmth which can punctuate even a sleet- or rain-festooned day. By dressing appropriately you can not only beat the elements, but remain comfortable all day long. This may seem an irrelevance compared to tackle, flies and fishing, yet each year I see anglers whose days end prematurely in abject misery, because of scant regard for weather change. The secret lies in donning layers – either opting for systems such as Patagonia's, or for a more personal, customized approach – so you can tailor what you wear to prevailing conditions, shedding or adding garments as necessary.

The other criterion is weight: lightweight cottons and purpose-made synthetics offer far

greater protection and comfort than perhaps the more traditional chunky woollies; 'shell' and waterproof jackets prove lighter and more adaptable over more familiar (waxed) apparel. It is a personal, but vital, consideration. If you can remain warm, dry and comfortable whilst retaining ample casting movement, you are, quite simply, going to fish better.

Now to the more tangible aspects of small-water fly fishing during April. As the pundits always decree, 'if you want the weather to change in Britain, just wait a minute'. Well, the fishing is like that too; I have known scintillating dry fly fishing on a day which started with methodical searches, sombre flies and ponderous retrieves, with hoar frost crackling underfoot. More usually though, during the early weeks, it is the latter approach which is preferred – traditionally, that is. I have no fear of flying in the face of tradition if it will catch me fish – and nor should you.

Trout behaviour under pressure

Let me say from the outset, black flies and Boobies are not the *only* medicine for early season searches; more often than not, this idea is due to the majority thinking this is so. Trout tend to rebel. Some years ago I wrote of the 'intelligence', or at least group-preservation instinct, of shoaling rainbows. It is worth re-iterating here.

During a period of my life when tuition, both in fly casting and practical fishing, was my daily occupation, we had at Nether Wallop Mill, a small (about 1 acre) crystal lake, stocked with seemingly innocent trout awaiting the machinations of eager fly fishing neophytes – sure enough, they surrendered. However, due to eagerness, exuberance and, occasionally, brute force, trout were lost. This situation often conspired to make life a trifle difficult; I could not – and neither could the pupil – catch anything, which was no help to an instructor's ego or credibility.

To tilt the balance once more in the fly fisher's favour, a further stocking of trout was required. Once catapulted into this quasi-freedom, the trout's usual naivety shown to anglers with fly rods prevailed; that is, until one of the 'old hands' intervened. Often (and I don't mean over a period of weeks, but years) a previously hooked and lost (or merely 'pricked') trout would literally push or side off a rainbow in pursuit of certain flies – obviously those which held a trigger of danger or were recognized as threatening due to previous encounters. I am convinced this would (and does) happen time and time again on a variety, if not all, waters at some point. It may also account for the sudden and rapid decline in a fly's effectiveness in a short period of heavy fishing pressure – a familiar pursuit on reservoirs during early season is the 'harvest of the innocents', but it also happens on small waters. Simply bear in mind that trout learn, perhaps not profoundly or deeply, but sufficiently to give us the run-around, creating a situation where it pays not to follow the leader or pack, or latest fly craze, trend or colour.

Presentation

It is also the situation of fishing pressure which often fashions technique. Given the much vaunted and reported weighted-nymph-and-lure-based strategies of early April, you would be forgiven for running with the pack. There is, however, a problem; leaded and large, bulky flies tend to make a fairly impressive entrance to the water – varying from an audible 'plop' to miniature wave, if this is multiplied the lake over – and, given the trout's susceptibility to at least a partial learning curve – then a problem swiftly amplifies to a point where lakes often 'turn off' completely, with few if any anglers catching fish.

It was at Rockbourne where I first realized the problem *en masse*. The remedy, I am sad to say, was not mine, but from the maestro, Bill Sibbons. We started to use lighter and smaller patterns on intermediate lines of No. 6 and found this system worked superbly. The heavier the angling pressure, the more bizarre seemed

the fly choice – 14s and 16s being the norm. That was fifteen years ago and nothing has changed, apart from some amendments and refinements to the tackle.

Given anything like early season angling pressure, I would opt, without hesitation, for this set-up (intermediate No. 5 and match 9ft to $9\frac{1}{2}$ft rod) – the Air Cel Ice or Glass Line has further refined the technique, offering a degree of camouflage to the required delicacy. Thereafter use a 12ft to 14ft leader tapering to 3lb b.s. standard mono (Drennan, etc) or 5lb reduced-diameter type (double-strength Tectan, etc). Now to the even more curious component, the fly.

Fly choice

More often than not I will tether a Phantom Pupa to the tippet – not perhaps the first choice of fly fishers, or the ultimate 'confidence' pattern, but work it most certainly does – and on most retrieves, ranging from fairly swift, foot-long draws on the line, to a steady but slow figure of eight. The late Dave Collyer's pattern of Phantom still works well for me, but I am experimenting with what I can only call my Jelly Nymph and enjoying some surprising results. Pheasant Tails are also good for this style, as indeed are Hare's Ears. The important, nay vital, factor is to keep the nymph small – 14s and 16s are *de rigueur* (or a short-dressed 12 when fish are larger). The method, however, is 'alternative'; after all it is little use having a method that defeats the norm if, in turn, that method turns into the very thing it was designed to conquer. Two main styles predominate – 'imitative' and 'attractor' (though 'aggressor' may be more appropriate). I prefer the former, though concede that the latter is probably a more successful taker of fish and often (albiet unwittingly) used more frequently than we realize. Aquatic insects can produce an extraordinary turn of speed, but seldom could they match some retrieve rates with various nymphal imitations seen on our waters. Indeed, I have yet to find a stickfly (or cased caddis) that swims midwater, embellished with a veneer of fluorescent hot orange or phosphorous yellow!

That said, how many of us are sure exactly what the trout sees in our creations? What we can cater for, however, is their depth, location and tendencies. It really is a question of what you feel happiest fishing with – I happen to prefer a Damsel Nymph to a Montana, though I am under little illusion that both summon the 'chase, catch and kill' instinct within the trout.

So fly choice can be catholic. Black, as mentioned earlier, is a favoured colour, but I don't believe it matters greatly whether it is in the form of a Green Butt Tadpole, Montana or Viva style. The colour combination is the deadly ingredient, with profile playing a supportive role, so my personal money is on the Tadpole. However, I am always prepared to change – and do so quickly if black is not working – to the opposite end of the spectrum: white or maybe orange, again in the Tadpole format. Quite honestly, for early season use, these are all you need.

Yet, even during this period of torpor, life, especially in the alkaline lakes, will be going about its business. There is a host of imitable (and often overlooked) food forms; for instance, immature damsel nymphs – generally a distinct yellow, golden olive coloration – corixa, shrimp, hoglouse, midge (both larva and pupa), beetles and dragonfly larva. Certainly there is enough to encourage an imitative and, importantly, effective strategy. During the last couple of seasons, a yellow-olive and smaller version of the Distressed Damsel has been extremely effective for me, as has Mick Williams' Datsun, an imitation of the bloodworm.

Other factors

However, dominating fly choice is fish location and depth. Similarly to March, it is quite possible to get things utterly wrong and fish your pattern too deep. My records suggest most activity will occur over water of 8ft to 10ft deep, with a fishing depth from the surface to 4ft as a narrow but seemingly effective band. Occasionally it is necessary to seek out the deeps and do a spot of bottom grubbing, but this does appear to be the exception.

Similarly, slow retrieves appear the more usual. Yet again my experience and records suggest a fairly constant figure of eight ranging up to a quite brisk 2ft pull-through movement, to be the more deadly – irrespective of patterns (save the dry fly). In essence, the pattern's ability is to grab the attention of the trout whilst movement encourages and, more importantly, maintains that initial attraction – something only speed seems able to do.

The other important factor is to be prepared to roam. So often remaining stationary, transfixed to one spot, will prolong an agony. Of course, 'hot spots' exist and they should be treated appropriately. However, and especially if the water is relatively new to you, by having a cast here and there, not only will a working knowledge of the fishery evolve, such as depth, contours, old weed beds, windward banks and bays, even just places which are likely holding spots, but you stand a much better chance of encountering fish. The one problem with this time of year is the shoaling instinct of rainbows; find one and undoubtedly you will find several, but quite why this is more prevalent at this point in the season I cannot say. By staying in one spot you have an extremely good chance of fishing over nothing at all – all day. I can recall an instance when one tiny little wind-lashed corner of a lake held what appeared to be nearly every fish in the five-acre water. I had spent the previous five hours looking for something – anything – then, just by chance, my fly settled amidst this huge school. Yet, I could just have easily remained static, fishless and convinced that the water held no fish at all.

That is the early season, and it would be unfair to paint a picture of sombre patterns and sinking lines – it is not all like that. Floating lines can be equally viable in the long leader/nymph strategies, but also dry flies – the one feature that many small waters enjoy is a good emergence of hawthorn flies (*Bibio marci*). I can only reiterate what I and, indeed, others have said before; a fall of this terrestrial is important.

But there are factors to bear in mind. First, only certain wind quarters will dump them on the water; secondly, they have to be in sufficient numbers to make the trout's efforts worthwhile; thirdly, you should not use a dry fly, but a *damp* one. The long, gangling legs of the natural ensure an unceremonious wetting, pinioning it to the surface film, which places the creatures *in*, not only *on*, the surface. This is where your artificial should be. And finally, where large colonies of hawthorn do land on the water and the trout start showing an interest, the localized 'fall' will tend to create preoccupation, with the trout tending to refuse other food forms. Sometimes great rafts of the insects can be found in tree-lined corners and quiet bays and, though this does not call for slavish accuracy of pattern, a close copy mimicking both outline and, importantly, aspects such as legs and thorax will outfish the more generalized imitations. And do not forget to degrease the leader tippet (the 1ft to 2ft section above the fly) often, as much as every other cast, rendering the nylon submerged and suitably dulled. This can often mean the difference between success and failure, as can accurate casting to rising trout.

That largely sums up April; in many ways a curious, individual month, with little accord with the rest of the season. The trout and, to some extent, anglers, behave differently, only to settle down for the remainder of the season. Perhaps its just a case of 'spring fever'.

May

May, that pause between spring and summer, was surely fashioned for the imitative fly fisher. Small stillwaters are no exception. Of course, it is easy to fall into the trap of delusion. Catching recently introduced quarry, even on nymphs, does not legitimize a 'fishmonger mentality'. Yet, there is so much more to small lake fly fishing and, given the now popular and widespread 'catch and release' or 'option' waters, anglers can give full rein to imitative styles and fish for trout which are often very selective

indeed. This type of water appeals to me more and more – irrespective of the controversy that this approach to fishing seems to attract.

But why should these waters be so very much different? Quite simply, because of the problems outlined in April, trout learn to avoid forms which summon danger. Often their first mistake is their last. Once released, having been fooled, a very much wiser trout is left to rue its recent escapade. The outcome tends to manifest itself in a far greater dependence on natural organisms. This is quite logical, because the fish is in the water longer and has to eat; and, once used to the ways of the midge, corixa, damsel, shrimp, olives and so on, starts to be able to be selective in diet, and sharp-sighted and wary of imposters. This ultimately fashions our approach with a fly rod.

Certainly the whole concept is a great deal more challenging. There is little in the way of 'chuck it and chance it'. You must develop a certain knowledge and understanding of what insects are likely to be active, the ticklish business of imitating the food form in both pattern and movement, and sufficient understanding of how best to achieve that with your tackle system. It all sounds a tall order and inordinately complicated. Actually it is not, once a degree of confidence is attained. Yes, of course it takes a little effort, but you will be truly fly fishing, rather than being quasi-imitative.

May is as near-perfect a time to start the crusade. Available to you will be the natural bounty of the lakes – possibly there will be just too much. However, as with rivers, there is a distinct tendency for one or two food items to predominate; yet, even on occasions of complete or part preoccupation, general patterns do work. Things are not quite as complex as they may at first appear.

The system

A move to a lighter line and more delicate rod pays dividends – yet still opt for a fast-taper design that will deliver long yet delicate casts. Often the ability to place a fly further than your comrades, and reach feeding fish at 25 to 30 yards range, is the difference between jubilation and dejection.

Let me say from the outset, with a reasonable casting style – if necessary, seeking qualified instruction – and a suitably balanced outfit, even of No. 5, these distances are realistically obtainable, with a degree of precision, coupled with finesse. As the most usual line for this type of approach is a floater – there are odd occasions which call for an intermediate, but these tend to be relegated to 'alternative tactics' – essentially the 'dry' line is your weapon.

Of the countless designs I have used over the years – even splicing and creating my own tapers – I firmly believe the Wulff Triangle Taper No. 4/5 to be the best all-rounder, closely followed by a 5 or 6 Moser Casting Line, and if you can get them, a No. 5 or 6 Ultra 2 sunrise-yellow longbelly (quite why this dreadful colour aids shooting, I cannot guess, but it seems to!). Not only do all these lines cast well, but they have a sufficiently refined taper to achieve positive yet delicate turnover.

This brings me to leaders; so often a perfectly good, long and accurate cast comes to nought – worse still, spooks a trout – purely because of a poor balance or construction. Not to taper a leader to some degree is courting presentational disaster.

Years ago we had to go to inordinate lengths to construct a large nylon-butt (25 to 18lb b.s.) fine-tippet leader. Mostly this entailed keeping a 2 to 4ft butt length section to which was knotted a proprietory 9ft tapered leader (generally Platil), then a further addition of 2 to 6ft tippet section of slightly lower breaking strain than the leader's tip. Not much has changed – the system has endured. The advent of longer ready-made tapered leaders has made matters easier, however. Normark, Platil, Masterline Siglon and Orvis manufacture leaders of 12ft to 16ft, which save a great deal of time, and though the initial expense is certainly a great deal more than a straight piece of nylon, the turnover and general presentation advantages far outweigh the few pounds for a small collection; and, by adding a tippet, not only is leader life extended, but tactical nuance can also be realized.

34   Danger point – a trout jumps and Mick Phipps quickly drops his rod tip to avoid a 'break-off'. Doing this gives vital inches of slack line and tip off which tends not to tear hook holds

Actual tippet strength is determined by several factors. First is the strength allowable for that particular fishery – some insisting on a 5lb b.s. minimum. Secondly, you should consider the size of trout likely to be encountered; and thirdly, insect species to be imitated. We often overlook this point. A large Damsel on long-shank leaded hook, on a fine-diameter tippet, is creating enormous hingeing forces on the leader during casting, which can seriously weaken nylon; conversely, a size 18 Midge Pupa tends to look like fluff on steel cable if much above 3lb b.s. is employed.

The second factor – large fish on fine nylon – can be dealt with comfortably, the double-strength and super-strong nylon types offering much reduced diameter for high breaking strain. But that is not all; if your tackle – rod and line – has been suitably fine tuned and balanced, then accidents are unlikely to happen. Indeed, on my 9ft No. 4 Sage, I would feel perfectly in control and in command with a 2lb b.s. tippet and a 5lb trout. It would be 'interesting', but I would remain confident of the outcome – given no huge barriers, such as fallen logs or Sargasso-like weedbeds. The same would not be true if I used the same leader strength and a No. 7 outfit. It is all common sense really.

Fly choice

Before venturing forth to the aquatic world, the odd word about the fisheries is called for. In many ways I am fortunate in living in the southeast because many waters operate catch-and-release systems of one form or another, Tenterdon Trout Water having used a basket-retention system for over fifteen years, and Cottington near Deal, and Springhill – to name a mere handful. Of course, the natural's imitation and tactics are not exclusively for catch and release; they are just biased to preoccupied or selectively feeding trout which can happen at any juncture through the season. May merely amplifies this condition.

Indeed, you can almost take your pick from nature's bounty. Pond and lake olives will be active as nymph, dun and spinner fall; corixa, shrimp, hoglouse, damsel and dragonfly nymphs will also begin to be active; midge, early caddis, as well as various terrestrials in the way of beetles, bugs, and protracted hawthorn activity – you have a vast choice. There are also other phenomena worth being aware of; indeed some are distinctly localized. Stonefly may be significant in the north and other suitable habitats; the mayfly may also offer sport. Then there are tadpoles – so often we neglect these immature frogs. Perhaps it is because they would appear of little use to the fly fisher and, though I confess occasions are rare, small stillwater trout can become aggressively 'switched on' to this margin-hugging amphibian. The word 'plethora' just about covers this abundance.

So what can you use to imitate this Pandora's Box of aquatic life? Certainly, wherever possible, matching the hatch is a good policy or, at least, matching the natural, be it aquatic or airborne. For this to happen, you have to know what you are looking for. John Goddard's splendid book *The Waterside Guide* will unravel many an insect mystery, which then can be imitated, and sometimes, of course, you can simply trust your own powers of observation. It is all too easy to fall into the trap of being way too technical about insect study. The whole business of matching food forms pivots on your ability to match the little form captured from the water, which you think fish might be taking an interest in and feeding on, and then matching it to a fly in your box in terms of approximate colour, size and shape. It is nothing more mysterious than that, and is certainly Latin-free and non-entomologist-friendly.

There can also be 'saving graces' in the forms of aquatics that are present either the season long or in such numbers that they are high on the trout's menu priority list. Corixa, shrimp, hoglouse, even damsel nymph and olive nymph and, of course, midge can be confidently imitated the season long – the first three being, oddly, my preference for a generalized approach.

For years I had a feeling of mental dissipation when confronted with corixae; I simply never felt confident when trying to imitate what appeared to be bewildering hordes of this little creature. I now realize my mistake: I simply did not have a pattern in which I felt confidence. Two seasons ago I sat down, looked at various naturals from an assortment of waters in an aquarium and got down to the business of imitating what I (not anyone else) saw. The result was a range of patterns helped, of course, by predecessors but nonetheless based on what I felt to be 'key' points. They have subsequently caught me trout from waters which tend to be fairly tricky at times when preoccupied feeding takes place. As I say, trust your own observations and, if possible, capture the insect, take it home (wives and small children beware!), study it, and imitate what you feel is relevant and important.

Observation

Observation, both of the natural and the trout's

35 *Anxious moments: Keith Bryant wisely slips a large net in the water and only then brings this double-figure (16lb) rainbow over it. Never sweep or lunge at a fish with your net – you may miss and catch the leader or line*

movements towards them is the central point in May. Almost irrespective of area and water, something will be happening, somewhere, at some point in the day. Indeed, very often you can get some really quite heavy flurries of olives, emerging and hatched. Curiously, this does happen more frequently on the rougher, more overcast days in the middle of the month, rather than those sun-scorched, spring-suffused calms we sometimes enjoy. Indeed, I have experienced really quite marvellous pond and lake olive fishing on days with a distinct 'chop', and towards evening as well. The remedy for such occasions is provided by a Duck's Dun (DBD) on a lightweight tippet (3lb b.s.), 12ft leader, cast either towards rising or moving fish, or across the wind and allowed to search. However, be careful of drag; this is as ruinous on still water as on rivers.

If this tactical disruption is to be minimalized, then some degree of line mending may be required in order to allow greater areas to be covered. The 'secret' is to allow the imitation to move with the water, not against it.

Presentation

Curiously, on calm, bright days, olives appear less inclined to emerge during the day, though ample dry fly opportunities exist, caused generally by midge. The Sparkle Gnat in size 16 to 20 is seldom ignored if cast accurately towards a rising trout. If surface activity persists, and the dry fly is stoically ignored, then it may pay to put the fly 'in' rather than 'on' the surface – this may sound like nit-picking but so often this fraction of an inch can be critical to success.

There are actually two ways of tackling this problem: from above, by cutting the hackle from the underside of a fully hackled dry fly in a 'V' configuration, or by using a parachute tying; or from beneath the surface by employing a floating nymph, ET Emerger or similar self-supporting fly-like suspender. Or indeed, a very sparse, 'short' nymph or pupa pattern, also the GE Nymph if olive patterns are absent can be confidently fished when no visible trout activity exists. It does appear that trout have a comforting policy of looking upward for their foodstuffs, so even a lightly dressed pattern, fishing only inches from the surface, can pull fish up to it. In all these instances, I would urge a slightly longer leader of up to 15ft and degreased along the tippet with fuller's earth sinkant.

There will also be occasions when your pattern will have to be fished deeper – in bright light and any number of climatic variations, and sometimes just because of plain sullenness on the part of the trout. These require a leaded pattern, ample sinking time and patience on the retrieve. If this style has to be adopted, I would once more opt for Nick Cooke's fully greased (Mucilin is best) leader technique, in order to detect takes 'on the drop' which happen and are missed all too frequently. This is where the imitative, ever-present 'confidence' patterns come into their own: Corixa, Shrimp, Hare's Ear, Hoglouse styles, Damsel Nymphs and other omnipresent imitable forms.

Retrieve rates

In terms of retrieve rate, on balance slow figure of eight is to be preferred to demonic stripping though there have been occasions when trout, for some unaccountable reason, enjoy the chase and, even with small flies (14s to 16s), a swift 2ft-long series of pulls can produce a response over other speeds. Simply, it pays to vary your approach and retrieve rates (shrimp, corixa and olive nymph have an extraordinary turn of speed).

Use of the Mayfly

A word about mayfly; when they are present, sport can be frenetic. Do not, however, be deceived. Trout, once used to this unmistakable giant cream and olive upwing, can become exceptionally choosy, and reasonably close copies of Mother Nature can work at a time when the 'they'll take anything' brigade are reduced

to frustrated, gibbering imbeciles. Dick Walker's Angora Mayfly Nymph is still the best imitation of this stage, but make sure it is tied as the originator intended – I have seen more travesties of this pattern than almost any other artificial. The correct dressing is a great deal deadlier. For the dun, I put my faith in the Lively Mayfly, though a Grey Wulff enjoys enormous popularity.

The mayfly is but an interlude, but what an exciting one it can be. And, before I forget, if fish are rising and steadfastly refusing mayfly dressings repeatedly, then try a small Black Gnat (size 16 or 18). This ludicrously small (in comparison) offering, is frequently taken – possibly an *hors d'oeuvres* to the mayflies as a main course.

Areas

Sadly there is no firm key to the best places. Insects' emergence or activity tend to be the arbiters of trout position. Weed or reed beds can often be a good locale, as are islands and deep corners and channels, though be prepared to fish in areas that, though they outwardly seem preposterous, nevertheless hold good, or show signs of insect activity. The trout will not be very far away.

Catch and release

I leave you with the decision as to its viability or ethics but, if practised, I implore you to respect your quarry and, wherever possible, release the fish without bringing it onto dry land. Nets, hands, hard banks and the stress of an alien environment cannot help but damage the fish so, no matter how tempted to gaze at your prize, try to desist. Use barbless or depressed-barb hooks and, if you have to land the fish, ensure that your net is soft and, more importantly, knotless. These are simple rules that ensure the trout's well-being and perhaps our sport in seasons to come.

CHAPTER SEVEN

Summer

Dog days and difficulties

WITH the far side shimmering, sliding in and out of focus, a collection of fly fishers somnolently pacing around and an orb beating mercilessly out of the deep azure softening to the horizon in the heat, you know you are in for a tough time. Realistically you tell yourself your chances are nil, yet there you are throwing cast after penitent cast into the hopeless heat.

There is no short or sure answer to the 'dog days'. Hope, tinged with optimism, is one defence against pessimism; that, and some degree of water knowledge. Even adopting the unusual or downright absurd may work when all else fails.

First though, we must consider the waters and the reactions of the fish to our efforts in such situations.

Choice of water

Selecting the right water is as important as choosing the right fly pattern. If your intention is a daytime excursion, the very last place on your list should be a shallow, clay-based pool with a maximum depth of 8ft to 10ft and no cover from trees, bushes or reeds. That is not to say these are not worth fishing or, indeed, do not hold trout; simply that the water, especially during the day, tends to heat up to such an extent that trout can't be bothered to wave a fin in defiance.

Instead, select fisheries that are reasonably trout-friendly at such times. Spring-fed waters,

especially chalk- or limestone-infused, are always a sound choice, as are any which have gone to the lengths of oxygenating and moving water about, such as Lakedown with its recently constructed waterfall and 'bubbles'. Bankside trees offer their cooling influence of shade, making the trout's summer world a more comfortable one. Depth is another factor which creates an easier way of life, though on one or two, the previous criterion keeps water temperature down precious degrees. Essentially it is the depth plus wind and wave action that allows the various levels to mix and disperse and thus avoids strong water stratification, creating oxygenated water instead. This can sometimes lead to the cooler water being pushed up into the unlikely shallower areas, but on the whole you should direct your efforts more to those deep areas; if only to get out of deep sunlight. The lovely thing about the water is its absorption and distillation of ultra-violet rays. Trout, lacking eyelids (a fact so many fly fishers forget), seek out the darkened water and avoid harsh light like the plague.

Yet, for some curious reason – and I have that maestro of the deep, Steve Parton, to thank for this information – the combination of depth and bright light makes hot or fluorescent orange a deadly fly colour scheme. This is a curious business if you consider most flies to be merely tonal after about 12ft or so, with colour (apart from a few) being almost redundant.

So with colour, depth and stupefying heat, I will take the plunge with tactics. The first tactic is not for purists; indeed, I have to admit

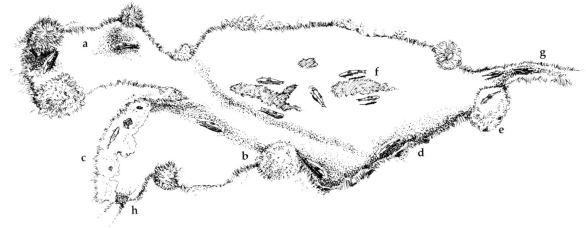

- *A lake in late spring/summer*

a spring or deephole
b deep gulley or 'chop off'
c scum/algae mat
d deep margins
e overhang tree
f weedbeds
g stream entrance
h outflow pipe

to things having to be fairly desperate for me to use the following flies and lines. However, we do go fishing to catch a trout or two and this procedure may help us do just that.

Using two lines

Having first ascertained the position of deeps, holes or troughs (old stream beds, etc), your priority is to select a line that will reach the area and fish the chosen pattern appropriately. Most of the time a Wet Cel II will suffice and, given various count-downs or using a stopwatch for perfect accuracy of depth and repetition, I have found between twenty and thirty seconds in water temperatures of 64 to 66 degrees Fahrenheit very reliable. On the other hand, some instances demand that the fly not only stays near the bottom, but is fished very slowly indeed. You are then left with little option but to use the Hi-D or DI lines of Airflo which at depth are extraordinarily tactilely suited, if a shade clumsy in casting due to their compensated descent rate.

In fact, by having the two lines, two deep-water options can be explored. With Wet Cel II, operate a pulling retrieve rate utilizing a figure of eight, short sharp tugs, hand-over-hand pulls, or even a combination of the three; or use the slothful progress of a Booby or suitably buoyant pattern to avoid snags, utilizing a figure of eight, interspersed with frequent pauses on the Hi-D. Both methods call for marabou-based patterns and you should always make certain they are, in fact, legal when you are fishing. If a fishery rule states a size limit of 1 inch or whatever, make absolutely sure that your fly conforms to that ruling. Incidentally, if you need to reduce the marabou tail length, do not use scissors or the seductive wiggle action will be ruined; instead 'pinch' the fibres out with your thumb and forefinger to the desired size.

For the Hi-D buoyant fly set-up, quite honestly anything other than the Booby is 'gilding the lily', but if you do find this really too offensive (as well you might), a less worrying option, erring to imitation is a foam-thoraxed Damsel or Montana Nymph which both fit the buoyant bill perfectly and are often taken as the fly drops through the layers, pulling the fly through a delicious, seductive curve as it does.

The more usual, ultra-slow figure of eight, interspersed with pauses, allowing the fly to undulate, is by far the most effective, and certainly, during oven-like temperatures, you will be able to position the fly in the sure knowledge that it rests in the cooler layers.

However, sometimes the following shock tactics are called for:

- Use of Pink/Purple Tadpole

- 'Ambushing' the fish

- 'Free-fall' tactics

Using the Tadpole

One pattern that 'shakes' the trout from their torpor and propels them into activity is the Pink Tadpole, which (and here I must be honest) has saved my bacon on more than one occasion. It is fished on the Wet Cel II using the aforementioned retrieve and can be devastating in its effectiveness, taking trout when an angler is convinced he is casting into a fishless void.

Two elements suit the fly: first, long-range casts, and secondly, fairly swift retrieves. There are, in fact, two distinct shades of pink – a violent fluorescent bordering on fuchsia, and a softer blancmange tone. Often one will work better than the other, so it is advisable to carry both (if you are brave enough to carry either!).

Another unusual variation on the Tadpole theme is purple. Similarly to pink, purple has for years been top of the steelheaders' colour choice in the USA, and as a steelhead is but a sea-running rainbow, I find it surprising that this colour has not evolved in our stillwater armoury. Certainly, over the last few seasons it has been a very successful pattern to change to when the going has got tough. There is even more logic in using the pattern in a deep-water role, when evidence from America regarding the trout's optical abilities testifies that olive, black, blue and purple are the most easily defined colours at depth – enter the Purple Bugger (if you dare).

Ambushing

Another line of approach which leans more to the tactical rather than the fly imitated is 'ambushing', and it has an extraordinarily close affinity to jungle warfare. But it does put the angler where trout are most likely to be; that is, resting in the shade of overhanging branches or, more likely, under the very branches themselves – anywhere, in fact, that not only has a cooling factor but a degree of calm away from bankbound storms. The problems attendant to this style of fishing are primarily threefold:

Agility   Fishing in such places will at best require a good deal of balancing and stooping, and at worst may require you to hang on to branches and perform other feats more akin to a circus act.

Rod control   The ability to cast and present your fly in such close confines – there will probably be no room for backcasts or indeed any type of rhythmic casting movements. Most likely presentation will be made by simply threading your rod or terminal tackle through the serpentine twigs and branches *à la* chub fishing, though sometimes a deft 'bow-and-arrow' cast can, in fact, be fashioned.

Fly choice   For placing through branches this should be a heavy Shrimp or leaded Hare's Ear type, as these can be relatively easily negotiated and placed through foliage. For 'bow-and-arrow' casting choose a lightweighted pattern, a slightly leaded Damsel being ideal as the inertia factor is not so great, thus making for cleaner, more accurate turnover.

- *Marabou-tailed movement*

The reality of the situation would suggest you are going to spend a fair bit of time up trees and tangled, and so you are. But it is surprising just how trout have a habit of concentrating the mind – especially the larger ones. And if you can combine all this with some degree of stealth, I can promise you some truly memorable fishing.

The real problems start though when the fly has begun its descent. Trout, when left undisturbed in places where they feel entirely comfortable and secure from the outside world, can be very gullible. Getting them to take won't necessarily be the problem; setting the hook most certainly will. So far I have smashed three rod tips into agonizingly expensive splinters due to over-enthusiastic striking.

Wherever possible ensure your rod tip is as low to the water as possible and just the merest lift will secure a hook hold, no matter how tenuous. The weight or body mass of the trout should thereafter set the hook more firmly. Then there is the small matter of playing the fish. You will have no other option than to hold it; allowing the fish any room for manoeuvre will be courting disaster. The first choice of rod will be middle-to-tip or medium taper (whatever you do don't use a tip-actioned rod or you will tear the hook hold), and as heavy a leader tippet as you dare is another must. I have found 11lb b.s. Orvis Super Strong to be ideal and, given tree roots and all, it is remarkably abrasion-resistant. The whole thing sounds hugely precarious, but if you need adrenalin in your fly fishing, there is that aplenty.

A rather more gentlemanly approach is to fish to the sides of bushes or similar overhanging flora, instead of actually going into the tree cavity. Often, by casting just as close as you can to the branches with a leaded Shrimp, Hare's Ear or Gold Head Damsel and allowing it to free-fall to the bottom, then lifting it smartly upwards and away from the trees, you can lure a trout from its hiding hole. However, it will be hell-bent on returning there, so the same tackle requirements apply.

Free-fall system

One tactic which has above all helped to overcome daytime, heat-singed flat calms and, moreover, is pleasurable, has been the 'free-fall'. It owes some of its style to dead-drifting a nymph on a river, merely allowing the current variation to impart animation to the fly; but in its still-water context, its execution was codified originally by the fly fishers of Queen Mother Reservoir at Datchet, and Peter Lapsley and especially Nick Cooke, who has made the method a 'fine art' form.

Like all truly effective operations, its base is simplicity itself, and can be usefully employed in most areas and situations, though flat calms and very light ripples suit the style best. The choice of rod and line is personal preference, though to free-fall this does lean to the light end of the spectrum, No. 5 or No. 6 system over No. 7 and No. 8. This is not due to artistic reasons, but practicality. The speed of response through the system is vital to a satisfactory outcome. Quite simply, a light line is thinner and less air- and water-resistant, so can be lifted a great deal faster from the water. My personal choice is $9\frac{1}{2}$ft or 10ft No. 5 Sage III, though most middle-to-tip 9ft to 10ft rods will suffice as long as the line rating is below No. 7.

The next element is the line. Whatever the make – and between the top manufacturers there is little variation be it Hardy, Air Cel Masterline, Cortland or Ultra and Airflo – just make sure the line floats and does so continuously.

Now to the leader. As I have suggested already, a better turnover will be achieved with knotless taper. Certainly there is no disadvantage and a good few advantages over a straight section of nylon. For this technique, the overall length should be about 16ft, which allows for the Orvis, Scorpio or Normark adaptors to be used in conjunction with the butt braided loop or nylon section to make the necessary length, or longer should situations demand.

Thereafter, the whole section is greased to float, including the fine tippet end and butt section, extending up into the fly line tip area. The whole leader system should float as high as possible. Mucilin (red tin) is by far the best, followed closely by Permagrease and Maryatt's Duck Grease.

The real shocks to the system (no pun intended) are the fly patterns. Given the sophistication of the tackle, the flies, by comparison, are extraordinarily simple and few in number. You could easily get by on the Gold Head Damsel and Hare's Ear Damsel, the Datsun, Free-fall Midge, Peacock Nymph and Golden Orb. There you have it; perhaps, if you really wanted to stretch your fly box, a few Yellow Head Pupae could be introduced but, in fact, you can subtract from the list rather than add to it.

The free-fall method

The method is disarmingly simple but – similarly to the patterns – deadly. Initially select a fishing area of good overall depth – ideally 10ft to 15ft – with deep, rather than shallow, margins or gentle gradients. This makes dams or areas that have been built up during construction with the spoil from earth movement which may also have created deep pockets or holes, even troughs and channels, all viable areas.

Having found a suitable location, the next step is the decidedly unfashionable aforementioned action of greasing the *entire* leader with Mucilin or Permagrease down to the fly. If a light to medium ripple sets in, then a sight 'bob' can be placed at the leader/fly line junction. These fluorescent pads are a positive boon in bite detection, with perhaps the best and certainly easiest to apply being the Umpqua Roll-on Indicator sold by Orvis.

Thereafter the cast can be made, always remembering to fish the water close at hand first – even by your feet, if you have been cautious in your approach – then fanning outward, gradually extending your casting distance. Try not to go so far that you cannot see the leader clearly.

The nub of this method rests on the dropping fly and the fly fisher's ability to detect a take. No matter how slight, subtle or insignificant – strike. The old river fishing axiom 'strike first, ask questions later' when nymphing is wholly appropriate. Often the familiar sight of the leader darting forward will signify the trout's acceptance of your artificial. However, it is far more likely to be the subtler variation on this 'alternative' theme.

The hardest thing in the world for stillwater fly fishers is to do nothing; their whole world revolves around retrieve, and this method pivots on the ability to cast and do nothing. No involuntary twitches, pulls or tweaks; just leave the system alone and glue your eyes along the leader snaking its way downward through the layers, and watch hawk-like for the slightest movement on the floating section. It is difficult, but the end more than justifies the means.

Generally the takes will happen as the fly sinks and can occur at any point during that process, from just as it starts up to the point the fly line is about to curve downward under the weighted fly's influence. The Golden Orb (Nick Cooke's Goldhead, but re-christened to avoid confusion), Mick William's Datsun, and the Free Fall Midge are all perfect in this role and, to be fair, most takes will occur during the descent through the layers.

However, there are occasions when two bites of the cherry are a good idea, and an *ultra*-slow retrieve after the free-fall may work wonders. I mean ultra-slow; if the sight bob or floating line leaves a wake at all, then you are retrieving too fast. This role is far better suited to the Gold Head Damsel or similar, and it was this form that gave me some scintillating fishing at Church Hill Farm on one particular sun-baked day of hopelessness one year.

The top lake had, for all the morning's fishing pressure, yielded three trout – it was a charity fun day sponsored by Gallahers. Rod after rod toiled away in the shimmering torpid heat with scant reward for not inconsiderable effort. Midday is not a time for jubilation and huge expectation. Having moved dutifully

36 *A 'Kiting' fish. If a large trout decides on a different route to the one chosen, try using a side strain – laying the rod on one side. This will generally turn their head*

around to my allotted area, I cast with the now-changed free-fall system, incorporating the Gold Head Damsel and the greased-up leader. Five casts later, out of seeming impossibility, I was the proud captor of two pristine rainbows; one taken on the drop, the other on a painfully slow retrieve. My neighbours were less than charitable in their various responses, but it did confirm the free-fall effectiveness at times when hope has a nasty habit of evaporating in the heat haze.

Using the dry fly

We have come a long way in stillwater fly fishing. Gone are the days of plain black and white lures, and the time when lines just sank or floated and nymphs were unprepossessing simplistic concoctions. Now we are enveloped in a welter of jargon, complication and micro methods; fine-tuning of our tactics is a latterday prerequisite. And yet on small stillwaters, most anglers have overlooked one of the most fundamental, simple yet deadly methods of all – the dry fly.

Certainly reservoirs and large sheets of water have rung to the clamour of 'new wave' dry fly stylists who have created almost a new dimension – angling philosophy – yet the small waters have been a 'shrinking violet' to this dry fly doctrine.

It is during those oily heat-filled days of high summer, with a torpor settling on the whole vista. The early fly fishing 'birds' catch the 'worms' (or trout!) and the midday angler rues his folly in coming out so late. Most depart for home by five or six o'clock, but if only they had waited just one or two hours more. Just on the edge of darkness, when that velvety cool settles on the water, then it is that the hunter is encouraged from the lair and the unsuspecting victim begins to emerge, hatch, scuttle and scurry. This is the time for dry fly on the small water.

The logic behind this method's effectiveness is twofold. First, the 'dog days' of summer tend to depress both trout and insect life to a near standstill; and secondly, there is the often overlooked factor of tranquillity. With the majority of fly fishers gone from the water, a degree of calm begins to settle, and certainly the trout tend to become less cautious and wary.

So often, in the process of fishing stillwaters – especially the small type – anglers make a huge tactical mistake: themselves. When stalking it is the cautious, careful-footed hunter who tends to deceive the quarry. Fly fishers often overlook the fact that, given a water sized around three or so acres, with ten or more rods fishing, the actual pressure on the fish is immense. Quite logically and reasonably, trout seek some form of sanctuary away from the mayhem of crashing lines and gaudy missiles overhead. This goes a long way to explain why smallwater fisheries have a habit of going utterly 'dead' in the afternoon.

If you take the scenario still further, then trout on small waters are subjected to very much more fishing attention than their reservoir kin – the survivors that is. Not surprisingly, if you further complicate matters by taking into account hot bright weather and rising temperatures, then the equation demands our fullest attention and tactical dexterity.

Having dispelled any complacency, we can begin in earnest. The dry fly, though essentially an evening tactic, can have its moments during the day – often on occasions when it seems nothing will work.

The system

The joy of dry fly fishing is that it needs little in the way of specialist equipment – a No. 6 outfit, and of course floating line, being perfect.

You might, if small flies persist in hatching, opt for a light No. 5, but it is not essential.

However, I should be guilty of mis-information if I did not mention two key areas – lines and leaders. After all the words, articles, urges and pleas, still fly fishers persist in using sub-standard floating lines – lines which should either have been pensioned off a season ago, are unworkable through lack of cleaning or care, or are simply so ill-chosen as to sink. Fishing the dry fly demands that your fly line *must* float – right down to the very tip. Here I would suggest that Mucilin (red tin) or Permagrease should be applied regularly to the fine, level tip, even on the high-quality makes. Dirt, scum and other waterborne nuisances collect on and particularly submerge this fine section, often causing it to rest *in* the surface film instead of *on* it. If not cleaned and greased regularly, this partially submerged section will delay the strike to a fish-missing degree. This fact has been borne out by bitter experience, with fleeting opportunities in ruins and rapidly departing trout. A good fly line, properly cared for, will pay for itself time and time again. The same goes for the carefully constructed leader. I would urge that a knotless taper of 12ft or more is an ideal choice.

Tippet size should again correspond with fly size, but co-polymide types of reduced-diameter nylons do have a hasty habit of coiling up on themselves if used in too light a breaking strain with a bushy dry fly – say a size 10 or 12 hackled/palmered Sedge. Standard mono for the larger sizes of dry fly is arguably a better option, though you can 'push' your breaking strain of Superstrong, Double Strength or Umpqua by using 8lb, to the ordinary mono's 4 or 6lb b.s. – indeed, it may be the better option if trout have attained a good size.

The real problems start to manifest themselves, not with the turnover of large flies, although this can be trying, but with the hooking and landing potential of the smaller ones – 16s, 18s and 20s – which are very definitely first choice on many occasions, and with the

37 Big fish action at Damerham. Damerham was one of the first small waters, and through Bill Sibbons' unique 'stalking' tactics has remained a clearwater favourite

compounded problem of, again, large trout. Obviously using $1\frac{1}{2}$ or 2lb breaking strain nylon is out of the question even if fishery rules permit, which is doubtful. Again the co-polys in 4 or 5lb b.s. hold part of the answer, but even these fished at range can lead to problems. A 'shock absorber' of some kind is a ready remedy, which leads me to the next leader system.

For years, when river fishing, I have used Roman Moser's braided leader system; indeed recently, more and more so on reservoirs. Lately, Roman has revamped the original design offering both floating braided polypropylene stretch types, as well as Kevlar braided non-stretch. Accompanying these is a separate Powergum shock butt, looped at each end, which joins between the braided butt and leader proper, thus doing away with the old style of knotting. It is a workable shock absorber and importantly, an easily connected system. My only variation away from the normal make-up, is to dispense with the original nylon tippet by adding a longer, heavier section – say 8lb b.s., then the tippet gives me overall a 12ft to 14ft leader. The other important feature of the Moser

floating braid is the enhanced turnover of even large flies. Even if you do not wish to leave the comparatively safe – and to be fair – less costly nylon, I would urge that you have some form of tapered design.

Turnover, especially when targetting or 'leading' a rising trout, is paramount and, I would argue, probably as important as fly design. The whole system need not be long, 12 feet being both practical in fishing and 'clean' in turnover, even in gusty conditions; and it is this speed and accuracy that will put fish on the bank. So often people go down the road of length equating with finesse, and whilst I would be the first to acknowledge the long leader's attributes, this is tempered with the knowledge of occasional tangles, periodic mayhem of nylon being blown back on itself, and wind knots – all equalling lost opportunities, and being factors largely nullified by a shortened leader. This Lilliputian system is no less delicate either – the angler is so often the perpetrator of that crime. Quite simply, aim your fly (with the rod tip) *above target*, allowing the cushion of air to soften the descent.

In terms of ointments, you need a good-quality instant floatant, such as Gink or Orvis Hy-Flote. Both benefit from being pastes which liquify with the hand's heat and allow exact placement – very important if you want perhaps only the thorax to float, or the wings even. However, I would advise that high-riding flies (other than emergers) are liberally dosed with Permaflote, twenty-four to thirty-six hours before fishing, or indeed, directly after tying, rendering them positively cork-like in their floating capabilities.

The opposite is also necessary – Sinkmix or detergent-injected fuller's earth can make a critical difference. It has been said so many times before, but degreasing with mud the last few inches up to a foot by the artificial, can be crucial. But this is not because the nylon is treated to sink – I have had too many occasions when treated nylon has floated to believe this implicitly – but that the surface is rendered matt and glint-free. However, it is advisable to re-anoint the tippet section every third or fourth cast, ensuring a constant coating.

Fly choice

Now to the flies themselves. Similar to wet, dry flies fall into two categories: attractive and directly imitative, though there may be crossovers when an imitative design can also attract through enhancement or prominence of a particular material, colour scheme or feature.

Often some quite outrageous pattern will work at the most curious of times; for example, black flies on some waters are particularly good on extraordinarily bright, hot days. Bright fluorescent orange dry flies again can be pos-

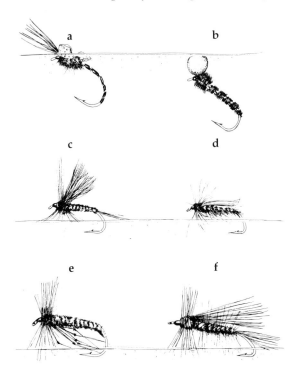

- Dry flies

a   Halo Emerger
b   Suspender (emerging)
c   Duck's Dun – low-riding
d   Bob's Bits – very low-riding
e   Hopper – fairly high-riding
f   Stimulator – very high-riding

itively magnetic to trout, especially on hot days but even on overcast high-summer days, when often you could do a great deal worse than just throw one out and leave it.

One of the hardest things of all in respect to this method is the aspect of 'confidence'. Certainly, if fish are rising, there is a logic or degree of planning that can go into the proceedings. However, this reasoning of a tactic – noting the natural, finding a facsimile, tracking a rising trout, then carefully negotiating a cast to the said quarry – goes totally out of the window if nothing whatsoever stirs the tranquil surface, indeed, when there is little to imitate; yet time and time again a trout will be attracted to surface patterns.

Arguably, the most pertinent requisite of this method – overriding the technicalities and tactics – is confidence; confidence that the lone fly just sitting there will work.

Careful observations and some detective work will ascertain the insect system on your particular water or locale, so a logical dry-fly box can be assembled. Indeed, it is often the case that certain patterns appeal to certain fly fishers – hence the mushrooming ranks of artificials. Again, it is all a question of confidence. Now to the fishing proper.

Daytime fishing

Essentially dry fly fishing can be split into two distinct sections – daytime and evening – there being very little in the way of parity between the two.

Apart from the aforementioned Daddy instance and bright orange factors, during heat-filled indolent days there is another minor tactic worth mentioning. On waters where common blue damsel fly exist (and there are very few small waters not graced by its presence), quite noticeable trout activity can be seen, centred around weedbed masses and hovering blue damsel adults. Often this occurs when quite simply the lake has 'died a death' in every other sense. The odd trout – and sadly, it is just that – can be deceived with a blue damsel imitation

GUIDELINES TO DRY PATTERNS

Attractors general patterns
- Orange Emerger hook size 12–16 Std
- Hoppers (black, scarlet, orange, olive, amber and claret). Hook 10–14.
- Daddy Longlegs. Because of their numbers and season long availability, a 'daddy' pattern in hook size 8 LS–12 Std shank is a good attractor pattern
- Raiders (simple seal's fur for hackleless dry flies (red, orange, olive, claret and black in hook size 12–16 Std

Olive imitations (pond and lake)

Dun	Hook	Std DE
● Ducks Dun	Hook	14–18
● Greenwell's Glory	Hook	14–18
● Adams	Hook	14–18

Spinner		
● Apricot Glitter Spinner	Hook	14–18
● Sunset Spinner	Hook	14–18

Caenis Species		
● Glitter Spinner	Hook	18–24
● Poly Wing Spinner	Hook	18–24

Sedge imitations
Realistic patterns

● Tent Wing Caddis	Hook	Std 10–16
● Depositing Caddis	Hook	LS 10–16

Impressionistic Patterns

● Elk Hair (olive, amber and brown bodied)		Std 10–16

DE = Down eye   LS = Long shank   UE = Up-eye

● Balloon Caddis (olive, amber and brown bodied)		Std 10–12

Terrestrials

● The B and A (beetle and ant)	Hook	Std DE 14–16
● The Super Ant (black and brown)	Hook	Std DE 14–20
● Borger Para Ant	Hook	Std DE 14–20

The Midges (chironomids)
Realistic Patterns

● Hackle Point Midge (black, brown, olive, claret, amber, red, orange etc)	Hook	Std DE 10–20
● Foam Midge (above colours)	Hook	Std DE 10–20
● Sparkle Gnat	Hook	Std DE 14–24

Impressionistic

● Bob's Bits (olive, red, black and claret)	Hook	Std DE 10–14
● Para Midge (above colours)	Hook	Std or curved DE 12–20
● Hare's Face Midge	Hook	Std DE 10–14

Occasional Patterns

● Borger's Braided Butt Damsel	Hook	Std DE 10
● Grey Duster	Hook	Std UE 14–18
● Lively Mayfly	Hook	Std DE 10–12
● Grey Wulff	Hook	Std DE 8–12
● G&H Sedge	Hook	LS DE 12–14

literally cast into the clear pockets of weed mats, then just left to resemble an exhausted or spent adult. Takes can be acrobatic and startlingly sudden. As with any large dry fly, the strike is vital and some delay is necessary. The problems so often stem from the startling nature of the take, which in turn causes a chain reaction with a hasty strike made too soon. The fact is it may be the only rise you will get during the day, so it does pay to fish hard for short bursts, then have a rest, rather than doggedly soldiering on, becoming lethargic in the heat, only to miss the rise.

Evening fishing
Evening, however, heralds the promise of much wider floating-fly opportunities and richer pickings. Curiously, this tends to coincide with our exodus from the water, mentioned at the beginning, yet trout start to rise on the now tranquil surface echoing the pearlescent colours of evening. As this is a time of heat and high summer, the olives, and to some extent, midge, play second fiddle to the sedge; and the lovely thing about the Caddis is the variety of ways it can be fished – static, twitched, running, or a combination of all three.

However, without trying to sound too dogmatic, it does pay to give some thought to tactics. By watching and analysing rise forms, a very good working foundation can be achieved as to method and fly choice. If the water positively erupts with near-demonic trout exuberance, fish a largish wake-making pattern – Sedges being ideal. If, however, you see those purposeful, almost languid 'nose and tails' or rolls – even heavy swirls – opt for a smaller design, either based on the static Sedge (accuracy to the natural to some degree is not a bad idea), and a Midge dressing, again in calm-water small sizes (16–20), or accurate designs tend to work better, or a Balloon or Female Caddis left inert.

But should you happen across those reasonably noisy 'sipping' rises, then an entirely different line of approach is necessary. I would say on balance that this feeding mode is extremely common in warm, muggy weather. The cause can be any number of natural waterborne occurrences, but my money would be on caenis fall or pond or lake olive spinners – both can be maddeningly difficult to imitate successfully, and call for light lines, fine tippets and very careful accurate casting.

The saving grace to what appears a complex situation is that clues tend to be scattered about in front of you; for example, spent spinners tend to stay put and allow themselves to be observed. This does at least aid fly choice. The fact that trout are rising, and probably in sequence if somewhat erratic, also helps in terms of cast direction and general route planning. It is left to you only to effect a good, and above all, accurate and delicate cast. As this instance often occurs in shallows or water margins, some degree of stealth is also an important ingredient. Keeping a low profile, possibly hidden behind bushes, is always sound dry fly policy and also enables often quite short, deadly casts to be made as trout come in closer.

Not all evening dry fly fishing is as problematic. In the case of the Sedge, you can have enormous fun experimenting with the move-ment of a dry fly. Try casting at range and with a fully greased leader, trying a variety of retrieve rates, getting the fly to resemble the action of freshly hatched sedge running across the water, then resting and repeating the exercise. This is ideally suited to the Elk Hair. Or, in the case of the egg-laying female, try twitching then resting in a variety of sequences – the Running Depositing Caddis being purpose-designed for this job. This requires a mixture of figure of eight, stripping, twitched movements on your part, in order to impart animation.

The static presentation, on the other hand, requires you do nothing at all – which is sometimes far more difficult than engaging in some form of movement. If your fly is refused when fishing in this manner, re-cast and, when a trout next refuses, try pulling on the line smartly, causing it to skate momentarily along the surface in imitation of a fleeing insect. Often this effects a response which is swift and deadly.

Another trick when fishing the Caddis is to make it 'run', by stripping downward with the line hand, whilst raising the rod hand and at the same time shaking the rod tip from side to side, achieving a stuttered, agitated running movement. The fly is then allowed to rest and the rod hand lowered. This is then repeated until the line is retrieved. It is an alternative method but one which, especially when darkness is closing in, can be very successful – but beware, takes are furious!

As the evening fades to the silky purple-indigo shades and bats begin their high-pitched hunting cry, there is another phase, and here generalization plays its role.

After hours' fishing

It does appear that, with the onset of night, trout traditionally lose their caution, and begin to search for food in unguarded earnest. This affects fly choice to some degree, as details become far less important, with vague outlines and colour being the overriding triggers. For many years on rivers, especially chalkstreams, my spinner patterns have been enhanced with

38 *Camouflage is a vital ally to the angler. Here Mike Perry blends wonderfully into his surroundings. Trout also like cover, making his approach and choice of tactics a winning combination*

fluorescent or reflective crimson and oranges. This, in turn, has affected my stillwater box, with most patterns being 'shot through' with one or both colours.

But reality on stillwaters would suggest there being little use for any other than a claret-based pattern, but again, I 'work in' some crimson, scarlet or orange into the dressing, be it a Hopper, Bob's Bits or similar workman-like dressing. I even have a claret/crimson-bodied Elk Hair that works in such circumstances, especially where caddis are at play 'after hours'. At present I am experimenting with magenta, purple and violet, but it is early days with no firm conclusions for or against as yet.

Of course, the burning question with the dry fly is timing – timing the cast to correspond with the trout's position, and the timing of the

strike. Of the first part (and to some degree, the second), I can only say that experience brings its own rewards, and you should be prepared to make mistakes and learn from them – and, of course, experiment. Striking can actually be calculated – at least loosely. The bigger the fly, the longer the delay; the smaller the fly the quicker the strike. Also distance fits into the equation: the farther you are from your fly then, again, the quicker the strike.

Once mastered, the dry fly fished before or on the edge of darkness, with the world fading to ink around you, is a magical end to the day, and one which can explode into a frenzy of white water and candescent leaping trout lighting up the sepulchral setting. The dry fly may, at times, be static, but seldom is it uneventful.

The hunter in earnest

The fly fishers' basic instinct

A primaeval element – the instinct to hunt, stalk, and capture prey by stealth and natural cunning – lurks in most fly-fishers.

This concept may seem doubtful when applied to serried ranks of reservoir bank-fishers, yet, in the cloistered surroundings of many small waters, prehistoric instinct can be given full rein; sooner or later, the urge to stalk and deceive the larger-than-average trout will become irresistible.

I confess to preferring this kind of fishing to all others. Selecting a trout and plotting its capture draws you in to your fishing, projecting you spiritually beneath the surface of the water into an alien and complex world. Respect for the quarry grows with every missed opportunity, feckless footfall, or hurried cast that sends a fish gliding ghostlike from sight, scornful of your intrusion. Such fishing is truly addictive.

Key elements in this fishing are:

- water clarity

- tackle selection

- aquatic knowledge

- tactics

- watercraft

Water clarity

The fisheries themselves vary from tree-screened pools to exposed waters covering many acres, but all have one thing in common – clear water. Generally the rock strata beneath are of chalk or limestone, so high alkalinity results in prolific weed growth.

These features are missing from the more acidic upland waters, and even from fisheries in the south created over beds of clay or sandstone, though pockets of either chalk or limestone can be found in most counties.

Stalking trout also calls for deep margins, or holes within seeing and casting range. Depths of 4ft to 6ft are desirable, plus channels of 8ft to 10ft, ideally with clumps of weed; though, in exceptional clear waters, it may well be possible to stalk individual trout in depths up to twenty feet. Indeed, one summer, whilst fishing in British Columbia, I and other members of the British Commonwealth team fishing in Kamloops were able to stalk, target and capture trout cruising depths down to 30ft in White Lake, the clarity being so pronounced. This, of course, is an exception and the whole concept of hunting in clear waters is self-limiting and the choice is, by and large, fairly polarized and specific. But, with new lakes being created each season, the list of fisheries where stalking is possible grows ever longer.

As a starting base, you will find at the end of the book a list of fisheries which I have found lend themselves ideally to this form of fishing. But rule of thumb would suggest that if you can see the bottom in 6ft of water the lake is suitable for stalking.

Let me first say categorically what stalking, or targetting, individual trout *is not*; it is not merely dropping a fly in the water and jigging it up and down for hours on end. Not only is this extraordinarily boring, but decidedly ethically questionable. It is also not an 'X marks the spot' type of fishing. Let me explain. Some years ago a fad arose, which was embraced by some luminaries of the time, of attempting, and very often succeeding, in catching trout anywhere other than the mouth. This, however you dress it up, is cheating, and although clear-waters and mouthwateringly-sized trout can set the pulse racing, due to the sheer closeness and visual nature of the discipline, it is, and always will be, a test of skill, deception, pattern selection and consummate patience, rather than barbaric sniggling.

Clothing

Now to requirements – travel light. Everything should be in a comfortable waistcoat or one of the new, belted stalker pouches. Even with a waistcoat, always carry the minimum.

Important weapons in the hunter's armoury

39 *A good L'Église fish makes a strong bid for freedom. Keeping the rod this high often forces a trout to the surface, so enabling a speedy netting operation*

119

are good-quality polarizing glasses. The late Oliver Kite thought they gave the angler an unfair advantage, but we mortals need all the help we can get. Just recently on the market, is an intriguing design from Tanner's Fishing Glasses which work on the same principle as a polarizing filter on a camera, by virtue of being able to be rotated, thus affording complete glare-free vision whatever the angle the sun is to your fishing position.

Another extremely important consideration is lens colour. Green or neutral grey are fine during normal light conditions, but when low light or extremely overcast conditions are experienced, there is a huge advantage in opting for a yellow or amber lens. My choice here is invariably the Cormorant yellow-lensed HLTs.

I would suggest that polarized glasses are so important to this style of fishing that it may even be a good idea to opt for carrying two pairs – a neutral-lensed pair and a yellow-lensed pair, and in so doing offer day-long comfort and enhance underwater vision to an extraordinary degree, even on overcast and blustery days as well as, in contrast, extremely bright days.

A wide-brimmed hat will also add to vision enhancement and is a tactical 'must' for this type of fishing. I tend to use two varieties – a battered safari-type trilby and a bone-fisherman's (Florida Keys, not an anorexic condition!) up-downer flats hat. My wife says my flats hat looks preposterous – and so it does – but for blocking harsh overhead light and thus improving vision it is superb. Odd as it may seem, the selection of the right hat and polarizing glasses – non-fishing items – is of more importance to me than the choice of rod and line for this type of fishing.

The system

Rods for this style should be between 9ft and 9½ft and fastish-tapered. You need, as often as not, short but accurate casts with leaded flies; a soft or slow-tapered rod would throw too wide a loop. Ideal line sizes are No. 6 and 7 – the ever-useful allrounders for stillwater use.

The overriding criterion governing the choice of rod is the size of trout you expect to catch. The object of stalking is to select better-than-average specimens. Once your fish is hooked, your tackle must be strong enough to cope.

I have watched, in a state of incredulity, an angler playing an 8–9lb fish for more than 75 minutes. At no time did he put the fish under any sort of pressure, so the trout dolefully swam about, tethered and stupefied.

Anglers like this do nothing for our sport. If you intend to land a fish, take the fight to the trout and make your tackle work. A rod tip kept high will subdue and absorb just about any shock. But I would say this about rod design, a great many of your battles will be fought 'hand to fin', in other words you will hook trout literally under your feet, and very often that is where the fight will be conducted. An extremely fast-actioned rod may well tear a hook hold, whereas a middle-actioned rod will absorb the plunges and tremors but, importantly, inflict less jarring notes on all but the most tenuous of hook holds and allow these close-quarters fish to be landed. Strangely, these last couple of seasons, I have been doing a great deal of my stalking with rods as light as AFTM 4 and 5, and not noticed any appreciable difference in fighting backbone when it came to largish fish. In fact, only a few weeks ago (as I write) I landed a 12lb plus rainbow in the peak of condition on my trusty Sage SP4 9ft No. 4 and a 3lb tippet, in conjunction with a size 16 fly. I forgot, you see, that I had picked up, inadvertently, my river gear, instead of the intended No. 6 which looks almost identical. I can record a happy outcome, with only minimal panic breaking out on momentary occasions.

Rules often dictate which line should be used. You may be restricted to a floater, but fear not! A fly can be presented quickly at depth by adding a sinking leader to your line – an instant and easy-casting sink-tip. Airflo and Roman Moser leaders are both excellent and come in a variety of densities. Particular favourites are the new lightweight Airflo sinking leaders and the Moser Diver No. 2 which, in effect, is a copper braid; braided leaders, even now, are viewed with a certain amount of suspicion, and yet the tactical variety that can be achieved by interchanging various densities is enormous, expedient and effective. Certainly it does overcome the problems presented by getting a small, lightweight offering down to deep-lying fish when attached to the floating line, but if I were restricted to one type of line, an intermediate would get my vote. Actually, any slow-sinking type will do, be it the Kelly Green Wet Cel or the suspicously similar equivalent in the Hardy range through to the Airflo Glass lines or Bob Church's version, which I favour.

Other contenders for all round usefulness are Hardy Slow Sink, Wet Cel I and Masterline's intermediate Gold series. There are, of course, many others on the market, but these are known to me and have achieved what has been asked of them. There are occasions, however, when getting that little bit deeper is essential to success, and here a Wet Cel II is an almost mandatory requirement, especially during the colder water conditions of early winter through to late spring, where your quarry may well be lurking a couple of feet lower than during the traditionally warmer weather of more usual fly fishing periods. Recently I have been using a Cortland sink-tip and also the Teeny Mini Tip, both of which have lain aside reservations that persisted with earlier sink-tip lines in the way that they used to cast, that is to say casting two densities of line at the same time generally led to a less than delicate touchdown; these rather more rarified designs, albeit still marginally awkward, offer nearly as good a presentation as single-density types. What, of course, they do offer is the control and vision of a floating main section which, on occasions, can be decidedly advantageous.

The choice of leader is critical and should never be underestimated. Having mentioned already the braided types, I will reserve this section for the universally more useful nylon varieties.

Often opportunities are missed through the leader being, curiously, a bit too long. This needs explanation, especially in the light of having previously urged the use of 12ft upwards. In this type of demanding fishing what you are trying to achieve is clear turnover when casting, and fly presentation that is both accurate and delicate. Keeping the fly line sufficiently far away from the fish to avoid spooking it suggests the use of 16ft to 18ft of nylon, but in practice leaders of 9ft, 10ft and 12ft are far better for achieving accuracy in this style of fishing.

If, and it is a big 'if', you feel trout are a bit twitchy, decrease tippet strength and/or lengthen the tippet to form a total length of 14ft. It is not advisable to exceed this, otherwise the nylon, hingeing in the air, can send a fly in all directions, especially if a heavy fly is used.

The aim is accuracy coupled with delicacy, and the easiest way to achieve both requirements is to purchase a knotless tapered leader of 12ft and either keep this length or add a tip section of matching strength.

Certainly a steep taper will enhance turnover no end. Suitable leaders are supplied by Orvis, Scorpion Masterline (Siglon) and Normark. Those by the first three companies are of reduced-diameter co-polymer mono; the latter's are of standard diameter.

The advantage of co-poly mono is that it offers high breaking strain without sacrificing low diameter and suppleness, combined with the distinct advantage of cutting through the surface quickly due to much reduced surface area, making the descent of a fly that much quicker. However, 5lb Drennan Sub Surface Green is an ideal nylon for those still suspicious of the co-poly types and, to my knowledge, this particular nylon and, indeed, breaking strain, has never broken on a fish unless an alien cause was introduced – a wind knot, a bruise or similar 'gremlin'. In fact, this particular brand and poundage is the 'favoured son' of many

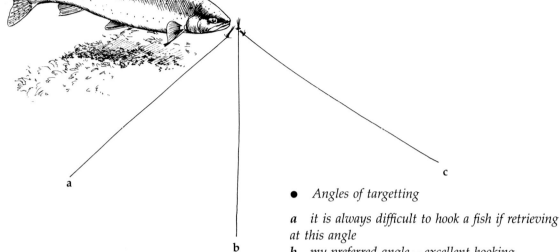

- *Angles of targetting*

a   it is always difficult to hook a fish if retrieving at this angle
b   my preferred angle – excellent hooking
c   good, and probably the most used. However, as the trout is facing the fly, hook-ups are a problem. Wait until you either see the fly vanish or feel solid resistance

notable fly fishers. I confess to preferring the less corpulent co-polys, but will, if necessary, raise my breaking strain to meet certain requirements and, in so doing, still not sacrifice low diameters.

Next on the agenda comes a capacious metal-framed landing net, which is invaluable not only for normal use but for digging a fish out of weedbeds – a task for which a triangular front-corded net is unsuited since it may 'cave in'. The other important aspect regarding net designs are transportation and ease of operation. My chum, Pete Cockwill, and indeed, many others, manage in Houdini-like style to use the very tough and accommodating Gye net. I can't; I just seem to get in a ghastly tangle and end up generally losing the very thing I am supposed to be securing. My present net is a telescopic sea trout style designed by Sharpes of Aberdeen, as mentioned earlier in chapter 1.

Tactics

Tactics for this style of fishing are surprisingly few. A great deal depends on you, the fly fisher, and your willingness to walk the fishery in search of trout rather than wait for them to swim past in an angler-friendly procession.

Around all our small stillwater fisheries you will come across monolithic anglers positioned all day long by known hot spots. Stoically they refuse to move, even when elsewhere there may be trout large enough to send them to a piscatorial nirvana. Still, these immobile anglers at least allow the nomadic fly fisher to take a greater share of the spoils.

Comfortable footwear is essential, preferably with soft soles that do not grate noisily on gravel to alert cruising trout.

Once tackled-up and ready to move, I try to ensure that some fly line is outside the tip-ring at all times, so that as soon as a trout is located a cast can be made. Speed is of the essence, especially if a trout is moving quickly. Also, holding the fly in readiness in your left hand further allows a speedy cast to your quarry.

Once you have a target, three main lines of attack are open to you:

- the free-fall method

- catch me if you can

- the ambush

Using the free-fall method when stalking

The idea of sending a nymph tumbling downwards towards an unsuspecting fish seems simple. It is not. What is needed is a very definite idea of the trout's position in relation to that of the dropping fly. Misjudge it, and insufficient time will be allowed for the pattern to descend to the right depth, and an opportunity will be missed.

A trout will move some distance to intercept an imitation, and will often follow the fly down. It is uncommon for the targeted trout to move upwards, but I have seen it happen. Far more likely – and this must be your aim when using the 'free-fall' method – is that your fly will cut across the cruise-path of the trout.

If you do miss a fleeting opportunity, don't worry; a trout's patrol route (especially that of a big fish) is jealously guarded, fairly regimented, and clearly defined. Stay in position, and soon the trout, having completed its regular journey,

will reappear to offer another opportunity. Indeed this can afford the fly fisher not just a few, but a whole day full of opportunities so long as your presence remains unnoticed.

There are one or two other points worth mentioning about the free-fall styles. Firstly, never underestimate your quarry – the fact that you can see them, means oddly, they can see you. Err to caution, keep your movements as minimal as possible and your overhead casts few. As the day wears on, you will notice that trout become ultra-cautious – the mere sound of a 'plopping' fly sending them fleeing in panic. Now is the time to look very carefully at your choice of pattern. I carry nowadays a whole range of different leaded styles, including the early morning depth charge – like Cockwill's Hare's Ear Shrimps, Wiggle Tail Hare's Ears and Ultra Damsels, together with a few Red Spot Shrimps in various colours, all embodying enough lead to reroof a church. These are always my first choices to get to the required depths, however, once a few lines have thrashed the water, and a few trusty brethren have, curiously, shot skywards and vanished, the more

- *Stalking – on the drop*

1   The trout intercepts the falling fly
2   if the trout misses, allow the fly to land on the bottom (if practicable) and wait until the fish returns on its route then pull the fly up in fly of its nose and 'jiggle' it

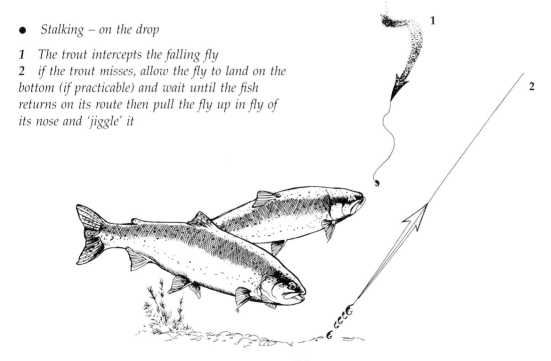

1

2

modest (yet equally devastating) smaller leaded bugs come into their own.

These originated with that stalker supreme, Bill Sibbons, and amount to tiny hooks covered with lead wire. I have subsequently added tiny little marabou tails, a pearly Mylar thorax cover, and covered them with epoxy resin. This has not only given them a lovely insecty sheen, but further enhanced their already fast sink rate. These tiny little specks are ideal when trout are suffering from piscatorial 'nervous dyspepsia' and, even in extremes of both weather and angling attention, can and do deceive some sophisticated quarry, but almost universally, takes will come on the aforementioned free-fall.

Catch me if you can

The initial stage follows that of the 'free-fall' in that the fly is allowed to drift down to the trout's cruising depth. Then, once the fly is level and perhaps a few feet – even inches – away, from the quarry, the retrieve is started. To this end, a fly that you can see is always an advantage, for instance, a light fly over a dark background or vice versa (white is an extremely good visual colour in a wide variety of conditions) or conversely incorporate a bright 'spot' of fluorescent colour.

The fly should be moved in either smooth draws or by fast, jinking retrieves away from the trout, tempting it to pursue or make an aggressive surging response. The object of both styles is to get the fly to the right depth initially, otherwise the methods are usually unsuccessful.

The ambush

The third and final major tactic, this is reminiscent of 'sink and draw' fishing, and it is perfect for following up missed opportunities, or fishing areas too deep to decipher whether trout are resident or not, such as deep holes or by the side of algae or scum mats. This style requires the fly to be allowed to descend to the bottom, or just above in heavily weeded areas.

Once the fly has reached its limit of descent, it is brought swiftly back to the surface just in front of a returning patrolling trout. The tactic is also employed to induce a take from fish sensed rather than seen to be in the area and, therefore, can actually work in quite murky water, indeed, it is often used to catch the larger trout inhabitants at L'Église in Kent.

If a follow is not forthcoming, the fly is allowed to descend again to the bottom and the curving upward movement of the fly is repeated slightly nearer to the bank until your chosen fishing area has been fully covered. Although somewhat random in its approach, this style has the ability to draw fish that would not otherwise respond.

Other tactics

Another alternative though minor tactic is based on the 'plopability' of a leaded fly as it enters the water. Having said earlier that this can

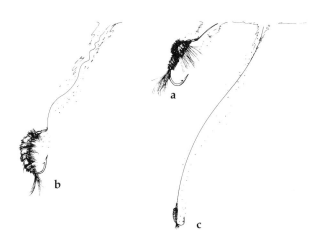

● *Fly patterns – different rates of descent*

a heavily-leaded Montana can 'hold up' in the water due to its bulky materials and hackle
b a Wiggle-tail Hare's Ear – this will sink rapidly due to its condensed shape; though it will make a disturbance
c a Lead Speck – though tiny, due to its aerodynamic shape and density this will sink extremely quickly and make comparatively little disturbance

'spook' quarry, it can, it must be said, be thoroughly advantageous, the noise alerting the trout and audibly suggesting food. Far from frightening fish, a 'plop' can positively galvanize trout into taking. Prime areas are where casting is cramped by the bank, trees, bushes or weeds, indeed anywhere where one has to almost resemble an orang utang's prehensile state in order to fish a fly. You will often find that a fairly comatose trout will spring into action and seize your fly in a trice. An instant response is essential, but be warned, very often the sheer speed of the quarry will have you striking with equal venom and smash takes are a very real possibility.

Other useful flies for stalking styles include Yellowhead, Wobble Worm (red, olive and black), Walker's Damsel and Mayfly Nymphs, the Gold Head Hare's Ear, streamlined and hook-weighted Datsun, Corixa, and the Varnished Midge. For the 'pull-off' styles, marabou-tailed flies seem to work best, Tadpoles (olive, black, orange and white), Distressed Damsel, and Cooper's Yellow, all being effective. For the 'ambush style', a combination of both types of pattern is required, though corixa and shrimp patterns are the mainstay, as they are for the 'plop' approach.

Quite honestly, strategy overrides the choice of fly. Carrying a small range of patterns in various colours encourages you to place far greater emphasis on locating and catching trout.

Another important factor is the actual taking time, because an overall pattern does seem to exist. In the mornings free-fall styles tend to be successful. The notoriously difficult midday period is better suited to the 'pull-off' and ambush tactics, while in the late afternoon and evening period a combination of the 'free-fall' (light permitting) and the 'pull-off' styles seems to work best.

The take

There are problems with all these styles in that you will seldom, if ever, feel a trout take the fly. Indeed, it is sobering to think how often your artificial is taken by a fish with no tactile indication on the line or leader. The problem must be magnified when fishing a large reservoir.

Water clarity is the saving factor, helped by the enhanced vision afforded by polarizing glasses. You can see the trout's reaction and respond accordingly. Yet, even with this distinct advantage, few people manage to strike correctly or quickly enough.

There are several pointers indicating that a trout has accepted your artificial:

● the unmistakable 'blink' of white as the trout's mouth opens and then closes on your fly. The glimpse of white is easily seen when you are fishing shady spots but it is less obvious in harsh light.

● when the trout's gill-covers open momentarily, though this is visible only at close quarters. At the same time the trout's head quivers.

● the 'easy-finned glide' – perhaps my favourite take. A trout surges towards the fly, sometimes changing direction slightly as it does so.

There are other, more subtle, variations of the take – a mere tilt or flick of the trout's head, or a flash of the trout's flank when a fish is lying deep, could mean that your fly has been accepted. At any momentary deviation from the trout's set cruising pattern, strike or lift without hesitation. Many anglers strain to see the fly, and mostly this is utterly futile. Far better to observe the trout's movements, striking at any irregularity.

Curiously, the most difficult fish to hook is a trout chasing a fly and coming straight towards you. There is something deeply mesmeric about the sight of cavernous white jaws nearing your artificial. So often the strike is way too soon, and the fly is whisked out of the trout's mouth.

Often a trout will continue to pursue and give you a second chance, but if you are too late, or prick the fish, you can forget about

40 *In the jungle. Trout like tucked, out of the way, quiet places. Never be afraid of fishing when vegetation is dense*

shrimp and corixae. These are truly interesting trout to fish for and often very demanding.

Thereafter the whole business is academic. I personally live for the take: that moment when the trout accepts what appears to be a natural item of food. Of course, hooking and battling with a large fish, especially at close quarters, is highly charged with excitement – a 'will he, won't he?' test of nerve. But, even with the fish of a lifetime, don't let the trout set the tune – you, the fly fisher, must be the conductor. As *The Hitch-hiker's Guide to the Galaxy'* advises – 'don't panic'. Playing a large fish, even on light line, is a tense business nevertheless, and I would urge and entreat you, if at all possible, get your line on the reel and play your fish on the reel. Far fewer specimens are lost this way. If it wants to run – let it, within reason – and always keep your rod tip up to absorb any sudden shocks. Try also not to let the fish 'churn' on the surface, those wild, thrashing water upheavals can loosen precarious hook holds. Once your fish tires and offers up its flank, dip your net and submerge the rim and bring your quarry to the net and never vice versa, tilt and lift and, hopefully, he will be yours.

You will hear many accounts of how large fish from small waters don't fight. Mostly these are erroneous and invariably bandied about by people who have never actually hooked a large trout. I can recall with woeful clarity, and indeed the manager at Lakedown Fishery will be able to recount a tale of, an utterly beaten, baffled, and bemused Jardine, when with 150 yards of line and backing out, an estimated 14lb plus rainbow and I parted company. I have seldom even had salmon do that to me, indeed, the last time I can recall a fish taking line at that speed was a bonefish on the Florida Keys. The comment of the century coming from P. Cockwill Esq., who, whilst standing by the side of me, and looking equally mesmerised, looked at my blur of a reel, saying 'I didn't know they made grey backing.' 'They don't' I said, 'that's my spool.' 'Oh ****' he said. Ah well … that's fishing.

catching it for a while. Put your failure down to 'adrenalin rush', and try for the fish again half-an-hour to an hour later. The trick is to wait until the fly is enveloped and the trout's mouth closes – 'white changing to dark'. Then strike with venom – upwards, not sideways, or the hook may not find a hold in the upper jaw, which is where you want it. Indeed, having mentioned all the various types of trout response, it is worth just outlining what you are actually looking for in terms of takeable fish. Not all trout are worth pursuing, in fact some are pure time-wasters. The worst of these are the fish that are going about their business at a positive dash, their minds firmly fixed on the opposite side of the lake. The ultimate stalker's trout is a 'dawdler' – a fish that is merely meandering and cruising in a sedate fashion. Another trout suitable for scrutiny with a fly rod is the out and out 'shrimper' – you won't miss it, invariably these trout cruise very close to the lake floor in the vicinity of weedbeds and periodically stand on their heads and literally 'hoover' through the green fronds in search of

CHAPTER EIGHT

Autumn and Winter

Fishing brownies

THE most enigmatic of the fly fisher's quarry must surely be the brown trout – quirky, sour, mean, ill-tempered, obtuse. Even now, with all our accumulation of knowledge and high-tech innovations, the brown trout remains the ultimate stillwater challenge.

Quite what motivates them and goads them into various responses is often only deduced by elaborate guesswork. Perhaps with so many other questions now answered and theories and myths exploded, it is best that we never know for sure. There is something deeply refreshing in mysteries, and I know of few fly fishers who do not willingly answer this siren's call. A big brown trout for most of us is a 'Holy Grail'.

Size, of course, is relative; but one factor about brownies is their unique adaption to waterborne situations. I can recall huge fish from diminutive brooks which were wholly disproportionate in size to the average trout; they were monsters by any standard. This is probably through 'bloody-mindedness' on their part – a sort of 'this is my tree root and no angler is going to tempt me away from it' attitude. So to the enigma you can add quite realistically 'defiant'.

It is a wonder that we catch any at all; and yet there are opportunities and techniques which can, on occasion, go some little way to ensnare the wily brown trout.

The problem diminishes a little on rivers, where there is at least some rhyme and reason to feeding and feeding periods. Mostly these are totally governed by insect emergence, or activity of some kind, be it surface or sub-surface. At least the overall concept gives we poor fishers some clues to the endless problem. Thereafter we must rely on our own powers of presentation to create the allure.

A certain amount of this applies on small stillwaters – pond and lake olives, midge, sedge and caenis hatches all have a role to play, and offer tantalizing prospects. By the time September comes around, a good many insects have 'shot their bolt' for another year. Hatches are, to a great degree, untrustworthy. You are forced into seeking other remedies such as 'staple' food forms and reactive patterns. This leads the benighted fly fisher to another difficulty in this equation: brown trout are not rainbows – they don't look like them, they certainly don't behave like them and they don't react in the same way.

I found this out in no uncertain terms on my first trip to the Emerald Isle. My fly box was bristling with all the modern reservoir wet concoctions – fluorescent waists, tags, cheeks and hackles, fluorescent 'Red-Arsed' Wickhams', Yellow-Tailed Muddlers, fluorescent-infused Bibios – and I quite expected to deplete Lough Melvin of her Salmonidae. On the second fishless day, I realized that things weren't going exactly to plan. Anticipating a third blank in succession, crestfallen, with my pride in tatters, I entered one of those quaint west coast tackle shops – the sort that sells dog biscuits, tea and more Guinness – where I purchased some proper 'floies sohr'. Guess what! I started to catch fish; importantly, brownies and their very close relations.

From that week forward I realized that brown trout probably see things rather differently from their more exuberant Pacific cousins. Loosely, if it looks drab, dark and edible – inspect it; if it's colourful – watch it, then avoid it. Certainly, though not a hard-and-fast rule, this theory does at least offer some thread of meaning to the escapade and a few crumbs when your fishing lies in tatters. The moral here is keep bright colours to a minimum and use only sparingly.

Although this relates to the larger waters, the reality is almost identical on smaller stillwaters that are stocked with brown trout, which seem to revert extraordinarily quickly to a 'wild' state of behaviour and assume a level of cautiousness that belies their pea-sized brains.

However, choice of water can be instrumental to success. Very few lakes concentrate solely on brown trout: expense and the fish's notorious lack of co-operation with fishery figures and rod averages tend to limit their geography and reduce density. Nevertheless, there are certain stillwaters which have become well known for brown trout fishing: Chalk Springs, Lakedown, Rooksbury Mill, Dever Springs, Avely and more pride themselves on their ability to produce real quality fishing for the discerning brown trout enthusiast.

This brings me back to September and the influence this month has on style and likelihood of success. After May and early June, July and August seem to be ultra-dour for brown trout. High water temperatures and harsh overhead light both have an effect, making the steadier and more cooling influence of September a far more reliable period to hunt in earnest.

Tackle for September

The tackle should vary from previous suggestions. As a matter of course I would go for lightweight No. 5s and 6s rather than higher, but this probably has more to do with fad. The most useful lines generally are floaters and intermediates (or slow-sinkers), though I have on occasions blessed a Wet Cel II or fast-sinker.

The one thing I have become fussy about, especially with floating lines, is colour. Having used a fluorescent yellow or orange one for years and felt no need to change, for some inexplicable reason I now tend to use a dark or semi-camouflaged type when stalking browns. This may seem illogical, but nevertheless I find myself going through the routine which is probably based more on superstition than on hard fact and reality. Certainly, if I am fishing round a good deal of shrubbery and overhanging trees, I opt for the less conspicuous line. River fishing, especially in the company of Phil White, has conclusively proved to me that fish are caught as a result. The actual colour need not resemble a peat bog or grassy field, but merely be less startling. Much the same could be said of nylon. How well I remember Dick Walker years ago, urging us to dip our nylon into silver nitrate solution to turn it black (actually Dylon, the hot fabric dye, does a good enough job, though you have to be careful not to immerse the nylon at boiling point). I thought this advice surplus to requirements, but not any more. Any edge afforded the angler will help in the 'chase', though I have to say that choosing a glint-free finish, either provided by manufacturers or by liberal use of 'mud' (fuller's earth mix) works just as well as using dye and is a great deal less troublesome. (Rubbing a leader with scouring powder works well too.)

Catching wily or 'educated' trout demands attention to detail. Obviously tippet diameter should be kept as low as possible; not merely to give the illusion of non-existence, but to allow the fly to hinge and move seductively in the water. Once more, it is the co-polymer superstrong and double strengths I find superior, although they do need a degree of attention to reduce their shiny coating. A new variety marketed by Umpqua from the USA appears a good deal more matt and has so far proven to be excellent.

In terms of tackle variation, that really is it. The only other point worth reiterating is the previously stated dictum of travelling light and wearing appropriate clothing. Ensure that your tackle is sombre and make sure you are too!

Now to the problematic area: tactics and fly choice. The real difficulty is that any variations on the already mentioned themes are microscopic twists that will convince a brown trout to 'take' rather than leave alone. For the most part these are instinctive reactions for a particular fish at a particular part of the presentation. Often there is simply no explanation for the things you did; from some inner primal recess the tactic emerged to create a subtle ploy.

However, there are one or two points worth mentioning, which I earnestly hope will form the base of your operations. The first group appeals to the trout's instinct to chase. Oddly, most anglers see the high-speed chase as the prerogative of rainbows. This is not so; brownies enjoy the 'catch-me-if-you-can' game every bit as much.

I have found that there are times when they will respond to a short induced movement and will simply feign disinterest if urged to travel more than 6 to 12ft; yet, on other occasions they will pursue hotly for yards. Daytime will see the trout respond better to the short induced chase, whereas in the late afternoon and early evening the longer one ensues, and at dusk, it seems to revert to the short again – or so I have found to be the case.

The other critical feature which affects both fly patterns, retrieves and styles is the brown trout's distaste of a wildly undulating fly. I find that they will chase along a flat plane (almost irrespective of depth); they will chase a climbing pattern (or ascending nymph *à la* Sawyer); occasionally they will hit a free-falling pattern – though this is less likely than with rainbows – and a static fly on or just under the surface is relished. But I have never seen a fly taken when stopped during a retrieve, even if started up again almost immediately (which is wholly illogical given the insects which operate with that 'stop-start' mode – corixae, shrimp, caddis pupae, damsel and dragonfly nymphs). I have,

however, witnessed trout diving headlong into weedbeds to flush out hapless shrimps, then drift back, mopping up the fleeing crustaceans at their leisure.

All these clues at least offer a degree of understanding of what is required and fly choice.

Fly choice and retrieval methods

Naturals – any aquatic form – if chased, will flee in panic. That at least gives us a clue to retrieval rate, and that is fairly fast.

First things first, however, and the induced take does seem to be the best weapon at our disposal during daylight hours and in teasing out specimen fish from their incarcerations amidst undercut banks, tree roots, deep hollows, holes under trees and other sepulchral lairs. Use a suitably weighted pattern such as a Shrimp, Damsel Nymph, Killer Bug, Pheasant Tail, even a Grey Goose, allow it to descend into an area of either known or instinctively suggested activity, and then in an easy glide bring it to the surface via the upwards sweep of the rod tip, in conjunction with the line hand pulling steadily downward so as not to lose control of the line's movement. This is probably the most consistent line of attack; certainly it allows the angler free rein to search the margins around the fishery if they are deep enough. The two largest browns to come out of Lakedown that I have heard of both fell victim to flies fished a matter of feet from the bank. Caution and gentle footfalls are essential when fishing in that manner – it really does pay to 'walk the fishery'.

The other retrieval method does require a sunk line of some description, depending on what depth the pattern is to be fished. Generally speaking I tend to start with Wet Cel II, working up to an intermediate once the light intensity has left the water.

Given the brownies' love of the chase, a hand-over-hand retrieve – as obvious as that might be – is often the best method. It can be slowed down or speeded up at will, and always there is that continuous movement of the fly that is generally so deadly. A figure of eight is, of course, another excellent approach – again fast or slow, depending on the day. I would opt for either of these over a pulling movement, which lacks their continuity.

A personal favourite pattern when using either the figure of eight or hand-over-hand sunk line is Dick's Damsel – the original Walker damsel pattern – which really has stood the test of time. I would also be at a loss without a black pattern – the Tadpole being a particular favourite, with a bright white version for evening work. Quite why white works so well in the low light I cannot imagine, but it certainly has proven the most consistent colour, other than black. Then, purely as a change pattern, I use a yellow-hackled Jersey Herd which has proven deadly over the years, especially in slightly coloured water. Another really 'oddball' pattern, which seemed to hold a fascination for the brown trout of Leominstead and remains so on other waters, though now somewhat out of fashion, is the Aylot's Orange. It might surprise people to find out that it still works, but then most of the old ones do.

Another fine pulling brown trout fly is John Goddard's Persuader, as is the Wormfly – oldies both! It does benefit the method to have a range of 'change' patterns. Trout, particularly brownies, being territorial, become bored and disenchanted with the same fly going through the same area, time after monotonous time, and a change will often provoke that all-important response.

As well as considering line types, retrieve rates and changes of fly, it can help to alter depth as well. If retrieving after a sinking time of say ten seconds (counting down), then try fifteen seconds and so on. This sounds rather methodical, almost mechanical, I know, but it is a pointer to success nonetheless.

Another important element is the retrieve. Whatever you do, keep pulling; if you feel taps or tweaks on the line (the trout mouthing the fly), just keep going until everything goes solid.

That really only leaves 'targetting' – a personal favourite, though only practical on clearwater fisheries.

Targetting

There is something intensely absorbing in pursuing brown trout with this method. The lovely thing is that brownies tend to favour particular areas or holes and are far less nomadic than their cousins. This, though, can lead to problems:

- 'education' – if you know the fish are there, you can bet someone else does too;

- if there are only a few fish in one area, the chances are they have been fished over and are fairly selective;

- a trout can show every outward sign of being perfectly happy and settled and yet be spooked and alert to danger all round.

I have witnessed on many occasions trout quite happily feeding yet ignoring, literally moving out of the way of, an artificial no matter how craftily constructed. That is when the fly fisher's greatest asset – patience – is an advantage. The ability just to stand or crouch reasonably concealed and *do nothing* is one of the hardest things that you can achieve. But it is time extraordinarily well spent; merely by observing the quarry a far greater understanding of the actual fishing requirements will be attained. The way that the trout moves, feeds and reacts – all will be displayed, with the added bonus that all the while it is accepting your presence as a legitimate part of the scenery, rather than a discordant note. You will generally know when this partial acceptance has taken effect as the fish will move in a determined and purposeful way, gliding and feeding easily, untroubled. That is the moment to make your move. It may take five minutes or five hours to reach this point, but is time valuably spent.

Quick-penetrating flies on fine tippets are *de rigueur* – the important thing is to achieve the depth without adding too much weight to the fly patterns – loud 'plops' and depth-charge entrances are ruinous. Nowadays, with leader technology, we can get the smallest and most sparse of patterns to the desired depth – Airflo lightweight, fast, and extra-fast sinking, are a godsend as is Roman Moser's All-Round Nymph Leader. Certainly these have opened up a whole new area and made deft little nymphs fishable at speed, near to the lake floor.

The important factor in this type of fishing is to catch the trout's attention, which calls for good judgement of sinking rate and underwater positioning of your fly and precise casting – not bad assets to have anyway! Once engaged, keep the brownies interested by pulling the fly away, often at speed, towards the surface. Don't stop until you see the mouth open and close – then strike.

So often I have brought a fish to the surface only to have it turn away at the last moment with a derisory and discourteous flick of its tail. This is generally a sign of an agitated fish, uncertain about what is going on and sensing a hint of danger. The best ploy is to rest the area for ten minutes or so, going back to it or re-casting when life has settled.

There are, of course, many types of fly for this type of fishing, the list is almost endless: Shrimps, Corixae, Damsels – all the old familiars. I favour some different types, if only to present fish with something fresh; something the now widespread use of goldheads could not do! So intense is their use that on some waters the fish literally recoil in shock as they drop through the surface – too many people are using them too often.

Not so the Grey Goose, Killer Bug, Sparkle Nymph and the Chalksprings Grub. All have a role to play, as has one other creation, the Deer Hair Shrimp. But the best fly is one fished with confidence, stealth and good presentation.

41 Keeping a low profile. By kneeling, a large trout can often be brought to the net a great deal quicker as it becomes disorientated, not knowing where the pull is coming from

Perseverance is another important ingredient in the quest for the enigma. And, just to prove how obtuse these fish get, the most successful fly on Rutland at present is a gold and silver Flashabou Tube. So much for sombre patterns!

But then that is the brown trout – a definite 'maybe' if ever there was one. Happy hunting!

Winter fly fishing

With a time of 'autumn mists and mellow fruitfulness', the auburn-tinged leaves and berry-laden hedgerows suggest a 'winter of discontent' to be spent reminiscing of spring days, youthful greens and a lazy evening rise with a confusion of rising trout. The traditionalist bids farewell to another season. For another breed, another season – an alternative one – is about to unfold: the winter fly fisher is ready to do battle with north-easterlies and frost.

Years ago, I felt that winter trout fishing – specifically rainbow fishing – was both a passing fad, to some degree lacking a sense of sporting tradition, and ethically questionable. Winter, after all, was a period of recuperation and rejuvenation – a time to tie flies and scan the winter-laden river surface for that speck of crimson-tipped float in my quest for roach and the usual foray for pike. Then I actually tried fishing for winter rainbows and found it to be enormous fun, often challenging and very much a pursuance of an imitative approach.

There are, of course, a good many variables to add to normal fly fishing circumstances, headed primarily by the weather; and though fish can be caught in some extraordinarily hostile conditions, it can be decidedly unfunny and often excruciatingly cold.

When to fish

The first tactic is to define the periods in which it is feasible to fish during winter. Looking back at diaries and analysing 'red-letter' days, two weather systems – both quite different – seem to predominate.

First, as you might expect, are those often balmy, 'soft' grey days, hinting at drizzle, which give off a gentle warmth which positively urges flies to hatch and become active. I did indeed say 'flies' – I have come across some reasonable hatches of pond olives on mild December days and some cinnamon sedge hatches throughout November. Of course, if you see the adult, then somewhere below the nymph and pupa must be stirring as well. However, hatch periods and taking times are alarmingly short, and often suddenly slip into an utter void when you can 'feel' everything has ground to an unceremonious halt.

This is also true, if not more so, of the second taking time and, of all winter conditions, the most likely to offer sport. I refer to those wonderfully clear, almost sparklingly crisp sunny days which 'crunch' underfoot and surround themselves with frost when the sun wanes.

It flies in the face of traditional expectation to fish at such times, but a clue as to why these periods are so often marked by good rises and earnest trout activity lies feasibly in the angle of the sun. Having lost a good deal of its strength, its more slanted angle to the water quite logically renders it a great deal more suffused and deflected than during the summer months, whilst still having a bearing on temperatures. It raises them a critical few degrees higher and encourages activity in the Insect Kingdom, especially at the top layers, and in turn, switches the trout on.

The one thing that has a habit of destroying sport totally is a wind. This might seem completely odd, given the previous conditions and the clarity it encourages, but nevertheless, there are occasions when a bright, clear, calm day urges trout to feed, only to be curtailed in a trice by a breeze that 'kicks in' and ruffles the surface. Trout will stop rising the second that wind bites; probably because these conditions indicate a northerly airstream when any wind will have an icy edge as keen as any Cossack's sword.

The activity period too can be depressingly

short. There is little point in starting much before 10 a.m. and seldom any reason to stay beyond 3 p.m. There are, of course, exceptions, but they tend not to prove the rule.

Where to fish

Here I have to say that we of the south tend to fair rather better than our brethren in the north, purely because of two major factors: a usually less hostile winter and the odd chalkspring-fed lake. It is, of course, not essential to have an alkaline water; clay-based water can be equally fishable and equally good, but during periods of hard frost they are often frozen over. This is something, by and large, that chalk waters do not do due to their more stable and constant high water temperature (48 to 56 degrees Fahrenheit). So choice of water can be vital. The question of alkalinity and stability also stretches to gravel pits such as Steeple Langford in Wiltshire, which lies in a chalk strata area. Indeed any gravel pit trout fishery, as long as it is open, is worth investigation.

Depth too is an important consideration, both in terms of fish location and tactical approach. The trout will often prefer the warmer bottom layers – hypolimnion – and it is essential that we reach such areas tactically. However, hot air rises and, given a constant wind direction, the warm lower layer will soon become the upper – epilimnion – layer. This may sound contradictory to the statement made earlier that winds during winter can destroy surface activity – this is so. Entering our conundrum now is another factor 'what is the upper layer?' and in this case it may not reasonably be at the actual surface, but a few inches down. What happens is a stratification, or a thermocline, and though the wind may drive the warm air surfaceward, there still remains a narrow, icy, surface wind-affected band at the top, making fishing perhaps a foot down or so much more effective than actually at the surface. This, though, is dependent on uniformity, both from the wind and, to some degree, the water's contours. The thermocline can, of course, tilt and alter, given various conditions and circumstances; and feeding trout will seek these warmer layers purely because insects will be more active. We, as anglers, are left with little choice other than to experiment to find such areas.

Clothing

Before venturing into tackle and tactical differences, a few words on a vital consideration – clothing and keeping warm. All too often this is not given enough thought. The dictum outlined in April of easily added or subtracted lightweight layers holds the key to happy, comfortable angling. The main essential is to keep hands, feet and head warm. Logically, a hat –

● *Water currents in winter*

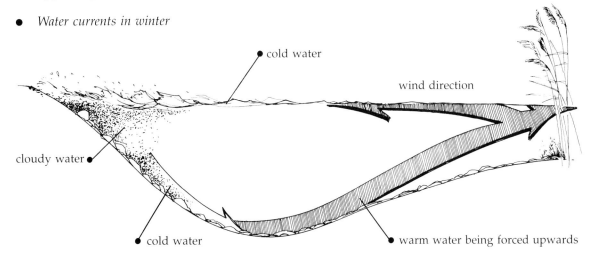

cold water

wind direction

cloudy water

cold water

warm water being forced upwards

tweed or felt – warm footwear and (bizarre as it may seem) I opt for neoprane chest waders which give my feet, legs and torso protection in utter lightweight comfort – the best I have yet come across are the Daiwa variety – and shooter's mittens. Detesting gloves and their insensitivity, preferring abject cold misery, I cannot advise on these, but if you cannot orchestrate and maintain a slow figure of eight retrieve with a chosen variety, then they are not right.

A waterproof – and I do mean waterproof – coat is essential, incorporating good windproofing qualities. These are rare and you may have to look outside fishing suppliers and venture into the world of walking and rock climbing to find suitable candidates. My Patagonia Watershed jacket and Touchstone wading jacket have both been totally reliable in some dreadful conditions and get my vote, but there are, of course, many others available. Also overtrousers, which can provide a very warming and protective layer in cold weather, are a very good idea.

Tackle

Tackle need not vary an iota from previous expeditions on small waters, but should err to the light-line approach. This is not through fad, but the practicality of dealing with 'thin' water – generally winter lakes, across the board, are at their clearest during winter months and bright sunlit conditions. Seldom have I fished anything heavier than a No. 6, with a No. 5 outfit being the norm, which is frequently augmented by a No. 4 system for small chironomid fishing.

The problem with fishing such light outfits is the inability to find suitable sinking line, because along with the main-line of attack – a floater – you will, on occasions, need the assistance of an intermediate, fast-sink (Wet Cel II) and Hi-D densities. Ideally these should not be used on No. 5 or No. 4 weight outfits, these being the preserve of the floating line, but few manufacturers carry No. 6 Hi-Ds. The only variety I am aware of is Hardy Bros, though

the Cortland (Normark) do carry some fast sinkers in low AFTMs which are well proven. Regarding the intermediate line, there are some distinct advantages in carrying a Fast Glass (Airflo) due to increased subsurface sensitivity.

The one thing, though, is to resist portraying yourself as a human hedgehog – rods sprouting everywhere. Judge the day on its merits and certainly you can formulate some vague idea of a line of approach. At most you need carry two rods – better still, one – which for overall fishing does make the No. 6 system more practical. However, a word of caution: takes at this time of year can be subtlety itself, with the trout making barely perceptible 'footprints' as to acceptance or rejection of a fly. A lighter line will very often catch you fish which don't even register on a heavier system. The reason is simple: there is far less resistance on both the terminal tackle and, importantly, the fly line itself; I have known No. 4 line shoot away like a miniature missile when a No. 7 would barely have twitched.

Another vital consideration is the angle the rod tip is to the water. Most of us (I am also to blame) hold our rods far too high above the surface. By keeping the tip ring a quarter to half an inch above the water, not only will more direct action be fed through to the pattern but a far greater degree of tactile senses will be experienced, allowing for very quick reaction to takes.

Tactics

This is a huge area with a great many crossovers from summer tactics. By and large, though, you will be imitating small flies, midges (chironomids); generally black and tiny with a size 18 often looking huge. There are the odd red and dark olive variations about, with a smattering of brown, but by far the biggest contingent are black. There are also a good few immature damsel nymphs abroad – especially in stable, more alkaline lakes. Again, these are small by comparison to their summer appearance and far better represented on a 14 l.s. or 10–12 std short hook, generally sporting a pale yellow olive coat.

This at least gives us some clues as to the tactical approaches, especially if you add shrimps, hoglouse and snail, also the odd comatose corixa to the list – which suggests a predominance of bottom-grubbing styles, interspersed with some middle-layer fishing. The damsels are often energetic on mild days, together with ascending buzzers (midges) and are a realistic expectation when conditions offer some surface activity to midge and even the odd pond olive. There you have the tactics in a nutshell; perhaps an oversimplification, but often we complicate things for complication's sake. So, there are three styles: one bottom, one middle and one surface.

Most of these situations can be easily catered for with a floating line. There is one specific tactic that is very useful where allowed (it entails using two flies and a great many small waters only allow a single). However, should

you be able to, utilize as long a leader as can be handled or necessary – at least one-and-a-half times the water depth being fished, (ie 8ft of water to a 12–16ft leader) – placing the dropper amidships approximately half way up. A quick method is to use either a 9ft, 12ft or 15ft pre-tapered leader down to 6lb b.s. super strong or similar low-diameter material, then place a corresponding tippet 6lb b.s. of the desired tippet length (6ft to 8ft) using this juncture as the dropper.

The point fly should generally be leaded or heavy-ironed and, for the greater part, be sacrificial – a Hare's Ear l.s. Black Nymph, Black and Peacock Spider, Damsel or Shrimp, even the Red Hook (Datsun) can be adopted. The 'working' fly is the dropper, which should either

42 *Fishing the upper Yellowstone, Wyoming. Though a river, stillwater tactics – long leaders and Midge* Pupae *– were the only way in which the native cutthroat trout would be caught*

be a short spider pattern, a Barden's Pupa or short-dressed midge pattern of some kind,such as the BP or Parcel String Buzzer. This should take care of any bottom-grubbing trout seeking out torpid creatures and intercept patrolling fish hunting the warmer thermoclines.

Still on the floating line, never overlook straightforward nymph fishing in rough conditions, especially on mild days, working the flies two to twelve inches below the surface. Though no trout movement can be seen, you will often be amazed at how many takes you can get just sub-surface with patterns such as the Barden Pupa (in an appropriate colour), Beardsley Pheasant Tail, or Short Hare's Ear.

As with the previous tactics, ultra-slow retrieves are required. Better still, just allow the pattern to work with the wind/wave action. If any retrieve is necessary, a slow figure of eight is the recipe.

But eclipsing all these in terms of fun is 'fishing the rise'. Though slightly incongruous, you can experience scintillating surface fly fishing in winter. The problem that most fishers have is understanding the size of fly necessary; at the very largest end of the spectrum a size 18 Dark Terrestial can be useful, but the pattern choice should centre around 20, 22 and 24.

Quite why, in this country, we have an in-built scepticism of anything smaller than a 14 or 16, I cannot fathom. For the most part natural flies, especially olives (upwinged dry flies) and midges (chironomids), are smaller. These are what trout expect to see and eat; and a 12 or 14 in their world must evoke some suspicion. During winter, it is my belief that the trout's suspicions heighten, calling for far greater attention to size. Colour is not such a problem, as most active surface insects tend to be dark. This could be due to 'thinness' of the water and angle of the sun, but small Black Midges on 20 (or below) hooks can be devastatingly successful. This, of course, calls for light but strong tippets as trout in winter, if anything, fight harder than in summer, which once more suggests the low-diameter double-strength types.

The actual fishing of the pattern is straightforward: wait for the rise, try and ascertain the direction the trout is taking, then try to ambush it with your diminutive pattern. Reading a rise can be reasonably conclusive. Look for the bigger bulge of the ripple in the rise's ring – this tends to be the trout's shoulder pushing water away and gives an indication of direction. For these infuriating 'up-down' sipping rises, an educated guess is about the only remedy. The one thing with such small flies is timing the strike. Do not strike too soon; you can delay for a while – even to the extent of saying 'God save the Queen' – and then lift.

Of course, all those methods require the fish

43 Jeremy Herrmann, one of today's leading fly fishers, shows exemplary style. Always concentrating and always keeping his rod tip close to the water surface

to be feeding or at least actively in search of food. Yet there are occasions when you can evoke a response from winter trout, but again I would urge you not to employ large lures; small attractors fished slowly seem to be far more acceptable. In terms of colour, black, of course, is a firm favourite, but there can be periods (quite lengthy ones) when trout will only accept white, even the surreptitious use of fluorescent green as a tag can become distasteful to semi-interested trout, only pure white being acceptable. There can also be decidedly orange periods, which is not surprising as the rainbow in its natural world has a voracious appetite for salmon, and indeed their kin's, eggs which more or less coincides with our late autumn, early winter and again, early spring – and of course, Salmonidae eggs are bright orange.

Once again, it is the searching of water layers that provides success, coupled with slow retrieves and mobile (marabou) flies; either a figure of eight or small stripping or twitching movements. Possibly the best line for this is the Wet Cell II, which can search a wide band of levels, depending on the descent time – pulling on touchdown = 6 inches to 2ft, 5 seconds = 2ft to 3ft, and so on. It sounds mechanical but can provide vital clues. Leaders are also important when fishing with such line, and I would urge length, once again seldom dropping below 12ft, operating with a tippet strength of 6 to 8lb b.s. (low diameter), or 4 to 5lb Drennan Sub Surface Green.

Leader length brings us to the last tactic. Like it or not, fishing the Booby – a buoyant fly on a sunk line – is deadly; and there are times when it can work when nothing else will. Simply, it places your fly hard on the bottom at times when it is essential to fish there and, more importantly, stays there. An ultra-slow figure of eight is the required retrieve, and keeping it constant for some unaccountable reason leads to fewer 'hang ups' with bottom debris. Don't cast the fly out and leave it; this

---

WINTER WATERS

This list is very subjective, based on personal experience and by no means exhaustive.

- *Albury Lakes*, Surrey   Excellent small nymph fishing

- *Avon Springs*, Wiltshire   Very good midge fishing and surface feeding

- *Avington*, Hampshire   Clearwater stalking throughout winter

- *Chalk Springs*, Sussex   Excellent stalking and small-fly opportunities

- *Cottington*, Kent   Excellent dry fly opportunities and midges

- *Dever Springs*, Hants   General nymph fishing and stalking

- *Lakedown*, Sussex   Good small-fly opportunities, especially near the surface

- *Nythe*, Hants   Clearwater stalking possible even on overcast days due to its clarity

- *Springhill*, Kent   Excellent midge and surface fishing

- *Steeple Langford*, Wilts   Superb small-lake and general fishing, and good surface midge

---

has nothing to do with fly fishing, and at best can be described as ledgering with a fly rod!

But for me the quintessence of winter fishing will remain those clear northern days washed with pale sunlight and surrounded by umber and amber, and the expanding ripples from rises where my 22 Black Midge used to be; a gentle lift and electric flight of a rainbow in its winter regalia – now that is fly fishing. Perhaps the winter isn't so 'deep' or 'bleak' as folk would have us believe.

EPILOGUE

The Future

I have often wondered how Skues, Halford, even Walton would have viewed today's fly fishers. Doubtless they would have marvelled at modern technology – rods so light they are a 'whisper' to cane and greenheart's 'shout'; lines that float day-long and are comparatively maintenance-free – a far cry from dressing and redressing the surface to make the silk float, then religiously drying them at the end of the day; leaders that don't rot or need pre-soaking to make them flexible. They might be forgiven for thinking they had dropped into Utopia.

But what of the ethics? The camaraderie? The Waltonian ethos of the 'Brotherhood of the Angle'? Here they may be just a little dismayed. Fun, I have always thought, is 'part and parcel' of the whole thing. That joyful wisecracking at a chum's (or, indeed, your own) inability to catch fish, hiding the angst that you are feeling – a form of piscatorial Samaritan's hand. Friendliness is the epicentre of fly fishing. It seems to be waning.

A number of waters appear to nowadays reverberate with rancour and dischord. 'Hot spots' either jealously guarded or prematurely secured, dallying with the fishery rules, if not downright contravention. The unmelodius 'chirrup' of portable 'phones, now in proliferation on small waters. I was taken to task in the angling press for my criticism of these bankside tele-communicators; people felt they should be 'in touch' with their businesses – and so they should. But if business is that important, they have no business going fishing.

Friendly gestures also seem on the decrease,

fly fishers often cocooning themselves in their own little world, seldom pausing except to change fishing spots. There are not quite the same wondering discussions, help and passing of hints or flies as I once recall. Attitudes have become a great deal more competitive, and in their wake, insular and, to some degree, singular. I would be the first to say the object of the exercise is to catch trout, there would seem little point in going otherwise! I don't enjoy blanks and know of few anglers who do, and to say they teach us something – bunkum! All we learn is how not to do it. On the other hand, I shudder at the 'fish at all costs' scenario; or 'I've paid my money, I am entitled to the trout'. Wrong – one is entitled to a pleasant day out, with hopefully like-minded individuals, enjoying an aesthetic sport, trying to catch trout by stealth, knowledge and guile. Trout, I would add, are not a bonus, more an integral part of the day's overall enjoyment.

It is, however, wrong to judgmentalize on how fly fishers derive their enjoyment, and hopefully I have offered a reasonably unbiased outlook. My preference will always be erring to the imitative, but now and again (and again) I find a long-tailed white or black, even yellow, 'thing' on the end of my leader. It just seems sensible. The one thing I would never knowingly do is to break the fishery rules. This is a cardinal sin – the heinous crime of fishing.

So what of the future? National economics will tend to be the arbiter of whether small lakes prosper or not, on this factor few of us have control. What of the rising growth of

realistic expectation. Generally there are insufficient natural aquatic foodstuffs to support and enhance the trout population in the long term. There are, of course, some waters that are extremely rich and can and do offer natural growth potential; most, however, that follow the dictum of catch and release tend to be a shade frugal in the insect department in the wide sense.

Yet the freedom of choice is there – it is something that a few years ago would not have existed and therefore must be praised. Indeed, I will support anything that puts our collective 'best foot forward', just as long as the respect for the quarry and ethics of the sport are to the fore.

In many respects we are our own worst enemy. As I touched upon earlier, how we are perceived by others is *so important*. We score continually, a huge amount of 'own goals'. Almost every occasion I step out of my car into the car park of a small water I am greeted by the sight of coils of discarded nylon; worst still, the epidemic does not diminish when at the water side. If there is one thing that will, and indeed does, summon universal disapproval from the general public, then it is this flagrant disrespect of both the world in which we fish and the creatures which share that world. For goodness' sake, take nylon home with you and dispose of it responsibly or, failing that, when at the waterside, cut it into harmless one-inch sections using scissors and please also remember to take any litter home with you.

Alexander, my son, is at the time of writing, aged four. We share a passion for fishing, just like hundreds if not thousands of other fathers and sons. What a cruel, callous act it would be if we were (especially Alex) not allowed to continue enjoying the sport of fishing that we love so.

To take away from the hunter the very reason for existence is the unkindest blow of all. With it a primeval legacy honed to modern sophistication would wither and die, and with this destruction would come the fall of the species and its environment.

We may be hunters, we may be bloodsports folk, but we understand the rhythm of water, the fish and the land's needs. We revere our quarry. Without the fish, what is to happen to water worlds? Will the wetlands survive for the next generation? Only time will tell. But the pursuit of that aim starts with that contemplative ethic of Walton's Piscator, the gentle respect and order of the Edwardians and hopefully the enlightenment and passion of the present fly fishers. Our destiny is in our own hands.

45 The ugly face of modern fishing – a magpie caught in strands of discarded line

the 'anti' brigade? Their voice and action is beginning to bite into the foundations of angling. We thought we were safe – we were wrong. The time has, of course, come when we have to act responsibly, and with one voice – splintered niche groups can do nothing; solidarity and unity wins every time. Joining the Anglers' Co-operative Association and the Salmon & Trout Association, possibly the British Field Sports Society as well, will allow that unity to be heard.

But, what can we do? 'Manners' as they say 'maketh the man'. I would paraphrase this to 'manners maketh fly fishers' for that is what we are – fly fishers, not merely fish catchers. This is an important aspect; how we are perceived by passers by, walkers or any other person in the vicinity of a fishery, is how we are judged. Dragging fish up a bank displaying no respect; joyfully and over-zealously clubbing the catch repeatedly, swearing, carelessly discarding line etc, all these things erode our collective platform.

Finally, that emotive issue 'catch and release'. Will this help our cause? Curiously, many non-fly fishers find it more acceptable to have trout killed, thus justifying the act, quite logically as culling or harvesting a crop, rather than see us play fish out and release them, often exhausted and inappropriately handled. I personally would defend to the proverbial 'death' catch and release on rivers, especially where wild trout proliferate.

Where I think we can come 'unstuck' is in being perhaps over-sensitive and practising catch and release when it is inappropriate to do so and almost for its own sake, or in some cases sheer avarice – wanting to extend the day and catch more trout.

In many instances the small stillwaters that encourage catch and release are ill equipped to do so. This is only due to basic overcrowding, given fly fishers' expectations of catching a number of fish. Trout are stocked to a level of

44 The next generation. My son Alex about to net a spirited rainbow. Fishing is fun for all ages – we must now preserve it that way

Fly Patterns

Peter's Tadpole
Hook   Std 10 or 12: L2A or TMC 3769 weighted with fine
     lead wire
Silk   Dark brown 6/0 Uni-thread
Tail   Long plume of black marabou
Body   Mottled nymph chenille (Tom Saville)
Hackle   Black (dyed) Hen – 3 turns

Duck's Dun (pond/lake olive)
Hook   16–14 TMC 921 or E1A
Body   Light yellow olive Hairtron or soft Antron
Silk   Primrose 8/0 Uni-thread
Tail   Grizzle hen or jungle cock spade feather 3–5 fibres
Wing   Two Cul du canard feathers, back to back upright
Hackle   Dark blue dun wound through thorax, clipped
     'V' underneath

GE Nymph
Hook   As for *Duck's Dun* (weighted in thorax)
Silk   Orange 8/0 Uni-thread
Tail   Three summer duck (dyed) or woodduck
Rib   Silver wire (extra fine)
Body   Olive goose cosset or dyed pheasant tail
Torax   Squirrel dyed olive/blended (Gordon Griffiths)
Wingcase   Two clumps either side of thorax of summer
     duck dyed

ET Emerger
Hook   18 or 20 Living Nymph (GRS 7MMB)
Silk   Primrose 8/0 Uni-thread
Body   Olive dyed squirrel
Back   Pearl Mylar or Spectraflash sheet (Piscatoria)
Thorax   As for body
Thorax cover   Dark grey ethafoam (or polycelon)

Hoglouse
Hook   10–12 TMC 9300 or Partridge L2A weighted with
     leadwire then flattened
Silk   Brown 6/0 Uni-thread
Tail   Partridge (brown) fibres mixed with fox squirrel
Body   Tan hare's ear plus (Flymail products)
Back   Thick PVC or clear flexi body
Hackle   Brown Partridge

CJ's Corixa
Hook   Drennan Midge S.10–8 weighted with lead wire
Silk   Primrose 8/0 Uni-thread
Butt   Silver 'T' shirt point on bend
Body   Cream Irise dub
Back   Marbled latex (Traun river products)
Hackle   Small bunch of summer duck and two fibres of
     GP tippet either side of body
Head   A build up of tying silk with a silver of latex
     wound down to the eye then dubbed back and tied
     down – the eyes are formed by T-shirt paint (Pebeo
     line). The whole lot is then covered in 5 minute
     epoxy

Distressed Damsel
Hook   TMC 9300 8 or Partridge SH1 8 (weighted with
     lead wire)
Silk   Dark olive or black Sparton or Danville
Tail   Long Black Marabou 2–3 inches
Body   Very dark olive irise dub or equivalent seal's fur
     blend
Hackle   Jungle cock saddle or dark badger hair or heavy
     cock (tied over thorax)
Thorax   As for body
Thorax cover   Flexibody – dyed olive (Piscatoria) cut in
     an elongated triangle and tied in three segments, the
     wider rear clipped to form two wing buds sloping
     down body
Eyes   Two red pearl beads (Piscatoria & craft shops)
     threaded as mono, the ends being singed to a ball
     shape melted against the beads using a cigarette
     lighter. A troublesome dressing, but worth it

NB The blend for the Distressed Damsel comprises 40%
Sooty olive seal's fur; 10% purple seal; 10% light/yellowy
olive; 10% dark red (Crimson Lake), 30% Lureflash Pearl
Twinkle cut into $\frac{1}{4} - \frac{1}{2}$ inch sections – place all the
'ingredients' into a blender and mix for about 10–20
seconds.

NQAL
Hook   TMC 3769 10–12 or Partridge SH1 10–12 (weighted
     – lead wire)
Silk   Glo Brite No 12 Fluorescent Floss

Tail 'Pinch' of black marabou – half to one inch long
Body Peacock herl
Rib Copper wire (fine)
Hackle Cree or furnace

NB Build up a large floss head, varnishing 3–4 times to preserve colour at depth.

Clifton
Hook TMC 3769 10–12 or Kamasan B.175
Butt Glo Brite No 12 Fluorescent Floss – used also as initial tying silk (varnish)
Body Peacock herl × 3 strands
Rib Fine copper (dark) wire
Wing 'Pinch' of black marabou (15–20 strands)
Head Glo Brite No 4 Floss, built up and varnished (3/4 coats)

Barden Pupa
Hook Jardine Living nymph (Partridge) S.16–20
Silk Black Micro (Sparton)
Rib Pearl Mylar or silver (very fine) wire
Body To match natural – depicted sparsely, black seal's fur, or a 'signature' mixture, either Black Midge or Blae and Black (available through Gordon Griffiths). (Dub ultra sparsely.)
Breathing filaments A 'pinch' of white Antran 'tied in' sloping backwards and clipped short

Sparkle Gnat
Hook TMC 16–20 Partridge or Hopper dry 16–18
Tail/shuck Two strands of Lureflask Twinkle
Body One strand (2 for larger hooks) of peacock herl
Palmered Hackle Grizzle hackle 'tied in' at the bend and palmered towards the eye

Gold Head Fourwater Fox
Hook TMC 3769 10–14 (weighted – fine lead wire). Thread gold bead (small size seems to fit hooks well) on to hook, follow by turn of lead wire
Tail Red fox squirrel body fur (taken from sides, ie underbelly) keep to $\frac{3}{4}$–1 inch in length
Rib Gold tinsel – fine
Body Hare's mask fur, well mixed to form a dark shade
Hackle/collar Red fox squirrel body fur placed in a dubbing loop and spun to create a hackle. 2–3 turns – whip finish *immediately* behind gold ball

Green Butt Tadpole
Hook Std shank 10 or 12 (weighted with turns of lead wire), TMC 3769 or Kamasan B.175
Silk Black Micro-thread
Tail $1\frac{3}{4}$–2 inch 'tuft' of marabou (colour depending on body coloration)
Body One and a half turns of fluorescent lime-green (phosphorescent yellow) chennile, followed by either black, white or orange sparkle chennile (lureflash)

Pheasant Tail (Troth)
Hook Std s.14, 16 (or short on a 12) TMC 9300 or Partridge L.2A

Silk Black micro
Tail Pheasant tail fibres (half body length) × 4
Body Pheasant tail ribbed with copper wire
Thorax Two strands of peacock hurl
Wingcase Pheasant tail

Phantom Pupa
Hook Std 12–14 or l.s. 14 nickel (Mustad 3908 n)
Silk Olive micro (Uni-thread, wisp or sparton)
Body Clear polythene strip or clear buzzer tubing over silver hook
Hackle One and a half turns of grizzle (or good quality badger)
Head Orange build up of silk or T-shirt paint coated in 5 minute epoxy

Jelly Pupa
As for *Phantom Pupa*, minus the hackle. The body comprises a strip of 'Silipos' gel which is obtainable through Silipos, 34, Chiltern Street, London W1M 1PH; over, if desired, an underbody of pearl Mylar

Golden Distressed Damsel
As for *Distressed Damsel* though using a size 12 hook and golden olive materials, including the marabou

Hawthorns
Hook TMC 100 10–12 or Partridge E1A
Silk Black Uni-thread 8/0 or Sparton Micro
Body/abdomen Blue and black signature blend or black polypropolene, ribbed with partially stripped peacock herl (2 strands spun as a rope)
Wing Two light blue dun hackle points
Legs Two peacock herl strands knotted. The knot can be toughened with a 'dab' of black T-shirt paint
Thorax As for abdomen with a grizzle hackle wound through
Thorax cover Black polycelon (lureflash)

October fly patterns

Carrot Nymph
Hook S.12 d.e. std. wet
Silk Brown or black 8/0
Body Orange Antron or rabbit (*Signature* blend – Orange Midge)
Tail 8–10 Natural red cock hackle fibres
Thorax Grey rabbit under fur (Blue/grey)
Wing pad Grey primary slip (Mallard etc)
Hackle Two Cock hackle stalks (black) either side of thorax

The Wickham's Variant (Alun Jones)
Hook 14–16 Std wet DE (Capt. Hamilton or B 175)
Silk Brown Danville 6/0
Tail Small tuft of Honey Hen (optional)
Body Flat gold lurex
Rib Gold wire
Body Hackle Honey Hen hackle

Wing Very pale hen pheasant, centre tail paired, or
   similar buff wing feather

Brown trout fly patterns

White Tadpole
Hook Std 8 (my preferance) or ls 10–12 (weighted)
Tail Long plume of white marabou
Body White Veniard's Glitter Chenille
Rib None
Hackle One and half to two turns White cock (soft)
   hackle

Dick's Damsel
Hook Ls 10 (weighted)
Tail Four to five Olive dyed goose fibres
Body Medium damsel 'Signature' blend
Rib Copper or brown tying thread
Hackle Olive dyed partridge

Grey Goose
Hook 14–16 standard
Tail Grey goose fibres
Body Grey goose fibres
Thorax Silver wire with grey goose over

Aylott's Orange
Hook B 100 G
Body Arc chrome – fluorescent wool (Real Peach)
Hackle Natural red – four turns
Thorax Peacock Herl

Wobble Worm (Lapsley)
Hook GRS 4 A (Partridge/Veniard) – shrimp
Tail Red marabou – plume
Underbody Silver flat Mylar
Body Red Seal's fur (sub)
Rib Silver fine wire
Head Nos 4–6 split shot painted red

Sparkle Nymph
Hook 12–16 Std Wet fly
Tail Partridge hackle fibres (5–8)
Body Dark olive or dark damsel 'Signature' blend
Thorax Dark green Irise dub

Chalksprings Bug
Hook Std – 1 × long 12–14 (weighted)
Tail Four to five pheasant tail fibres (cock)
Body White angora wool (not fluorescent)
Thorax Beige Irish dub

Fly patterns – dog days

Peacock Nymph
Hook Drennan traditional wet s.8 (leader wire weighted)
Silk Black 8/0 Uni-thread (Veniard)
Tail Four to five pheasant tail fibres
Rib None

Body Peacock herl taken from blue eyes
Thorax Bronze peacock herl
Thorax cover Blue peacock quill

Golden Orb
Hook B100 G Few turns of lead wire if desired
Silk Fluorescent Floss Globrite, colour optional
Body No 7 or No 2 are good
Head Large diameter gold bead

Free-Fall Midge
Hook L.2A 14 and 12
Silk Black Uni-thread 8/0
Tail A 'pinch' of white marabou or arctic fox
Rib Fine copper wire
Body Peacock herl (bronze)
Head No 5 split shot, darkened black

Foam Damsel
Hook Ls 10 2 × long
Silk Primrose Uni-thread 8/0
Tail Small tuft of olive marabou
Body Dark or medium damsel my 'Signature blend'
   (Gordon Griffiths)
Head Yellow plastazote ball clipped to fit

Deer Hair Shrimp
Hook K4A (Partridge) s. 10 or 12
Silk Black, orange or yellow Uni-thread
Rib Copper wire
Tail Grey partridge (optional)
Body A mix of hare's mask and natural deer hair,
   dubbed over lead wire
Back Spectraflash sheet (Traun river)

Gold Head Damsel
Hook Ls 10 2 × long
Silk Yellow 8/0 Uni-thread
Rib Gold wire (fine)
Tail Plume of olive marabou
Body Medium damsel, my Signature blend
Hackle Grey partridge dyed yellow
Head Large bore gold bead

Street Walker
Hook Ls 10 2 × long
Silk Black micro 8/0 Uni-thread
Rib Optional oval silver (fine)
Tail Purple marabou
Body Black chenille
Head Magena; fuschia chenille or Fritz

Pink Tadpole
Hook Ls 10 2 × long
Silk Black (as *Street Walker*)
Rib Fine silver wire
Tail Blancmange pink marabou
Body Silver chenille
Hackle Grizzle palmered

Dry-Fly Patterns

Borger's Braided Blue Damsel
Hook   Light wire DE dry fly s. 10–12, TMC 921 or
    Partridge GRS 3A 12
Body/abdomen   Braided nylon (Leeda backing) marked
    with blue Pantone pen and ringed black
Silk   Black
Wing/hackle post   White polypropolene marked blue with
    Pantone pen
Hackle   Grizzle
Thorax   Davy Wootton's S.L.F. dubbing

NB   Singe the end of the braid to avoid fraying and for
additional realism.

The wingpost thorax cover is first tied on the shank in
two sections with a loop facing the bend. This loop is
brought upright and the hackle wound at the base (5–6
turns). The post is then brought forward to the hook eye
and laid down splitting the parachute hackle.

The B and A
Hook   14–16 light wire dry fly TMC 921 or Partridge GRS
    3A
Silk   Black uni-thread 8/0
Body   1st segment: Black twinkle (Lureflash); 2nd
    segment: Signature blend Black terrestrial
Back   Black polycelon
Legs/Hackle   A bunch of black deer hair, flared either side

NB   The deer hair can be clipped if desired, to obtain
more realism. However, uneven lengths offer the trout a
better target.

Hackle Point Midge (system pattern)
Hook   12–18 living nymph GRS 7 MMB or TMC 2487
Silk   Orange micro, signature blend
Rib   Panel string split or carpet backing (the nylon
    strands that hold the weave together)

NB   Obtain at night to avoid stressful domestic relations!

Wing   Two light blue dun or white cock hackle points
Thorax   As for body
Wingcase   Amber/ginger feather fibre
Hackle   Orange or natural red cock hackle wound
through entire thoracic area, then 'V' clipped underneath

NB   Alter colour and size to suit the likely hatch.

Glitter Spinner
Hook   Light wire DE dry 12–20 TMC 921 or Partridge
    GRS 3A
Tail   Two paint brush fibres divided
Body   Apricot signature blend
Wing   A mixture of Traun Magic wing, pink and clear,

also several strands of Pearl Twinkle, clipped to size
(along length of body).

NB   Other colours: Chestnut, light or dark olive and
white. Very small sizes for Caenis

Depositing/Running Caddis (egg-laying)
Hook   TMC 200 12–16 (10 for Great Red)
Egg sack   Fluorescent orange SLF
Body   Amber Sedge Signature blend
Rib   Very, very fine gold wire
Body Hackle   To suit body colouration, dyed brown
    Grizzly
Wing   Amber elk hair (to match natural)
Head   Dark deer hair clipped to shape

Orange Emerger
Hook   Drennan emerger 10–16
Butt   Medium pearl Mylar (take well round the bend)
Body   Fluorescent orange (deep) seal's fur or sub
Wing   White cul-du-canard flanked by two slivers of
    Pearl Twinkle
Thorax   As body
Hackle   Natural red, wound through thorax, three to four
    open turns

NB   Again colours can be altered to suit insect
emergence

Lively Mayfly
Hook   10 or 12 Cptn Hamilton L2A
Silk   Orange
Tail   Three pheasant tail fibres
Body 1   10–12 deer hair fibres
Body 2   Buff/yellow/fawn wool or blended rabbit

Balloon Caddis
Hook   10–12 Std light wire
Silk   Primrose
Body   Antran/polypropylene dubbing in olive, tan or
    amber
Wing   Deer hair/elk hair dyed chestnut or natural
Head   Polycelan re-doubled and tied down over thorax
    region

Sedge Pupae
Hooks   10–12 nymph 2 × ls
Silk   Cream or primrose
Body   Abdomen: Amber Irise club; Thorax: cream or
    yellow Irise dub
Collar/Hackle   Cree × two turns clipped top and bottom
    and positioned between thorax and abdomen

Pond and Lake Olive
Nymph   Pheasant tail and GE Nymph in sizes 14 to 16
Emerger   GR Hare's Ear (with blue dun tail and hackle),
    DD Emerger
Dun   Greenwell's Glory and DD
Spinner   Walker's Pond Olive or Apricot Crystal spinner